PART-TIMER

A Compelling Account of Serving in N.Ireland
During 'Op Banner'

Mark Cardy

ISBN 978-1-915962-96-6
First published 2025 by Compass-Publishing UK

Edited by Mark Cardy
Typeset by The Book Refinery
www.TheBookRefinery.com

I dedicate this book to all the men and women who have given their time and service to 'Op Banner', the veterans that went through conflict and are still suffering, and to the many who have given the ultimate sacrifice.

Contents

Foreword

This book by Mark Cardy is a very personal, compassionate and at times funny account of a life spent as a Part-Time member of the Ulster Defence Regiment. It outlines the dangers, both on duty and off duty; the training and the camaraderie you only find when you share such hardships and experiences with those you serve alongside.

For me, the written words from Mark Cardy brought me back to a time when my own father and mother served in the Ulster Defence Regiment. Both served in Craigavon, Banbridge, Portadown and Lurgan and Mark's recollections mirrored theirs in so many ways.

As a soldier myself I spent much of my time serving across the globe, that included time in Northern Ireland as part of Operation Banner. However, I never endured the relentless dangers faced by many in the Ulster Defence Regiment off duty; I was never faced with an enemy who would aim to murder you at home, at your place of work or when you were enjoying time engaged in hobbies, sports or community activities.

Reading Mark's initial manuscript you could be forgiven for believing this was a normal way of life and I suppose for many it was. However, the reality was that it was a highly unusual way of life. Not only did Mark and his comrades protect the people at night or throughout the weekend, but they also held full time jobs in what is known within military circles as 'civvy street'. In simple terms Mark highlights how the Ulster Defence Regiment stood between the terrorists and the terrorised and many paid the ultimate price for this service and commitment.

The book outlines the genuine sense of loss for many within the Ulster Defence Regiment when it was amalgamated with the Royal Irish Rangers. This resulted in Part-Time members of the Ulster Defence Regiment to Part-Time Members of the Royal Irish Regiment Home Service. Yet, without missing a beat Mark and his colleagues stepped into their new role and continued with the tasks and training given to them.

As peace took hold, and the need for the Home Service was no longer required, men stepped out of uniform and they began a new role focused on their civilian employment. Post Traumatic Stress Disorder can always be found within those who have suffered traumatic events. Yet being continually exposed to danger, perceived and real, can bring about the same debilitating outcomes.

Mark Cardy must be commended for his frank outlining of how his own mental health suffered due to many years of military service. Even though he didn't notice until years after that service has finished the effects remain the same. Therefore, this book is an important piece of the puzzle in shedding light on the mental health epidemic facing many former part-time soldiers.

As time goes on and memories diminish it is important that books like this are written by men and women who served with such incredible dedication. As I look at the grainy images of my father, who served 8 years in 11 UDR after 22 years in the Ulster Rifles, or those of my mother who died in service while a Private in 11 UDR, I am reminded of what service really means.

Mark Cardy is one of thousands who donned the uniform when the need was greatest. He never stood alone in those dark days yet at times he finds himself alone as he deals with the effects of his service. By writing this book he ensures future generations understand what men like Mark did and the price they paid for doing it. They brought about peace and should be remembered for it.

Doug Beattie MC

Introduction

Bombs regularly on the news, Action Man, tight security and searches in most large shop entrances, War films on television, shootings of security force personnel. When I was growing up this was our/my world, and we never thought of it as anything other than 'Normal'.

I left the Army almost twenty years ago. I may have left the Army, but the Army has never left me. I know you have most probably heard that phrase before? But hopefully by the end of this book you will understand just what that means for me and put into context just what that phrase means.

Why did I write this book? Op Banner finished in 2007. In the following years, most people remembered or knew of 'The Troubles', but with the passage of time it has been forgotten, pushed away, and is trying to be rewritten, by people who were not there, or were there, but are on the Republican front. 'The Troubles' are being whitewashed away, by the Media, the Government, and others. When the Government/Media speak of the Iraq/Afghanistan wars, they talk about veterans/heroes/fallen of that war, and also their PTSD.

PTSD does not seem to be recognised for those who served during 'The Troubles', but over twice as many British soldiers died in Northern Ireland than in Iraq and Afghanistan combined, and when it comes to PTSD, I am not saying that the soldiers of Iraq/

Afghanistan do not have it, I know they do, however in Northern Ireland 'We Served', had the threat whilst on duty, but we were and are more under threat whilst being off-duty, with Under Vehicle Booby Traps, Close Quarter Attacks when undertaking daily routines, one never knew when your enemy was watching and plotting to kill you; when walking down the streets you never know who was in the crowd watching. We live every day amongst people who want to murder us, and for safety we can never show that we are off-duty security force personnel!

Being a British soldier is very proud, and in most countries it is proud and good to show that you are fighting for, and defending your nation, but in Northern Ireland, we dare not show that we are in the Army. No pictures in our living rooms, trophies hanging in the Hall. No travelling to work in uniform or even hanging your uniform on the outside clothesline.

It is nearly 20 years since 'Op Banner' ended, and since our Royal Irish Regiment Home Battalions were disbanded. In this book I would like to let you know and feel what it was like, during my service years, from March 1987 to April 2007.

I was born in 1968. The Troubles/conflict began officially in Northern Ireland in 1969, so I have never known anything else!

Northern Ireland was, when I was growing up one of the poorest provinces in Britain. We did not have much, but we are very happy. Since some areas of the province did not have much, for the people in Belfast and Londonderry for example, some felt they had little to lose. When Troubles prevailed and property and streets destroyed.

If the Troubles started today? (2025), people have more assets, owning their own homes, cars, better jobs, more material things. Perhaps it may not have started, or if it did? Would not last for long?

In the 1970's and 80's, going into town, Mum's bag getting checked on entering each shop. Going into Belfast and having to go through the 'Clack, clack, clack' revolving one-way turnstile and having bags, coats checked before you continued. Bombs exploding on a weekly basis, emergency news flashes on the TV, people being shot. This was normal life!

People living on the mainland, hearing about Ulster on the news - all they saw was Belfast with boarded up shops, bomb ruined shops and businesses, curfew's at night, Army patrolling along every street, and if not then terrorists like the IRA and UVF were parading, patrolling, setting up illegal Vehicle Check Points, and life was just about surviving.

Myself, I saw programmes set in England, where life looked so free, with so much entertainment, great looking interiors of houses, no worries, so much wealth. It was so different from Ulster, so different that I thought it was just on film, or was being acted out?

The UDR and RUC lived and worked in Northern Ireland, and because so, were the best people to defend the public against terrorism and terrorists who lived and operated in the same areas in which we lived. With that came the threat! As the terrorists knew we were the greatest threat to them. Paramilitary terrorists were and are the biggest threat to us, only not in an operational manner, but in a personal way! The terrorists wanted to Kill UDR and RUC Personnel. And it was easier to do this with a part-time UDR soldier, or an RUC reservist, who had a regular job along with the security force career.

We couldn't change timings and places of work, and had set routines. Additionally, the part-time element of the security forces, could gain (whilst off duty) so much information and feed this back to the Intelligence Centres, which could get the 'Suspect Terrorist' arrested, or a terrorist operation compromised.

In the 2020 book *Undercover War* by Harry McCallion (who'd been in the Parachute Regiment and the SAS, and completed a number of tours in the 'Northern Ireland' Theatre) quotes in his book.

> 'A Favourite tactic of republican terrorists was to target off-duty members of the RUC and UDR when they were at their most vulnerable. Among the most dangerous assignments that could be given to a member of the Troop in Ulster was to act as a substitute or decoy, standing in for a member of the security forces who had been targeted for assassination. Those who volunteered for such missions required the coolest of heads, as well as steel in another part of the anatomy.'

Those who joined the RUC and UDR, especially the part-time element didn't have a choice to step in and become the member of security forces who was targeted for assassination. As soon as we signed along the dotted line, we became THAT target for assassination. Due to this threat, we had to become professional. On duty to capture/kill the terrorist, and off-duty to protect ourselves, and if an incident arose, to kill/escape the attacker.

We became so professional at our roles in Internal Security, that members of the RUC were head-hunted by the USA for their coolness in 'Contact', Professionalism in operations and arrests, and such a degree in the 'Forensics' to find/get/preserve evidence. The UDR (which became The Royal Irish Regiment in 1991) became so professional in this warfare Theatre (Internal Security), that I am confident to say, is in 'The Special Forces' category. I know we were not 'Special Forces' in 'Arctic-Warfare', 'Jungle-Warfare', 'Desert-Warfare', and even in 'General-Warfare', we didn't not come close to the rest of the 'Regular Regiments', never mind some of the better ones. But in our theatre we were professional. We had to know how to avoid a 'Contact', and if it happened, how to react. Off-duty, as was said earlier, we were targeted for assassination, so we carried our own pistols as Personal Protection Weapons, and learnt to use them, thus dropping the threat in front of us in less than 3 seconds (any later, and we would be dead).

We avoided being detected as an 'off-duty' soldier and were skilled in hiding/not showing that we carried a firearm. We worked out actions on if being targeted/followed/threatened and attacked. I would go as far to say that even 'James Bond' wasn't as switched on as we had to be. Bond sometimes put his pistol in a drawer or somewhere or went to places that he was expected/attacked, whereas, we had the pistol attached to ourselves 24 hours a day, and tried never to go where we were assumed to be. We had to think like the terrorist, to avoid being targeted/attacked by the terrorist.

When the troubles began the UDR and RUC had little knowledge of how to contain and stop the violence. Official IRA members where known, then there was a split in 1969, where the Provisional IRA was born (A phoenix out of the ashes, as they would put it). The IRA (PIRA) became very professional over a short space of time, and likewise, the UDR and RUC became professional, and professional on how to operate in the terrorist war. 'Internal Security' theatre the British Army will label it. The Troubles as the Media would call it. 'The Conflict' in the world view. And 'WAR' by the Republican terrorists.

'The Troubles' was guessed by the Government/MoD/and the Media to last, at the longest, 3 years, but it lasted ten times that, it lasted 3 decades. The IRA were thought to be a simplistic group, which would be easily contained and caught, how wrong they were. The IRA got so proficient, that in my and many peoples' views, became the best and best organized terrorist group in the world!

On joining the Security Forces in 1987, there seemed to be two conflicts going on. I'm not talking about the Protestant and Catholic conflicts, but what the public knew, and what was actually going on. The news broadcasted incidents that were happening in the public eye. The RUC were reporting to the media - incidents, arrests, seized articles that they wanted to be made public. But the Army only disclosed what the public already knew. They never made public a large majority of what was happening (I would guess that over 80% of what was going on in 'Internal Security' was not shown to the public), for instance the shoot-outs at the border I read in daily 'Northern Ireland Reports' (A 24 hour Army Internal print-out of incidents around the Provence) of 'Contacts' between Army (quite often special forces like the Commando's or Para's) and Republican terrorists. Injuries to the Army were never made public. Injuries or deaths to the terrorists were never made public. You would think that the Republican terrorists would like to make this public, as they could put this forward as 'the shoot to kill' policy of the British Government? But they did not want to make it public, as the firefight was started by them, and they lost the short battle, and members killed. It wasn't good publicity for the IRA or INLA. Also, the public never knew of the threats. Threats of large IED's coming into the towns and cities, threats to security force personnel, Threats to contractors, and people who supplied Barracks and Police Stations. The terrorist's wanted publicity, as they wanted to 'terrorise' the public, so by keeping it quiet, they were not achieving their aim!

After leaving the army, perhaps over 10 years after leaving, I was diagnosed with PTSD. I most probably had it during my army years, and did not know it, as we were so busy, getting on with life, patrolling, training, working during the day and family.

As with most men, I feel a failure admitting to having PTSD. Surely a man, especially an army veteran shouldn't suffer from PTSD, we think, we should be above it, and it is a weakness to admit PTSD!

War was never declared in Northern Ireland, but it did happen and was a costly one, on lives, property, money, and the future of our loving country.

1

Joining the UDR

I moved away from Lisburn in 1978. Ok let me put the dots together. I grew up in a council estate. That's not a bad thing, but it is my roots!

In the late 60's my mum and dad married, and managed to get a council house in the new council estate of Milltown, Derriaghy, just outside Lisburn. Dad started a business in the last years of the 1960's, and after few years wanted to better himself and our family, built a house out in the countryside.

In the late 70's. He was seeing a client in Ballinderry 1976/77, and there was an old house/site for sale. My dad bought it, and was going to renovate the existing house, but it wasn't possible, or maybe it was quicker, easier, and cheaper to raise the house down, and build on top of the foundations. My dad built the new house, and we moved into it in the summer of 1978, before it was fully finished!

I started p7 in my new school (Ballinderry Primary) in September, and made new friends, some of whom became lifelong friends. Life in the country seemed so different. No sectarianism, which I was used to. What is going on?

One day soon after I had started school, out of the blue, Trevor cycled from his house (about 2 ½ miles away) to mine. I was outside playing/ pottering about in the back garden, and he cycled in. Since then Trevor has been a great and trustworthy friend. We played together in p7. When we went to secondary school in September 1979, we were in different classes. We still mated about, but weren't quite as close, as we had other friends in our classes. Anyway, we still hung out together on the bus, sometimes the playground, sometimes we met weekday evenings (I cycled up to his house). Now and again on a Saturday afternoon.

After leaving school in 1984, we lost touch, and went our separate ways (work/family).

3 Days after I had left School, I started work in my Dad's business – kitchen making! I suppose it had and has good prospects, but I wasn't getting any fulfilment from working there. I thought that my life ahead was looking very boring and empty. A job, and ahead of me, probably a car, work more, get a wife, house and children, but am I going to go through life not having the satisfaction, that lies in my heart. I didn't know what I wanted. Perhaps this is what life was meant to be? You get through life, with the small victories, perhaps with other victories such as good possessions, good movies and good holidays.

I passed my driving test at the start of 1986, and during the summer of 1986, I decided to touch base with Trev again. We got on well, and went out drinking the occasional Saturday evening, and to see new films in the cinema.

Trev had some replica pistols and rifles, and I was amazed at how realistic they were. After a few weeks we started talking about the army, and he was talking about the UDR. I said I thought the UDR was wick, and not trained properly like proper soldiers. He disagreed with me, and we had a few debates about it. I thought the Territorial Army was better trained than the UDR. And then he admitted, he was in the UDR! A part-time company in the UDR. He told me about the training they did, weekends away, duties and patrols. How did I not know? Trev said about how they can't be overt about it, can't talk openly about it, with the threats/risk. Trev said he hadn't been in the UDR long. Just a few months now, and would I like to join also? I still wasn't sure how good the UDR was, and perhaps the T.A. was better to get into, in a part time way, if you know what I mean? But the T.A. only trains! Whilst the UDR trained, and patrolled at nights and weekends.

I was working in my Dad's business, and felt obliged to stay there, so my options weren't to join the regular army (I didn't think I was fit enough, for the regular army), but I now have the choice of joining the part-time army. Maybe the T.A. or the part-time UDR? I talked with another great friend from school (Steve), whose father was in the RAF (which he had recently left). I stirred something in him also, but he thought he'd rather join the T.A than the U.D.R. I liked talking to Steve about this, not only because his Dad had a career in the RAF, but also during the last school years, Steve and Dave (both parents in the RAF) physically trained hard as they both wanted to join the military. Dave went onto being in the Military Police, and Steve with his dreams of going into the Royal Marines/Commandos, got side-lined. Steve went onto the tech (Technical College) after leaving school, going onto being a successful architect and owning his own business! Although I know if you asked him now which path he would take if he went back in time? I know he would have made that plunge into the Marines, Steve is very fit and has the mind for being a good soldier!

He and I talking about the T.A. made my mind up, I wanted to join the part-time UDR. I asked Trev, how I went about joining and he put me in touch with the recruitment Corporal in his company.

I met the man very soon after making that decision, and think it was less than two weeks since I'd asked Trevor to get in touch with him for me. The recruitment Corporal talked a little about the UDR, the roles they did and training, courses, then he took my name and details, and said he'd be in touch. Trev at the moment was enjoying 'B' Company 11 UDR, loving the patrols, but now has decided to go full-time in the UDR.

I wasn't the fittest, but was carrying no weight, so I had to start doing a bit of running, training, in order to pass the fitness test during recruitment. Trev told me the timings for the basic fitness test,which you must pass. You run a mile and a half squadded and then had to run a mile and a half unaided. You ha to do the second 1½ mile run in under 11½ minutes.

I got my Adidas trainers out from the back of a cupboard, and started running a 3 mile circuit from my home. I went running around 3, sometimes 4 times a week, and it didn't take me too long to get up to that accepted level,but I wanted to get far better, so that after doing any fitness, I was not knackered for what training came next! When I got good at the 3 mile'r I started running 4 miles. I ran the 4 miles from Trev's house, as it was a hilly run. Yes it's all roads, but from his house it's all up and down hills around the route, thus giving me good training. Good training as it's a hard circuit, and I was making my timing faster and faster. I got up, or should I say down to below 24 minutes (less than 6 minutes per mile) per run.

During the time I was waiting to get processed, Trevor was waiting for the next full-time recruit cadre to come up. He got dates for the full-time course before I got any word back form the recruitment Corporal about my cadre! During this time, I had many second thoughts. Could I go to work early the next morning, after having done a nights patrolling until 3 in the morning? Will it take away some of my freedom at weekends, as I might have to go in and train/patrol or whatever? Would this change me? (typical? given time, doubts seep in) lots of questions.

Added to that, after a two or three months, the 'B' Company recruitment Corporal, got in touch with me saying that 'B' Company (Lisburn) is full, and whilst I would still be in 11th Battalion, I will be in a different company, in a different town and County. It was Portadown, where they need men. Well, that was another spanner in the works. Taking so much of my time on duty, and hours travelling to and from Portadown. Could I handle it? Trev said that Frankie (another friend, a couple of years older than us, but a good friend of Trevor's) was also joining, and he was going to Portadown also, only he'd just got word of his dates for joining (and I haven't yet). I decided to not pull out, but to join, and if I didn't like it, or can't hack it, I can always leave!

I got word to come in on a Saturday morning, to Thiepval Barracks, Lisburn, to do quick tests, and complete paperwork, such as my name, age and personal details.

I went in, and was nervous, didn't know what to expect. On entering Thiepval Barracks, there were so many soldiers walking about, and in Land Rovers, going to the Naafi. It was a different world here. Imagine! Just a couple of hundred yards away from Lisburn, where civvies, normal people, going about life and not thinking of the troubles, army, and here I am, feeling like I am in a foreign place, with so many English people. It feels like I'm in England.

From the guard room I got brought up to 'B' Company lines, where I saw others coming for the tests. I stayed silent, and didn't talk to anyone else. I didn't know what to say! One of them came up to me and started to chat. I chatted back, but kept the conversion short, as I had my mind more focused into what would come first. The fella chatting to me I got to know later, as he was on the same recruit course as me, and the same Company. He became known as 'whitie' (nicknames, I'll come onto later).

When we were waiting there, there were soldiers from 'B' Company walking back and forth by us, in and out. They were carrying SLR's, which looked very long and thin, and looked different without the magazine attached (I was used to seeing one on my Action Man (were the barrel normally got broken. Lol)).

We were all brought into a room in the main 'B'Company Building, with tables, and on them – paperwork. The tests were quite simple and quick. Maths, English, and another form asking for more information about me, like health, fitness and allergies. We were all finished quite quickly, and then I was back in civvie world.

I immediately drove to Trev's house and told him all that has happened. He said not to think about it. Easier said than done. I just have to wait. Trev got onto his full-time course, in the first few months of 1987, Frankie also got onto the part-time recruitment cadre around the same time.

Just after Frankie got recruited, I got word that everything was great. I was to come up to Portadown on 21st May to take the Oath of Allegiance to the Queen. I asked if that meant I've joined, or do I have to wait more? The recruitment Corporal said I was provisionally in, attached to a Company, until I have passed the recruitment course. I can go to training on Tuesday, or Thursday evenings, and maybe if there is a Company training weekend, I might be able to join in on a Saturday, or sometimes during any Company/Batallion training. He never gave me much information, just in case he got the facts wrong. As he was in 'B' Company in Lisburn, and never knew all the facts of what goes on in Portadown Companies.

I am really looking forward to what lies ahead.

When 21st May came Frankie was already in, and Tuesday 21st was luckily a training night, and he was going in that evening. Frankie said he would give me a lift in and a lift home again after the training. I was excited, and at the same time anxious. When the evening came, Frankie collected me about 6:30pm (1830hrs army time) and we travelled in. It seemed a long drive, and I knew that I couldn't find my way to Mahon Road, Portadown, if left to my own devices. We were on the M1 for quite some time, going past a few junctions, slipping off at junction 11 towards Armagh, and then came along what Frankie called 'Northway' which I later found out, was actually called 'The Northway'. Then round a roundabout, up another main road, under a foot bridge, and immediately after that, we come off that road onto a slip road, up onto another road, turned left, and then along another road (how on earth will I ever remember this ?). At the end of that road we staggered across to another road (when will this stop, where will it end?), then I saw it, and Frankie pointed it out. Mahon Road Barracks.

We drove up to the front gate, where Frankie showed his I.D. Card (Mod.90), and we entered. We pulled up to the left, just beside the guard room. We both went in, where Frankie signed in, and I signed in also, but I never signed in on the UDR signing in book, but signed in as a visitor, as I wasn't yet in.

We then went up to the Company Lines ('D' Company). It will be another half an hour or so, before I had to go to the C.O.'s Office to meet the Battalion C.O. and swear my 'Oath of Allegiance'. Frankie introduced me to one or two people in the company, when we entered.

I couldn't understand. The company building was a portacabin (well two or three joined together). But the UDR Regiment has been so well established, or should I say, going for so long. Why didn't they have a big army red brick building, like in Thiepval barracks? And there were other sets of joined portacabins outside the main drill square, on two sides. Frankie told me one was 'E' Company, one was 'A' Company, and down there (pointing to the bottom of the road, as 'F' Company, a new full-time company, which Trev was now in. Are these temporary buildings whilst a new 'big block' was to be built?

I felt so nervous. Wasn't sure what to say to each person Frankie introduced me to. It was a training night, so everyone was getting changed into uniform, and getting on with things. Frankie got into uniform also, and when it was time, led me to the main battalion HQ building, which was a modern type angular roofed building, that is pebble dashed. We went along a corridor, up the stairs, and along a better kept corridor, to an office, the Battalion Adjutant's office. We stood for a while. Not long, but it felt ages to me, until the Battalion Adjutant came out and invited me into his office. Frankie saluted him and let me know he'd see me back in the lines (Company lines that is).

The adjutant welcomed me in, and explained that I'd see the Battalion Commanding Officer (C.O.) and he'd take my oath. An easy task, and I could go back down to the company lines, I asked if I'd get a uniform tonight. He said I don't think so, probably another night soon, when the clothing store was open. I felt good about that, as it was as good as saying that I was in!

I went into the C.O.'s office, which was a casual time. I wasn't marched in or anything like that. He chatted to me thanking me for joining the UDR, and that it was a good regiment to join, and a great battalion. The Op's, training, and future is good, and we are doing so much for the country. I took my oath of allegiance; I received my army number. He then thanked me and said to return to your company lines.

I walked back to the Company lines, taking in so much. Once back in 'D' Company lines, I sat chatting to a few others in the platoon room (16 Platoon), waiting for Frankie to finish training. They were doing weapon handling training, and had been doing it in another room of the company lines. I thought they'd be in a different building (One for the weapons training?). Frankie was a member of 16 Platoon.

The platoon commander greeted me, welcomed me, and invited me to come along for all the training nights, until my recruits course started. He said every Tuesday and Thursday night is training nights, and we'll see about weekends? I asked if I can come on Thursday and asked about uniform issue. He said 'Oh Yes! Hopefully get your uniform on Thursday, or maybe next Tuesday?'

That night and the following training night, I got to see the barracks a little more. Past the guard room to the left was a 25meter outdoor range, with a heli-pad very near it. Frankie had already talked about the heli-pad before I had been to the barracks; as on the 8th May, he was sent down to guard it. That night there was a helicopter coming in. Frankie thought it may be royalty of some important politician, but it turned out to be something far different. It was the helicopter, that the S.A.S. was using. That night was the night of the Loughgall Police station shootout, where it was attacked by the IRA ASU (Active Service Unit). But unknown to the IRA, there was a Section of S.A.S. Soldiers waiting on them. They waited until the IRA started attacking the station, with the intent of destroying the Police station, and taking police officers lives.

The S.A.S received no loss of life. The IRA lost 9 of its members that evening.

The IRA thought they were going to be as successful in their attack, as they were on 11th August 1986, when they attacked the Birches Police Station. The IRA's motive is to destroy remote R.U.C. Stations, and prevent anyone from rebuilding them. Create no-go areas. The IRA did destroy the Birches R.U.C. Station, and it was never rebuilt. The Loughgall Police Station attack was different! Different in that the IRA not only wanted to destroy the station, but also murder those who are inside, at time of attack!

Frankie was saying that the helicopter came in, and quite a few S.A.S. men jumped out, leaving their weapons onboard the Puma Helicopter. They then went up to the Sergeants mess, for a well done mission, debrief, and to rehydrate.

On the Thursday the following week (after my meeting with the C.O.), I went across to the main building, the clothing store (well! I never went alone, other soldiers from 16 platoon needed some clothing changed) I got One complete uniform (I'd get a second after I have passed the recruits course). At the time I was below 10 stone (quite skinny), and the uniform seemed to be hanging off me (it soon become my nickname 'Raggy Doll'). I kept the uniform on, and returned to the lines. That night I met the Company Commander, who took me into the office, chatted about the process in front of me. I asked if I was to be in 16 Platoon, and he said he would find out. Have to see which platoons need the manpower.

That evening I was told "when you join the UDR, you join for life", I thought that was meant in the context of threats and risks to my life from the IRA!

I was in the middle of joining a company that is based in Portadown, Co. Armagh (The Orchard County). It sounds like a country place, all nice and peaceful. But in fact Portadown Co. Armagh is in the notorious 'murder triangle'. Portadown, Craigavon and Banbridge.

The area of responsibility for the Portadown Battalion Companies, is Lisburn ('B' Coy), Portadown ('E' Coy), Lurgan/ Craigavon ('C' Coy), Banbridge ('D' Coy).

The area covered by 'D' Company is Dromore to Dromara to Loughbrickland to Tandragee to Markethill, to Loughgall to Aghalee, and back to Hillsborough. The area covered by each company is called 'Tactical Area of Responsibility' (T.A.O.R.).

The risk and threat doesn't seem to be annoying me? I am now starting to feel part of something, it is this feeling my heart wants and has been yearning for. I am starting to feel, like I belong here, here in the army.

Training on Tuesday and Thursday evenings? The company always had training every Tuesday and Thursday evening. One of the platoon's (there is three) would be operational each evening, and so, the other two platoons can be training. The training program, would be decided by the Company and Headquarters, into what training the Company/Battalion needs to be updated, renewed. Or a new training objective, new tactics and new equipment.

I was able to come in Tuesdays and Thursdays, as my recruitment course was a month away. I was also allowed to come in for training weekends the company had on, but there were none before my recruit's course.

I was able, and did come in to help when there was a company 'Camp Guard Weekend'. Company camp guard?

During the week, the UDR full-time companies looked after security of the Mahon Road Barracks, but from Friday evening 2000hrs, until Sunday Night 2359Hrs, a part-time company looked after the barracks. I got to come in, not as an active soldier, but to help out, with CCTV's, the front desk and administration.

One Saturday I came in for a training day with the company. We were being trained on the Wynthrope Theory of finding IRA Hides in a field.

The Wynthrope Theory? It's where the IRA would hide weapons, moving from and to a bigger hide. Hides? What are they? Well, the IRA have lots of weaponry, and very few know where they are. If more people knew where they are, then during interviews/interrogation, the suspect would give it away and so lose all the weapons in the big hide. There are only one or two IRA personnel in each area knew of where the 'hide' is.

If the IRA wants to use a weapon for an attack, then The CQMS of the IRA, would go and get it from the main hide, and move it to a transit hide, which probably will be waterproof and concealed. Later that day or week, a 'Player' (the name we give to persons that are in Paramilitary organizations) would come visit that hide, move the weapon/munitions to a further transit hide – for the attack! Another player would be instructed to get it from that transit hide, and leave it somewhere else. The player conducting the hit, would collect it from the last hide, carry-out the attack and soon after, leave it back to the 'hide', or perhaps another 'hide' to be collected later. It might not be a gun, but could be a UVBT (under vehicle booby trap) to be planted under a car that belongs or is used by an off-duty police officer, judge, or UDR man. After the hit (being a shooting). After the incident has blown over, and things cool off, someone will collect it from there, and leave it to the next transit hide. Later, it will be collected from there, and perhaps left into another transit hide. Eventually taken back to the main hide.

If any Player is caught in these movements, no matter how hard the interview/interrogation is, the player knows nothing of any other chain of players and attacks. They were only given the one task. Lift it from – bring it to.

The place that is the last in line for attack is probably, just the weapon pushed into the middle of a hedge, or under a wall, behind a door, but the 'transit hides' (where a rifle/pistol is held) The weapon may be there for days/weeks, is quite often was a piece of plastic 'soil pipe' (just like the pipe that takes water from your household toilet) dug into the ground, with the lid on it. These items can be purchased from a hardware store, without suspicion. A soil pipe about a meter long? With two stop ends.

That is the type of hide we were being trained how to spot (some years later I actually found one, of which I will talk later about). In order to catch the terrorist, we had to think like the terrorist. How will a man know where a hide is? If the player is to lift a weapon, and take it elsewhere. The hide has to be located. The player will be told to go to a certain spot, look for a prominent object, and maybe from that object/prominent building or tree, look at something else, and the hide is 2' away from it. E.g. Go to a gateway opposite the farmhouse lane at No.? on ? road. Look into the field and see a dead oak tree, look to the left, and see a disused yellow wheelbarrow, and the hide is 3' to the left, below the blackthorn hedge.

Anyway, back to the Saturday training day. We got a classroom lesson on this, and then it came to doing a practical exercise for the training. The Company PSI (Permanent Staff Instructor) had put in a 'Training Hide' in a field, not far outside the barracks. Of course, the PSI had consulted with the farmer of a disused field.

We got our equipment, loaded the Land Rovers and left the barracks. Travel about a mile or so to this field. We were outside the barracks! So we had to be armed. We had to have loaded rifles. I was trained up with the weapon handling drills, but shouldn't be out of the barracks, and shouldn't have a loaded rifle on me.

But because of the treats, the company let me take my rifle, load it with a full magazine, and go out training with the rest of the company. Imagine that? I haven't passed my recruitment course yet, but I am 'out' on the ground.

It is amazing the trust and comradeship within the company. And I am now part of them!

Weeks have passed, and the recruits course is here. It takes place in the battalion barracks where you will be placed, as each battalion, has slightly different training, as to the roles, patrols, and tactics of that area. It will last 1 & ½ weeks. From Friday evening, through the week, and pass out on Saturday. You may ask why one and half weeks? As regular army is at least 6 months? There are lots of reasons for this! We have a regular job, and to take any more time off isn't possible for everyone, and if we were to take any more time from work, workmates and others will start to question why, and knowledge of an individual joining the Ulster Defence Regiment will become more known.

Because it is such a short space of time, we are not brought down to basics, as in a Regular Army recruitment course. As in learning to wash yourself, washing and ironing clothes.

We are also not taught everything that a regular soldier is trained in and for, like grenades, missiles, and generally G3 Warfare training (modern open warfare). We are of course trained in general soldiering, but mainly in 'terrorist warfare' that we will be operating in. This short recruit course may be short, but is a bit like doing a driving test. We are taught everything to make us operational, safe, secure, and how to do our duties. But to learn patrol tactics, soldiering in the 'internal security' theatre, you couldn't learn until you are actually out on operations. Like a driving test? You don't really learn how to drive until you have passed the driving test, and are out on the road. Like the driving test, where you have been practicing driving before the test, but learn proper driving after.

Before the recruits course we are provisionally taught weapon handling, a bit of fieldcraft, signals, first aid, so when we join the recruit cadre, we are not green (in knowledge), and hit the ground running.

We all came in to Mahon Road Barracks on the Friday evening (23rd July). Looked on the notice board in training-wing, where there was a few sheets of paper, with our names. We found out which billet each of us was staying, what team each potential soldier is in, and the names of everyone in each training team.

We had to quickly dump our kit on our bed, get changed into combats, and go to the main hall for 'introduction'. There were normally about 30 recruits on each course, and one or two recruit courses per year. The manpower turnover rate was quite high. Some soldiers perhaps only staying in for a few months, as they don't like it. Some for a year or so, and some stayed for decades.

We went into the hall, for welcome, introduction, and information of what the recruits course entailed. That was reasonably short and to the point, and straight after, went from there into another smaller hall. This time we got a Full Lecture on threats, risks, and what can happen. We got shown very graphic pictures of some of the bombs and Incidents, which have killed troops. Such as The Warrenpoint bomb of 1979, where 18 British soldiers lost their lives. During the time when we are shown the very graphical pictures (nothing hidden or censored), one of the recruits got up, and said quite loudly "I don't need any of this shit. I'm not signing up to get blown away" and stormed out. We all looked around each other in disbelief, saying to each other 'what fuckin country is he living in? Where has he been for the last 20 years?"

The recruitment cadre and training revolved around 'Op Banner'

Op Banner. It is the operational name for the British Armed Forces operation in Northern Ireland from 1969.

At the start of 'The Troubles' areas of Northern Ireland became Military State, but that shouldn't happen! It can't happen! As there is no official war on. This might start a 'Civil War', and the Press will have a field day if it continued. So the government had to hand back 'control' to the Police (RUC), in which the British Army assisted them in the mission to restore peace. This mission was to be called 'Op Banner'. And in that way, it isn't a military state, but the army helping out the RUC in keeping civil peace.

And also, the army cannot do whatever they want, or feel they need to. It has to be sanctioned by the local government and the RUC. On each recruitment course, We learn about our role, the UDR's role, and what we could do to help/assist the RUC and government.

We also learn about the 'cards' we lawfully have to carry on our person whilst out on the ground on operations. Like the yellow card, green card, blue card and others (all about the size of a regular playing card).

Mainly 'the yellow card'. It is the most important card we carry. It is, as I mentioned, about the size of a regular playing card, and on it was the 'Rules of Engagement'.

It changed every now and again, as new jurisdictions/incidents give questions on the use of lethal-force

It gives guidance on when and if we must open fire, use lethal force on a person. We went through numerous scenarios, and get questioned as to whether we could use lethal force in each scenario or incident. The bottom line is – we cannot use lethal force, unless there is no other way to stop a person/persons endangering someone's life, and ONLY when someone's life is endangered, and there is no other way to stop it.

I will give you a scenario where we will be questioned. The scenario is played out in front of the recruits. An actor (soldier) dressed in combats, with a balaclava on, holding a AK47 type rifle, comes in. He is carrying the rifle by his side. We are questioned 'Can you Shoot HIM?'. The answer is 'NO' as he does not pose any threat to life at this point, if challenged "Army! Stop or I will shoot!", he might stop, and do what he is told? He might be just carrying a weapon to another person, or perhaps he found this weapon, and is trying to find a security force member to hand it into? Can't shoot! If he is carrying it holding the pistol grip, with butt in shoulder (the actor showing the stance/walk). Can we shoot? NO! there is still no threat to life. If challenged in this scenario, he turns and lifts the rifle. Can You Shoot? NO! or is that a YES! No, as he hasn't yet pointed the rifle in our direction, and there is still time to further challenge him? Or YES, as there is only split seconds before he swings the rifle towards us/me, and if I do not take action now? Mine or others' lives will be in danger! If this man fires a burst of shoots at your patrol, then turns and runs away (actor acting!) can you shoot? Some of the recruits say YES we can IF? He has hit/injured/killed any members of our patrol or public! But the answer is 'No' with a capital 'N'. It matters not whether he has missed, killed one, or killed and injured many! 'the threat' has passed – he is no longer a threat, but if he is running towards a cover position, and might continue to engage us? Discussions and training on the yellow-card, right to shoot, isn't just for the recruit course, it is constantly trained throughout each year, in classroom and training areas.

I believe we (UDR/Royal Irish) are the best trained regiment in the world, into when/when not to use lethal force (through training and practice)

During my service years I found various 'yellow' cards from different years, and you can see the changes. The 1978 version states that you can use lethal force on someone 'about to plant, or planting a bomb', the later version states 'someone planting a bomb', then in later years 'detonating, or about to detonate a bomb'

Weapons Handling Tests (WHT's)

Mainly we got trained/tested on the SLR Rifle and Browning 9mm pistol.

These are the two firearms we are to be carrying on operations in Northern Ireland

The SLR rifle is the main rifle used in the British Army. We get trained and tested on all the weapon handling drills. Stripping down the rifle, cleaning, and how to clean each part, reassembling the rifle, and then loading, unloading, stoppage drills and carriage of the rifles. Most of us already knew most of the drill, as we were taught within each company as our pre-course training. One of the hardest parts of the SLR handling, was the cocking (making ready) of the rifle. The cocking handle was very hard to pull back, and I'd heard of a few men failing the recruits course, because they couldn't cock the SLR!

The Browning 9mm pistol. It's the standard pistol used by the British Army, but what I didn't know was that it wasn't a regular weapon in the regular regiments. The pistol is mainly carried by officers, and special forces. It is the UDR's alternative weapon, as all ranks used it. Perhaps on escort duties, protection duties, and of course off duty, as in personal protection (not everyone got them, or wanted them)

During the recruits cadre We are taught fieldcraft, battlefield first aid, physical exercise (lots of that), signals (as in basic radio use), patrol drills, Northern Ireland laws, our roles, and roles of the RUC. LOL and of course marching, and drill.

With signals (radio) and first aid training, we are taught in readiness of a 'contact' (when the terrorist attacks us, IED's (Improvised Explosive Device) or shooting). In signals we are taught how to put through a 'contact report'. This scenario is if your Team Commander gets knocked out, and you are nearest to the radio, and so – it is up to you to give the ops room an immediate contact report. Example: "Hello Zero (the ops room) this is Tango Two One Bravo ('D' Company, second platoon, first Section, second Team) CONTACT (make that important) Scarva Street (location) shooting (type of contact) one casualty, The other team is going in depth. OVER (finishing my piece of conversation)". It's not as in-depth an 'immediate contact report' as a team or Section Commander would give, as a Commander will give more detail, and send teams in depth to kill or capture the terrorist/s, request other agencies such as Nightsun (helicopter with searchlight), ATO (ammunition technical officer (bomb squad)), QRF (quick reaction force) and others depending upon the incident. We (the private soldier) just need to send enough information, The ops room will choreograph the rest. First aid, we are taught to expect the worst. Leg getting blown off, shot through the chest where a lung is shot. All the training throughout the week is so packed together, and is all, to train us for the Northern Ireland theatre.

We had to pass them all, in order to pass the recruitment course, to become operational. Especially weapon handling, and shooting tests. During the week, we were brought down to Ballykinler a couple of times, for practice, and qualifying tests.

When we swore allegiance, we were getting paid when we came in for training duties. We were all grade 4 soldiers.

On the recruits course, we all did grade 3 training, and tests. So when we left recruitment, we all are qualified grade 3 soldiers. We wouldn't be moved to grade 3 or paid as grade 3 until 6 months of signing-on. To go further into grade 2, will take another year, and you had to have passed all the tests of that grade, to achieve that grade. grade 1 will be a further year after getting grade 2 promotion. I achieved grade 1 about a year before I technically should have, as I was passing the tests with grade 1 grades even when I was a grade 3 soldier.

With regards to weapon training and range work, I never knew this, or never thought of it! But the UDR got so much 7.62 & 9mm ammunition (for the SLR & Browning hi-power). It got far more than any other regular regiments, as we were constantly in patrol state, constantly on operations. We were never in training state. Yes! Of course we did train (constantly). But our main role was OPS, on patrol, protecting the country and people.

During my/our recruits course we made lots of friends, or came to know everyone, and bumped into them during your service years, or perhaps in civvie street. Funny enough, during the training week, we were doing physical training. We were in pairs (random) running back and forth across the drill square carrying your partner in a fireman's lift. I was partnered up with Honey Monster (who would become a very close friend and shooting team mate, a few years later). I was about 9½ Stone, and Honey Monster about 16. Well? When I was carrying Honey Monster across the drill square, my legs were buckling under me. I was determined not to let it beat me! But within common deductions, I was about to crumble! Honey Monster came up with the plan! He carried me across, put me down. Then I run around him (looking like we are changing), and Honey Monster carried me back again. The DS Staff never noticed, but I felt bad about giving Honey Monster all the work (he was very happy about it, as I was quite light). This reminds me of Sammy (18 Platoon) during our service years. His left eye didn't have great sight, and may fail the regular annual health tests? But he beat it! When reading the eye chart with his right eye, he covered his left eye, with his left hand, and when it came to reading the eye chart with his left eye, he lowered his left hand, then raised his right hand, and covered the same left eye. The MO (Medical Officer) never ever caught on!

Before the recruits course, my dad (Andy) was against me joining, for a few reasons, and had said he would not be attending my 'passing-out' parade on the Saturday. But surprisingly (to me) my mum, dad and sister attended, and stayed for the refreshments after. He actually bought quite a few UDR items (like mugs, UDR Crest, and UDR tie). I was so proud he was there, as I wasn't looking forward to a future, were he wasn't happy with my decision to join the UDR.

2

Threats: Life Being UDR

As soon as we took the Oath of Allegiance to Queen and Country, we were a target of terrorist organizations. Our lives have changed whether we like it or not. We were under threat. The Regiment over the years learnt and were constantly learning how to minimize the threat.

Perhaps 'minimize the threat' was not the correct term to use, as the threat was always high. We learnt lessons throughout the years of how to ensure we maintained a low profile and not stand out, changing habits, places we went, to make us difficult to target and attack.

I must not divulge that I am in the UDR (outside close friends and family), for fear that someone might disclose it, the information be overheard, and passed onto the "wrong people".

Don't stand out! We were not permitted to wear any part of our uniform when coming into duty, or leaving the barracks. When carrying kit/uniform, don't carry it in a service kit-bag., Never have the MOD90 (Army ID Card) easy to see in your wallet, always have it behind other cards, or in a separate pocket in the wallet. Don't purchase a car that is easily identifiable, making it easy to spot, easy to follow, and if your car was out of the ordinary - it could be noted either entering or leaving the barracks or Police Station.

A few months after passing the recruits course, Paul, who joined on the same recruit cadre as I was in, had a picture taken in his civilian workplace. It was a group photo that had the small workforce out the front of the business premises. However the photo had come to the attention of the headquarters of our company. Paul was pulled into the Sergeant Major's office, and given a right bollocking. Why? It's not like you couldn't be in a picture? And some pictures do, from time to time, get into a paper! It was the way Paul was standing! He was standing 'At Ease'. He most probably didn't realize that he had done it, as it had become so natural to stand 'At Ease'. When on duty or training (which most times was during our standard army week).

Whilst on duty (ops or trg) we would get told off for standing slouched, hand in pocket or leaning up against a wall, and this got inbuilt, and you automatically stood up straight, sometimes at a rigid ease. I still do to this day, as I learned to stand 'At ease' over the years for hours and hours, and it became natural, relaxed. You know you're not going to get rebuked for it (whilst on duty). But off-duty! This position got you noticed, and in the workplace picture, Paul did stand out!

In order not to get spotted and targeted we must ensure to stay invisible to the enemy or their sympathisers. Going on and off duty, we were not permitted to wear any part of our uniform. This wasn't strange to us, as we were told as soon as we signed the dotted line, but it was so alien to us, when we went over to the mainland, a Garrison town, and saw men and women walking, driving along the streets, wearing their uniforms, and strangest of all – unarmed.

In the rest of the world, one is proud to be in the Military, as I am, the difference being that I am not allowed to show it. We were not allowed to display pictures of recruit course, winning team, or any other proud moments from our army life.

We were told (from the start) that if we wanted to hang pictures, medals and awards - make a shrine in your attic. Make a room there for them, and go and worship them whenever you want, but don't put them on show.

My friend and colleague Nigel went to the cinema in Belfast. On his way in, he got patted down by the security guard on the door. He felt Nigel's ppw, and asked if he was authorised to carry this? Nigel replied 'yes' and continued on through. Nigel got a bad feeling! He and his friend bought tickets for the cinema, and went in to watch the film. The previews and advertisements came on, and just before the film started, Nigel's feeling got a hold on him. He told his friend, and they both got up, and left.

Nigel found out the next day, that the doorman had contacted the IRA, and they quickly got an ASU (active service unit) set up, got guns, and were coming over to kill him. Luckily for him, he left before they had arrived.

This was how we should feel and act. Using our sixth sense. We had to be totally aware of everything going on around us, whether on or off duty.

Talking about uniform, we were told not to dry any part of the uniform on the outside washing-line. Someone could see it, pass information back to a Player. Once again, if anyone entered our house (reading the electric meter etc) there couldn't be any symbols, photos or emblems on show. Those things meant we couldn't show how proud we were, and what we had achieved. Northern Ireland must be one of the only countries in the world where we can't wear our uniform in public, show off the achievements we have made in our service (photos, trophies, medals), and no one gives us compliments, or thanks for our service.

In the house, in addition to being prohibited from hanging up trophies, we had to be that extra bit secure, as we knew home, was where most of the attacks on our lives would happen. Close the curtains before switching on the light (this minimized being shot through the window).

If I switched on the lights in the room, that would alert the gunman to get ready, as I'll be at the window anytime now to close the curtains. But if I close the curtains first, the gunman would not see me coming, then I (the target) am covered. No clear shot!

Out on the streets, walk like you belong. Be not utterly clean and well shaven, but look standard, slightly slouched, and look nothing like a soldier. Don't set patterns, like going shopping to the same shops/supermarkets on daily or weekly rota. Alter social places such as pub or coffee shops. Vary your timings and locations.

Although for us part-timers, we couldn't vary one aspect – work, workplace, and timings. We had to be vigilant, check under the car, look out for any oddities when coming or going, be ready to react.

In the car. Don't regularly use the same routes, vary routes, and keep watch for suspicious vehicles parked or following you. Look out for someone watching you as you are on the final few hundred meters away from work or home. Don't always drive straight home. Park beside a house a little away from yours. Switch off headlights (if urban area) a street away, so it's hard to monitor you. Take off seatbelt a few hundred meters away, so you can react and debus from the car. If carrying a ppw (personal protection weapon), know where it is, how to draw and use, know where to hide it.

Anywhere. Always have 'actions-on'.

For instance: Actions on a car tailing me. Don't drive home, as it'll show where I live, try to get the VRN of the car following. Drive around, different roads that you know and the following car will get tired and break away. 'action-on' someone standing about near your home or work. Get good description of the 'dicker' what he's wearing, times and location. Action-on getting attacked when you are getting out of the car at home. Know whereabouts on your body you have your ppw. Have in your mind where to run to (defence or attack positions), have follow up plans made as well. Is it only one gunman? Is there a second accomplice, a car, am I going to get a second attack? So many actions-on. Actions-on throughout the full day, for everything! I/we have to stay alert, be on our pins for something happening. Our lives depend on this. And hopefully we can foil/kill or capture the Terrorist.

These are only some, of the threats whilst off duty. On-duty is a different level of threats. Threats to the section, team or individual soldier. We have to be ready for any form of attack. I have to be ready for any form of attack. From the life-threatening physical attacks, to the simple verbal attacks.

On a personal level whilst on duty, I carry my SA80 rifle sling in the closed position, but I always (even when training or on the range) have my sling not pulled in, not tightened, so I can put it in my shoulder, use it without the sling being released. I carry my torch (that I am using on patrol), at VCP's in my left hand, right hand is on the pistol grip on the rifle. On the torch! I carry it with the body of it out the top of my fist instead of the bulb. That way I can use the torch as a truncheon, or throw it if needed. When on foot patrol, I switch off 'The safety catch' on my rifle. This sounds dangerous, but I still have to cock the rifle, aim it, and squeeze off the trigger. I know through training exercises, that whilst in the heat of 'the contact' it is so easy to, cock the rifle, rifle into the shoulder, aim, squeeze the trigger, and trigger does not squeeze? The safety catch is still ON! By the time I release the safety, go to squeeze the trigger again, the danger has passed, and in those brief seconds, either myself or another could have been killed.

On patrol we have to be as unpredictable as possible. Foot patrol when the terrorist may think we should be mobile, mobile while they think we're on foot. When driving down a road – just stop, turn, and go a different direction. As well as being unpredictable, we have to guess/predict what is ahead of us. Will it be easy going?, verbal abuse?, stoning?, petrol bombs, whatever? That sounds like we have abusive operations/patrols the majority of times. In fact, the majority of our ops, we have very little trouble, and if we saw some ahead, we tried to avoid it, but the threat was always there.

As the IRA said to Maggie Thatcher "You have to be lucky every time! But we only have to be lucky once"

I have to put the threat/risk into some sort of prospective. The UDR has full-time soldiers, but we were part-time soldiers, with day jobs. No! We are not reserve forces, but regular soldiers. Our serial numbers have the same prefix, our rank, courses, are in the same arena as a regular British Soldier, but we were a greater threat to the terrorist as we lived in the same towns/areas as them. During the day when at work, we still used our eyes and ears to spot 'players' (terrorist suspects, or associates), where they were, who they were with. Time location, and added information. We passed this info onto the Int-Cell, for them to form a bigger picture. In effect, we were 24hrs on duty (not many people knew – we were under military law 24 hours a day). The downside to this, was that the terrorists wanted to kill us even more, and we set normal life patterns, which meant it gave them more opportunity to kill us, like timings of going to work and coming home. They were mainly set times, most of us can not vary.

So, we have timings of going to and from work, timings of going to and from the barracks (during the week, there is a pattern, of how many times we went in, and it was similar timings).

There was also the pattern of 'haunts', such as shops, churches, collecting family members, pubs, clubs and people we see. In this world we had to be so stringent, added to that was now – to vary our timings as much as we can. Vary our routes to and from work, to and from the barracks. Not only that, but we had to be aware that we could be attacked, most likely, just before we arrive at work, home or wherever else we might be going. We had to think of 'actions on' if we were attacked. For instance I took off my seatbelt, when about 500m from home, so I could disperse from the car if attacked.

The threats would not cease, even if and when we leave the regiment!

3

In the UDR

I passed the Recruitment Course. I had my passing-out parade on the Saturday, and as unbelievable as it sounds, I can go on duty, out on patrol from the Sunday on!

It was at the start of the week when I took my first patrol.

Patrol evenings routines usually flow like:

Around 1800hrs to 1900hrs, everyone arrived at the barracks for duty. As soon as you enter the front gate of Mahon Road Barracks, you stop, and go into the guard room, where there is sign on/off books for each company.

We sign on with name, rank, time and reason for duty (ops, trg or admin). Then go up to your company's building (company lines), and get changed into combats or training gear for the duty ahead.

Quite often the Patrol 2IC (second in charge) would already be in, circulating, gathering names of who was on ops that night. The Patrol Commander was getting the patrol orders ready, and gathering information from the ops room and Int-Cell, of anything to be added or changed in the patrol, and establishing if Int-Cell needed us to look out, or do a task for them.

After getting changed, we head down, in ones or twos to the armoury, to sign out rifles and ammunition (each of us had his own personal issue SLR, and we get issued each ops duty with

30 rounds of ammunition and two magazines). It's a process of walking down, around the back of the guardroom, guard rest room, and through a fenced off area of the armouries (full-time & part-time), and through the heavy door of our armoury, not inside the actual armoury, just into the room which the two armouries are. In turn we sign our name, number, firearm type, serial number of the firearm (you get to remember your own rifle number quite quickly), 2 magazines, and 30 rounds (20 ball, 10 tracer). We load the rounds into the two magazines on the benches that are on two walls of the room. The magazines are to be loaded, 2 ball rounds 1 tracer, which gives the top round in each magazine a tracer. How do we know it is a 'tracer'? the tip bit of the projectile (bullet) is coated in red, indicating that it is a tracer round (phosphorus, and will light up red after around 50 meters from leaving the muzzle). After loading mags, and putting out slings onto the rifle. We then go back up to the company lines and find out which team you were in for tonight's patrol.

Our ops nights were usually a patrol of 8 to 10 soldiers (1 section, made up of 2 teams, 4 or 5 soldiers per team), and we used 2 Land Rovers.

The rank and make up of a patrol was - Section Commander (full-Corporal), and his team consisting of : a driver, normally 1 Greenfinch (female soldier) and 2 more soldiers in the back. The second team was a team Commander (Lance Corporal), driver, and 2 or 3 soldiers in the back. If we had an RUC man out on Patrol with us, he was normally added to the first team.

When returning to the company lines, the patrol 2IC (the Lance-Corporal) usually made out the list of teams, who was in charge of which team, the drivers, soldiers in each team, who was carrying which bit of kit (if needed), and any other relevant information.

By this time, the selected drivers (it's normally the usual soldiers who drive!) would normally have already gone to the company Stores and got a work ticket for the Land Rover.

A 'work ticket' was a hard plastic green folder which had the land rover keys and documentation in it. The driver signed for the 'work-ticket' of the vehicle, got a Sergeant or above to countersign, completed a POL check (petrol, oil & lubricants) of the Land Rover, and filled the petrol tanks if necessary.

The driver then knew the vehicle was ok to take us on patrol. Then, after getting the work ticket, he lifted two seats from the store. One for himself, and one for the commander. Yes! the seats! In the front and back of the land rover, there were just seat frames. The back cushions are there, but not the seats. They were kept in the company store.

Normally each company had soldiers on duty throughout the day. Some will POL and fill the Land Rovers that were being used later, and complete any checks needed, perhaps bringing them over to the M.T. (military transport) to be repaired. This saved time for the designated drivers on the next patrol. Although the driver will still have to do his POL checks, as it's his responsibility, and if during the patrol the Rover runs out of juice? The driver is to blame, as he must not have carried out the checks.

Once they have completed the POL check, then they drive the two Rovers over to the company stores (at the back of our company lines) for the relevant team members to load the patrol kit.

The documentation (work-ticket) is changed on monthly basis, and each evening/day the driver would put his name on the next line, date, (a Sgt or above has to sign it to allow the driver to use it), times and dates starting, miles on the mileometer, and at the end of the night, finish time.

Everything flowed quite quickly. As soon as we (the soldiers that are in the back of each L/Rover) have returned to 'the lines' from the armoury, the patrol Land Rovers would be sitting near the company stores, for us to load. Quite often, the designated drivers would be away at this point to get their own rifles, this keeps the conveyor belt operation of the evening moving quite fast.

The general patrol kit needed, was signed for by the team commanders. It consisted of two back seats for the land rover (2 wide cushions (plastic-type leather type covers)), a large basket (it's a large bread basket you would see in a typical 'bread delivery van' that holds lots of loaves of bread). In this basket: A call-trap (large square steel box, containing scissor-action of hollow steel pins to puncture tyres, making then flat quite instantly), 2 borollic torches (handheld box torch, that had three colour filters. This torch will be used to stop the traffic at V.C.P.'s (Vehicle Check Points) One to use, one spare, 2 right angle torches (hand held small torches (2 x A batteries)) for the team commander, and whoever is 'the chatter' at the checkpoint, calling the cars in, and checking them, A large Red 'Stop, Checkpoint, Headlights Off' sign, fire extinguisher, Land Rover jack & wrench, 2 x yellow blinkers (as you would often see, on roadworks, or lane closures

We would normally have one Greenfinch on each patrol, and she would kindly put together a 'Tea-Break Kit', consisting of two hot water flasks, tea bags, instant coffee, sugar, tin of condensed milk, army issue bickies, and if we were lucky, she made a few sandwiches. It was one of those tasks that never got 'thanks' but were always appreciated.

Greenfinches? Our female soldiers. The UDR was the first army regiment to have female soldiers in an operational role (1973). Although they were unarmed (until the SA80 came along) they were an integral part of our patrols. When on 'the ground' (out on patrol) the Greenfinches (normally one per patrol) would do much of the radio work, they helped at checkpoints by doing 'scribe' (paperwork for each vehicle being searched), if we needed a woman searched, and help in lots of other areas. In the barracks? She would help in the ops-room.

Whilst the Rovers were being loaded by each team, the team commanders prepared everything else that they would need, including documentation for the patrol, lists of soldiers in each team (rank, surname, Ni-Pin number (first letter of your surname, and last 4 digits of your army number), and skills being used on patrol (such as a team medic).

The reason for this list of soldier names and Ni-Pin's was simple. If a Land Rover got hit, then the ops room would know the soldier's and identity. The same with Cas-Vac's.

Personal Kit: I haven't mentioned what kit we each carried: On the clothing side. We were issued with black army boots (x2) They were sufficient, but only just. Over 90% of us (in 1987) wore the boots without complaining. Lol. As we hadn't had to pay for them! The boots were like imitation leather, which when it started coming apart, were like cardboard. They weren't waterproof, but we didn't really mind this, as we would only be wearing them for about 8 hours. Although within a few years, the majority of us, like the rest of the British Army, bought their own boots. The investment paid dividends when it came to wearing them, in training, and in Ops.

When I joined the regiment, I was issued 2 pairs of denim trousers. That's what they were called, even though they weren't technically denim. We called them 'denims' so we all knew what we were talking about. They were 'green' trousers. When we passed-out, we got issued 2 pairs of combat trousers. They were DPM (disruptive pattern material (camouflage)). Whilst training or patrolling in urban areas we wore denims. When on rural ops, or rural training, we wore combats. We wore thick woollen shirts. scratchy ones, that took a bit of getting used to, and Army Jumpers. The jacket was the single layer DPM Jackets. It wasn't long before I joined, that the Issue Jacket was a double lined Jacket, like that used during 'The Falkland's War'. They stopped being issued because when they got wet, the jackets retained the water, got very heavy, and it didn't warm the body, in fact it did the opposite! It made the body cold, and perhaps hypothermic. The army then moved towards what the army in Finland do – layer up. Many thin layers. Better than a few thick layers! One can add, and take off, as needed. Like I said, the British Army were slowly moving toward the multi-layer clothing but just hadn't done so yet. Perhaps they were trying to issue all the current kit out, before changing? Of course – berets. we only got issued the one, and when I passed-out I got issued with the 11 UDR shoulder titles, and a black UDR cap badge. The black cap badge was used when we were on rural ops to kill the shine of the gilt badge. We had 58 pattern webbing (the same as the rest of the British Army). We were also issued long-johns (trousers, and a long-sleeved t shirt), but didn't usually wear them until winter.

As for going out on ops, we signed out our SLR's; 2 rifle magazines (20 round box magazine) and 30 live rounds (10 of which are 'tracer' rounds (red tipped, and when fired, after 50-75 meters leave a red streak behind them. If we had a 'contact', the soldier that saw the attacker/s shouted 'watch my tracer' just before he released a round (to give an indication of enemy location), we looked around and watched the tracer round streak towards the firing point of the enemy). We loaded our magazines 2 rounds, then 1 tracer, which made 2 magazines of 15 rounds. It's a 20 round mag, but loading up with 15 puts less pressure on the magazine spring than a full 20 rounds, and so – the magazine lasted longer. This meant that our top round in each magazine (first one fired) was tracer. This also meant it was easy to check your magazine hadn't lost a round (perhaps you had dropped it, or a round had popped out whilst in your magazine pouch in your webbing. You look at the top of the magazine, and you should see the top round, with a red tip. The rifle sling? It's the same canvas sling that was used on the Enfield .303" No.4's. when we were training, or doing drills, we put the slings on front and back loops. You're probably thinking, "What other way is there to put you're sling on? "In Northern Ireland, in a public situation, in a riot situation, if surrounded by people – you might get your rifle snatched from you. So we attached the sling onto the back sling loop and made the other end into a slip-knot, and put it around our wrists. That way, if we dropped the rifle, or someone tried to take it from you, it was still attached. Why the back loop of the rifle, and not the front? If it was on the front loop, then the sling wouldn't hang down as much, and look neater, but if it was attached to the front loop, the rifle could be taken from you, and swung around, having the rifle pointing at you, and you could be shot . Horrible thought I know, but this was reality. On all operations (urban and rural) we wore it around our wrists. You also never knew? When the op ask and location may change?

In our combat jackets we had to carry 2 x battlefield first aid dressings. They were a brick shape (smaller). One went on the left arm (back of) pouch in the jacket, and the other, into the top right hand pocket. We were trained, that if we came across an army casualty we should use the casualties first aid package, and not our own. It was a waterproof package, with a rip edge. The inside of the cover was shiny, clean and opened out so you could use this to patch to stop air getting in (as like a lung wound). Inside was a large cotton bandage with sling bands (To make a sling, or secure the dressing)

By law, we had to carry our 4 cards (yellow, green, red, and blue) in our jackets.

Back to our patrol evening: having got changed into combats, got our rifles, loaded the Land Rovers, and it was nearing 1930hrs.

1930hrs. we all dressed into the 'briefing room' in the company lines. It was a locked room, due to the montage photos of suspects (players) around the room (carrying their addresses, car registrations and any other relevant info about them). Once we were all in the room, the Corporal (section commander taking the patrol out) gave us his orders for that evening's patrol. The set of orders were written the evening before, or perhaps two nights prior. They were written by the Corporal leading the patrol .

He came in that evening (last night), and went up to the ops room, and Int Cell, and correlated what the RUC would like us to do, to cover, to patrol, as we must remember that we are not making out patrols for our own benefit and mission, but must work to 'Op BANNER' in which we are protecting, helping the RUC in their protection of the Northern Ireland community. He also got information of current threats, suspicious people, and IRA movements and tactics from the Int Cell.

This may all be changed on the night of the patrol, if anything developed that we needed to help out on, or the RUC required us to investigate some suspicious activities.

The briefing started with our mission. And it was common to hear 'overt patrolling, to deter terrorism', Then the ground (area) we were working in that night.

Remember. When I joined, the 'D' Company 'T.A.O.R.' was Banbridge, Gilford, Loughbrickland, Dromore and Dromara. One of our main area's was the A1 Road. A main road from Lisburn to Newry, and quick and easy for suspects, and arms to travel to and from the border.

Between 1984 & 1987 Colonel Gaddafi had sent the IRA many AK47's, and tonnes of Semtex explosive. It was delivered to Southern Ireland, and from time to time, there were deliveries up North, and it quite often came via the 'A1'. The IRA had so many small arms, that they were selling some of them, to the Loyalist Paramilitaries (but not the Semtex).

On one occasion in 1987, the UDR received information that a batch of small arms was being moved to Belfast, and quite likely on the A1.

3 UDR (Ballykinler Battalion) (Rathfriland Company) had set up checkpoints, at various timings along the A1. Our Company had done VCP's along the A1 at various times, and 'B' Company (Lisburn Company) had done the same. 'B' Company got a catch. One evening they were doing a VCP, and an IRA suspect (player) drove into it. Well? On the A1, the traffic was thick and fast, so if you were doing a VCP, you had to use your sixth sense and only stop the vehicles that you thought may be suspicious. The rest you waved on, letting them flow through, but the tactic of the IRA, was to send a known suspect down this main road, and of course we would stop him/her. This would become a magnet for the patrol. Logging, searching, and getting as much information about

the players movement (that included even taking the mileage of the vehicle). In concentrating on this vehicle, we would wave on many more cars than we would normally do! The stopper would still try to stay vigilant and on pins, but with getting a known IRA suspect, it was human nature to think you'd done well, but the IRA's tactic, was to send the car with arms/explosive about five or six cars after the 'known IRA man'. That way, by the time the patrolling section, pulled in the car, got a member to search, greenfinch to scribe, a few cars had passed through ,and once the stopper calmed down, with his job back on track – the vehicle we hoped to catch had passed through – unnoticed!

Well, the section commander that evening twigged on, and when a car with a known IRA suspect came in, he instructed the stopper to pull-in the next 6 cars, for searching. The rest of the section probably didn't like this thought, as it'll would take up a lot of time, and man power.

One of the cars had a man and woman (looking like a married couple), with a baby secured in a car seat in the back. We (the UDR) were just lucky. We were well trained in vehicle searches. It was done thoroughly. The child's car seat was unbuckled and lifted out. Below back seat was a consignment of AK47's, magazines and rounds of ammunition. Int Cell indicated that that consignment was destined to go to the loyalist paramilitaries.

I still wonder to this day, if the information that Int Cell had received, had come from the IRA? That way the IRA got their money, the Loyalist's had bought the firearms, but they never received them, so it seemed like a victory for us, but took the pressure off the IRA!

We never stopped the carriage of munitions from 'the south', only catching the odd one or two!

Back to the briefing: After the ground was explained, we got an Int brief. A person from the battalion 'Int Cell' came over to gave us the intelligence of what was happening. Activities/attacks in other areas in Northern Ireland (if relevant). What was happening in our area, regarding IRA tactics, new info on any attacks that might take place (e.g. like it is expected that a member of the security forces is going to get an under vehicle booby trap, and to be very vigilant and continue to check our cars before we get into it). The Int man would repeat the known suspects names, car registrations, where they were seen, and what they may be up to.

I memorised a couple of cars and registrations of players within the first couple of weeks!

The section commander would take over the briefing again, give us the patrol details, as in where exactly we are going, what we are doing (VCP's, foot patrols, lie-up positions and break-times), and if we needed any specialist equipment out with us, any attachments to the patrol (like a dog handler, Police officer, or another, to help us, collate information)

After the briefing we would be straight out on patrol! We go together (in L/Rovers), down to the guard room/front gate. Get out, go over to the loading bay. The team commander would load each of us up. (where we would cock our rifles, and show they were unloaded and safe, then let working parts forward, release the springs (army terminology for, let the cocking handle spring forward, squeeze the trigger (pointing at the loading bay). Then load a magazine of 15 rounds into the rifle. The rifle is loaded, but not 'ready'.

To make 'ready'? Is to cock the rifle, bringing a round into the chamber. The safety catch is still on, but all it would take, to release the safety catch, is your right thumb, aim and squeeze the trigger.

When we go out on the ground (active patrolling) we always have our firearms 'loaded', but not 'ready'.

Out on patrol! We now have to 'switch on' as they say!

The commander, instructing the driver where to go, what we are doing. Also keeping radio connection with the 'ops room' letting them know our location every now n again (Sit Rep (situation report)), when we're stopping and setting up a VCP! Giving the ops room location of the VCP (six figure grid ref) we are about to start. Even though the ops room have a copy of the patrol plans, and we are probably sticking to schedule and timings.

The timings and location may change, or perhaps the Section Commander doesn't like the location?

The driver of the lead rover, made sure the second L/Rover was still behind. He also looked out for any irregularity in the road in front (an unusual vehicle that looked suspicious, Something that looked out of place (may be a bomb, waiting for us to pass) and any players)

The two soldiers in the back of the land rover, had the SLR's pointing out the back (In case of engagement (CONTACT)) and kept a look out, and were ready to react to a situation or incident!

The second L/Rover was basically the same.

Incidentally! The second Land Rover! The off road hard tyres we used on the L/Rovers, gave a distinctive whirring sound when we drove along a metal (normal) Road. Although we left a good distance between L/Rovers for security, to enlarge our depth of patrolling, if you saw a L/Rover passing, you could count to 3, the second one passed.

This meant that the second L/Rover was normally the one targeted, in a bomb or shooting.

In April 1990, on the main road between Downpatrick and Ballykinler (training camp and ranges), 2 UDR in L/Rovers were going to Ballykinler. The second one got hit with a massive covert IED (Improvised Explosive Device)(command wire detonation). Four UDR soldiers were killed

Life in the Land Rover wasn't always as serious as I have just made it out to be! Of course we took our duty very seriously, but there was still massive craic, banter, and nonsense talk. In a normal workplace, you may get to know other colleagues and workmates, but not to the same degree, as being on patrol, training, and with the men and women of the UDR.

At the end of a patrol, we return to base (RTB), de-bomb (unloaded the rifles, unload the magazines, put all the rounds into the plastic round box they came out of), put patrol and ECM kit away, Land Rovers get parked up in their places, and of course, the CQMS (company Quartermaster Sergeant) checks all the kit we brought back, to make sure they are all returned, and nothing damaged.

We came in from the patrol around 0100hrs. Quite strangely, I think we are the only Battalion (part-time) that came off patrol at 0100hrs (that is C,D & E Company). All the rest came in at 0230 or 0300hrs ('B' Company (Lisburn) also came off the ground 0230hrs)

After de-bombing, getting kit away, we could get changed. There was no de-briefing, any de-briefing needed, was given the next evening we were in.

Whilst we (the teams) were getting changed, to head home, the Section Commander wrote a debrief for the ops room, detailing the patrol, timings, any findings, and any other information that the section commander thought relevant.

As a private soldier, I only had to come in for the training or ops nights. A team or Section Commander, came in the day before the patrol, went up to the ops room to receive the tasking for the next evening's patrol (it could change, and sometimes did, even right up until we were leaving the barracks to patrol). The ops order (what the RUC would like us to cover), and Int-Cell request may be: overt patrolling in Banbridge to deter terrorist movement at the start of the night, completing a couple of checkpoints on roads coming into Banbridge from Newry direction, then one or two checkpoints on the A1 (main arterial routes from Lisburn to Dundalk), followed by overt patrolling in nearby villages.

The Section Commander and team commander would then come back to the lines, to write a set of orders, giving general locations (ground), a list of times, grids of possible VCP's (checkpoints) we would probably be doing.

In addition to the set of orders, the section commander needs to authorise the kit list required(especially specialist kit (such as night sight, if we are conducting a foot patrol in rural locations)) to the CQMS. This is called a 'warning order' for the upcoming operation.

My first patrol

The first few weeks I travelled in and home with Frankie, and we took turns in each car! This helped me to get used to the different routes we use to get to Portadown. Sometimes we go the main roads from home – A26 to Moira, then the M1 and M12 to Portadown outskirts, then the Northway, Brownstown Rd to the barracks.

Or perhaps a rural route: Aghalee, Aghagallan, back roads around Craigavon (various roads), into Portadown. Or Moira, Lurgan, Craigavon, Portadown. We had to vary our routes, so stop us being dicked, targeted, and probable attack. We couldn't change them one after the other, as that was setting a pattern! We just needed to choose a different route on that evening. If we got a sixth sense even when we are on a route, we will varied from it. I have known times when I was coming home from a duty, and perhaps driving a certain direction – got a bad feeling – and completely altered the route – even doing a U turn.

On my first night on ops/patrol I was quite nervous, I don't know why, as I had been coming in a couple of months now. Perhaps because it was my first time on patrol?

I wasn't treated any different to any other soldier, and that surprised me, as I am the NEW boy! It is probably due to the number of people that leave and join throughout each year, and I am just another number?

My role tonight? I was in the back of the first Land Rover, and was just helping set up each VCP, take cover, be security for the VCP. I was learning, watching all the team, what they are doing.

On VCP's tonight, the driver was the 'chatter-up' talking to the drivers of all the cars that come into the VCP, The team commander was watching everything that is happening, and was on the radio communicating with other teams and the ops room, The other soldier that was in the back with me, is doing 'stopper'. I set the 'Stop – Checkpoint – Headlights Off' sign on up the road (how far mattered on the roads), then returned to a grass bank overlooking the stopper. He had got a red Barlick out of the patrol box, when a vehicle was coming towards us, he would swing his hand that has the torch in a big windmill action, to show, slow and stop the traffic. When the vehicle came to a stop beside him, he would ask the driver to put the lights onto side-lights, continue slowly up to the back of the Land Rover, where the chatter would ask him his name, destination, where he was coming from, and perhaps if he has seen anything suspicious in the last few days? If the driver, passenger or vehicle appeared suspicious, then he would ask the driver to pull in. The vehicle would then be searched and logged. The driver and passengers details would be taken, and each individual may get searched, the team commander asked the ops room to check this vehicle (by registration plate). The Greenfinch would log all the details down. Time, location, vehicle description, journey details, driver and passenger details, and any other information. These details would be attached to the commanders de-brief that he handed in at the end of the patrol.

I heard where we were going, in the briefing before we went out! But now, I haven't a clue where we are. I just had to get used to all of our TAOR. It was all a learning curve. We are on a broad main road, and it looks like a road that I think I know going to Newcastle Co. Down. I asked the stopper if it was that road? Of course he said 'yes' and took the piss out of me for a while, and let me believe we are going into Newcastle, perhaps getting an ice cream. We are in Seapatrick, doing a VCP on a main road between Gilford and Banbridge. Tonight we are doing VCP's on some of the main roads around Banbridge, taking our break (about 15-20mins) out on the ground, where we pull the Land Rovers into a secluded spot, so that nobody sees us (that way, if any terrorist knew that we are on the ground, in the Banbridge area, he wouldn't know where we are, and so, leaves him unsure if we will stop his movements and actions. We want to be hidden so not to be attacked.) It was a normal patrol tonight, and nothing out of the blue happened.

My heart was beating tonight, and I felt so alive. Even though I (myself) wasn't doing much tonight. When I got home, I am still so awake. I hope I'm not this awake after every Patrol. I'm bound to burn out.

I hadn't established myself yet, I was just a private soldier. If anyone tells me to jump, I'd ask," how high?" I knew the people in my platoon, but I haven't got to know these people yet, and the same applies to me. They haven't got to know me yet. For the first few patrols, I am like the last kid in a school class picked for a football team! I'm just put into teams, where someone hasn't turned up for duty tonight, and I'm just filling the space. After the first few patrols, I started to bed into one of the teams/sections, as they now know that I always come in (reliable), and won't fade out! And they know that I am wanting to work, and am not a slacker. It was Davy's team I got onto most (he is normally the 2IC in the Patrol).

We are getting to know one another, and one of the first nights, just as we loaded up near the front gate. Just as we are driving out (we're not doing top-cover yet, as not all the top-hatches are safe, and not all (but most) Land-Rovers have the cheese wire cutter bar, running up the side of the windscreen).

Davy turned round to me and asked "Are You a Christian?". I was hit for six! I am a Christian, but did not want to appear as a wimp, I replied "NO! Of course not! What made you think I was?". All eyes in the Land Rover were on me (except for the driver). Davy just said, "We thought you are", and nothing else was said on this topic the rest of the night. This was a Monday night. We went out to our TAOR patrol area (Banbridge and Dromore). But I didn't like my 'NO! Of course not'. This played on my mind for the next few days. I kept thinking of Peter denying Christ three times. I never thought I would ever deny Christ. Tuesday night we were training. Now it is Thursday night! Another duty night. By coincidence (I don't believe in them!) I am in exactly the same team. We loaded up at the guard room, and on our way out I said "Davy! You know that the last night I said I wasn't a Christian?", and suddenly, all eyes in the team are on me, including the driver. I felt like I was in the spotlight! "Yes" Davy said, and I replied, "I am a Christian, and have been from first year in secondary school!". Davy said "we thought you are!" and nothing more was said after that. I thought I was in for a piss taking night, but nothing was remarked about me being a Christian. I knew from that point on, that I will never deny being a Christian again.

I am in 'D' Company, and 16 Platoon. There are normally 3 or 4 platoons in each company. In D Company we have 3 platoons. Which means we are (as a platoon) on ops every third night. The rota just moves throughout the week as 1st Platoon, then the 2nd Platoon, then the 3rd, then back to the first.

It was on a rota, like this:

Monday – 16 Platoon, Tuesday – 17 Platoon, Wednesday – 18 Platoon, Thursday – 16 Platoon, Friday – 17 Platoon, Saturday – 18 Platoon, Sunday – 16 Platoon, Monday – 17 Platoon

The weekends are not in the normal ops. At weekends we have another rota, as in Company Rota's. 1st weekend we will take over camp-guard (looking after Mahon Road Barracks), 2nd weekend we guard the officers (not just officers from the UDR) in their cul de sac on the outskirts of Portadown, 3rd weekend is a training weekend – perhaps in Mahon Road Barracks Saturday and Sunday 0800hrs to 1700hrs – or perhaps a mini-camp at Ballykinler or Magilligan Point (Friday evening to Sunday evening), and the 4th will be an operational weekend.

We have training evenings every Tuesday and Thursday.

I came in for nearly all the duties, and this meant I got only one day a week off. My typical rota would be

Monday-ops 1830-0130hrs, Tue-trg 1830-2330hrs, Wed-off, Thurs-ops 1830-0130hrs, Fri night camp guard 2359-0800, Saturday- camp guard 0800-1700hrs, Sunday- camp guard 1700-0100hrs, Monday – off. Tue-trg, Wed-ops, Thurs-Trg, Fri-officer guard 1830-0130hrs.

We got paid up to 19¾ duties each month. The only times we could get doing more, is if you were on 'dole-patrol'. This is a nick name made for anyone who hasn't got a regular job, or may have had to leave their job because of a threat. They can get up to 30 duties per month. We also got to do more than 19¾ duties, if there was a big threat out, and we are needed, or (it happened to me three times) we got a 'call-out' where we had to drop our main jobs, and go on duty for a number of days, because there was an imminent threat of attack, on town centres or security barracks.

Let me explain duties, or length of duties! A duty was 8 hours long. So if I came in for a training duty, and was in from 1830 to 2330hrs, I got five hours, In for an ops night 1830-0130hrs (7 hours), both gave me 1½ duties. The most hours in the day you would be accounted for, was 8 hours (1 Duty), so if you were in for 12 hours, you would only get 1 duty. The army day began at 0800hrs, through to 0800hrs the next morning. You could only get 1 duty for each day.

We got paid a travel allowance each time we came into barracks. If I remember correctly it was 11 pence per mile. To and from home. Distance from home to barracks was calculated on a standard journey length (not distances on a longer 'varied route').

In Northern Ireland, as it was in active operational role, for the British Army. Any British soldiers based here, got free board, and free food (in the cookhouse). That entitlement included us (the UDR), but to qualify, we had to be on an 8 hour duty (a full 1 day's duty). We normally received these meals, on our weekend ops and training.

4

Craigavon

Craigavon was a new town. The plans were for it to be a city. Designed, planned, and construction started in 1965.

It was a new town between Lurgan and Portadown. All roads were in cuttings to reduce pollution and sound. Hotels, parks, golf courses were planned!

Cycle paths, roadways criss-crossing through the full area, joined with roundabouts for traffic to move quickly. Walkways, Shopping areas in the new estates and a central one, all built. The thoughts and plans for the new town/city were perfect, but the execution was terrible.

The council calculated that council housing estates should last 30 years, and after that, be renewed, but that meant that houses were constructed very poorly, with bad materials, and it went out to the cheapest contractors. The estates were to be an overflow from Belfast and other populated cities. They paid families to move into the new estates, but no sooner had they moved in – received the money, than they moved back to their former housing areas.

The outbreak of 'The Troubles' in the late 60's, early 70's resulted in sectarian violence and segregation.

Many of the houses built were substandard, and later demolished, other estates had emptied, as occupants moved back to Belfast.

When I joined in 1987, Craigavon was a dangerous area to patrol, the IRA Active Service Unit (ASU) was in nearby Lurgan, and also the Mid Ulster UVF were close too. Craigavon is a maze of roads, roundabouts, footbridges, embankments, which was difficult to patrol, and easy to be attacked from. If we were attacked, it was difficult to establish from where. The ground was hard to go offensive and fight back, due to the embankments, footbridges, alleyways, foot and bike paths, and the labyrinth of streets.

We had a Police station in Portadown Centre, Lurgan Centre, and one in the heart of Craigavon. This was the Legahory area of Craigavon. Our rolls in 'Op BANNER' were to help and protect the Police, and assist them in their duties.

My Company's ('D') TAOR (Tactical Area Of Responsibility) was Banbridge, Dromore, Dromara area, but violence, attacks, and threats were escalating in Craigavon, so not long after I joined, our battalion had to 'up' the patrols in the Lurgan/Craigavon areas.

'C' Company were responsible for Lurgan and out to Craigavon, and 'E' Company were responsible for Portadown, The Birches, and back to the outskirts of the Craigavon Area.

In 1987 we hadn't yet got a personal issue body armour/flack jacket, later to be called the CBA (Combat Body Armour). If we planned a patrol in the Lurgan/Craigavon area, we would sign out (from company store) four body armours (a flack jacket, with a bullet proof plate on the centre of the chest, and centre of the back. As well as two riot helmets that have drop-down visors (per 4-man team, or per Land Rover). It would be another year or two years before we got our own personal issue combat body armour and helmets. As I had said before, when on urban patrol, we wore the denim green trousers, on rural patrol combat dpm trousers, but soon after I had joined, the army noticed that if you were wearing army green trousers in a riot situation, if you got hit with some liquid/fire from the petrol bomb – it melted. So very soon, we were wearing combat dpm trousers in all the patrols, and on-duty activities. We were now, only going to wear our army greens whilst doing admin/training and suchlike.

Do we get our faces cammed up? Not yet! At this time we only got cammed up when in covert patrols/lie-up positions which were mainly in the town suburbs or countryside (rural). If we were cammed up and were about to come into the public, we would de-cam. At this time (1987) we wore army green trousers when patrolling villages like Dromore and Dromara. But if we were to go to Lurgan/Craigavon it would be all DPM. Jackets and trousers

We also signed out more radios if going to Lurgan/Craigavon. We had to ensure we had good comms with the ops-room, also good communications within our own teams and sections when in the area. We had to have good communications in case anything happened, if we needed to steer teams/sections in depth/ cut-off/ defence. Also so we know where each team was located.

When we patrolled, we tried to get as much depth on the ground (area we are working in). For instance if my team was going down a street, being overt, we most probably would have a second team snaking in and around other streets, for the support of the main team (us), hopefully catch any terrorists that may be getting ready, or attacking us!

When I joined in July 1987, the biggest threat, was the vehicle borne IED. This was the full back of the van, filled with homemade explosives. A detonator, set in some Semtex, which will set off the whole explosive. Likening it to lighting a fire! The detonator was like the match. It would start fire at it's primitive state, Semtex was like the firelighter or paper, which will bring more fire and heat which will light the coal or logs. It is very hard if not impossible for a match to light a bit of coal, just as a detonator ignites the homemade explosives. Semtex is the firelighter, which will ignite the main charge.

In 1987/88 the explosives were quite primitive, took a bit of time to make and mix, and was easily smelt (ammonia or almonds). Around 1989, the IRA found a new explosive mix, that was really easy to make, cheap, had a high explosive value, and was always reliant.

Toyota Hi-Ace's (smallish delivery van) were easily stolen. We constantly got warnings by Int-Cell, of a White Toyota Hi-Ace (they were also very popular) being used against Police Stations, or army establishments. "The threat was 'imminent' and was going to happen" this is what we were constantly told. It was almost a bit of a 'cry-wolf' scenario

My first experience of Craigavon was a mobile patrol to the area during the day. It was a Saturday. Location was mainly on the Brownlow Road, Lake Road, and main roads that attach Portadown to Lurgan. Such big main roads, all dual roads or carriageways. But the weird thing was that they were almost empty roads with little traffic. Weird? As I thought that this type of wide road would be bustling with traffic!

Craigavon was a fantastic plan, but it (as yet) just hadn't worked. Doing VCP's on these roads looked so safe, as they were empty roads, quiet, with only background noise of life ½ a mile or so away, but this was dangerous location. We had to be on pins when setting up and running VCP's.

I was really anxious when travelling towards, around Craigavon for the first time. When I joined in 1987, we didn't use armoured vehicles, although there were two or three armoured Land Rovers in our Mahon Road Barracks. These were only used in extreme circumstances, like a riot situation, or in areas where attacks were imminent.

The Land Rovers we used were Series 4 Land Rovers (basic controls) with a Makrolon (fibre Glass) shell. Unlike Belfast, we weren't permitted to do top-cover (standing up in the back, with our heads through the hatch, with our rifles up also, to have good sight, and reaction), as not all of us had helmets. The top-hatch's on our Rovers didn't always have securing bolts, so if it got windy, or the vehicle hit a bump – the top-hatch would flip back on us! In our Land Rovers the two men in the back, on each side, would have the SLR's pointing out the back, across our legs, with the cocking handle folded out (ready for use), and sights flipped up (set at 300m).

My heart was beating faster than normal with a little adrenaline flowing, as I wanted to be ready to react if anything happened. There wasn't as much talk/banter in the Rover, as the whole team/section felt the same. The team commander had to watch around, keeping track of where we were on the map, listening out on the radio, keeping us safe. When we were setting Up VCP's the commanders had to be aware of getting a good VCP location! Where we couldn't be seen from a distance, not on a bend, where there was risk of a crash, good enough where we can create a Static Position, with a chicane (The two staggered Rovers, one at each side of the road, so a car/vehicle can't escape through). Good cover positions, good cut-off locations, everyone ready to react if something goes down. The team/section commanders were listening out - ready to make us move, if we are called for, in reaction to an attack elsewhere in Craigavon. Or any suspicious activity seen. Also! we had the threat/risk of the Mk 12 Mortar!

The Mk 12 Mortar is a home-made (terrorist-made) horizontally fired Mortar, which is dug into a hedge/embankment. It was a command wire launched weapon; the command wire will run out 10's if not 100's of meters away.

With the distinctive whine of the army land rover tyres, the players (terrorist members) could hear when we were coming. Wait until the first Land Rover goes past the mortar – wait for two or three seconds, then initiate the ortar (pressing the button, or connecting the wires). The second land rover will get the full of the blast.

The Mk 12 was so well planned, constructed (over quite a few years) that it is even armour piercing. I am not allowed to write about what way, how it is armour piercing, but the IRA had learnt about it off military weapons like the Russian PRG7

We always had to be aware of it, and adjust our patrols to make it hard for us to get attacked by one. It was a constant threat in Lurgan/Craigavon, and Banbridge when the threat rises.

When going to Legahory Police Station, we debus from the land rovers on the main road, which is about 500 meters from the station. We can't drive up to the police station, as it is too predictable, and we might get attacked. Perhaps in the form of the Mk12 Mortar set up to take the second land rover out, or perhaps a sniper shoot.

To lose one soldier is bad luck, to lose two or more in an attack, is bad commanding and patrolling.

We move in strategic foot-patrol (trying to be unpredictable) up the smaller road, towards the police station, with the Land Rovers following.

When we near the station, we go firm and take all round defence, watching out for anything, and protecting the Rovers that are coming through.

All round defence ? We are taught from recruitment about all round defence. Mainly whilst on foot patrol. In a pair (2 men) we would look out for each other. I would watch the windows, junctions, people around my mate (opposite side of road), and he would do the same for me. Coming up to junctions, I would go firm on the junction, watch for a threat, and my mate would pass through – go to the corner at the other side of the junction, go firm and protect me as I come over to that side of the road. However we can't just go firm at each corner, we also have to be aware that there may be a booby trap somewhere on that corner (perhaps in a waste bin), and had to be aware of overlooking windows that we might get shot from.

Bring that strategy up from a pair of men to a team (four men), and the same thing is happening. Pairs going firm, and the other pair going through. Raise that strategy to a section level (2 teams) and the distance has increased. We have to become more unpredictable in our movements, but still watching – looking after the other team. If we are channelled (as in going into a police station/ army barracks) one team will go into cover positions, observing all areas away from the police station, whilst the other team run in, and if it is a high risk area like Craigavon, each person would run with a weave, to be unpredictable if someone was going to shoot at us.

The front gates of the Legahory Station is manually opened by the policeman on duty at the gate. The land rovers go in, we (the second team) stay in cover, as we are the nearest team to the station. We let the team that was furthest away to enter through our defence. Then we quickly run in.

The Legahory Police Station. It was the first time I had seen this Police Station. And it looked like a temporary station. Unfinished. Portable, and a bric-a-brac look.

The police station was at the edge of a typical Craigavon housing estate, and is at the side of a type of village square. There was a doctors opposite it, across the road from the doctors, was a small shopping complex of the 1960's/70's, with an alleyway, public bar with darkened windows, a hairdresser, and a couple of vacant shops.

It looked like a shopping precinct that had materialized from the mid-seventies. Virtually no change to the buildings, decorations and furnishings. There were still a few CCTV's around it (I doubt they worked) that are exactly the same as a typical CCTV sign. You know the ones, a rectangle box with box steel around the sides and top to protect it from the rain.

The police station was surrounded by a high fence about 7 or 8' high, then about 3' inside the wire a grey block wall that is about 7' high. One set of double gates at the front. Solid gates that you can't see through, about 6' high. Inside you had a quite small brick station (single storey) with portacabins / mobile buildings attached to the sides. One of which was the canteen. There were probably plans to build the station into a decent building, but it wasn't cost effective, or realistic because of the troubles, and threats to the contractors that would be working at them.

On our way up to the police station from the main road, we were on a winding road, not a small road, but a new type modern street road, which had just been planned and made to wind, as it rose up the hill. Alongside it was the walkway. That walkway soon cut into the ground and passed under the road which curved to the left at the top of this gentle hill towards the shops and police station.

As the road curved to the left, to the right was a derelict housing estate. It was very strange, and in lots of ways 'eerie'. When I said derelict, the roads were still there, and in excellent condition, there were the steps up to the houses, again excellent condition. At the top of the steps were concrete raised flower beds, in good condition, with plants still in them (Perhaps more weeds, than flowers now), but as to the buildings? They were gone. Nothing. Not even any sizable rubble, just a few loose bricks here and there. It was also so very strange. All the poles and streetlights were still there, untouched, and still switched on from the evening – to the morning.

There were plenty of other derelict housing estates like this around Craigavon.

So making our way up to the police station, we had to stay aware of the houses and buildings overlooking us to the left, the undercutting walkway, and the raised derelict estate to our right.

The first time I approached Legahory Police Station when on ops/patrol, it was dark (September or October), the streetlights were yellow, and quite old, which although giving light, it is not great light. That was good for us to move in, as it was harder for the terrorists to see us, but at the same time bad, as we couldn't see into all the nooks and cranny's as they were quite dark and hidden. It felt so risky and so strange. When we are on ops in Banbridge and other areas of our TAOR, there is banter/chat/laughter, but here on duty tonight there was no chatting, no banter, just silence/hand signals and a feeling of pressure and suspense that something will happen.

I had been many times training in 'the Village' in Ballykinler where there was realism, and you know you will get attacked at any time soon. But here moving my way up towards Legahory cop-shop, it felt so sinister/dangerous. You hope you will react/respond if we are shot at, or an IED detonates?

Although you were with, and in a team, it felt quite lonely, as there was no chit-chat or voices. Everything was so quiet. So quiet that I can hear my breath, hear the movement of my SLR across the webbing, and hear every step of my boots upon the pathway. It being dark, not beside anyone (each soldier about 10 to 15 meters apart), adds to the isolation that is felt.

The derelict estate to the right had good roads, and was easy for the terrorist to engage us from there, or detonate an explosion (IED) from there, and make a quick getaway. We had to move up this road as unpredictable as we could. Pairs and teams leapfrogging each other as we move up.

When each soldier stopped and went firm, he must quickly check his position for a possible booby trap/ hidden IED (improvised explosive device) and if he wasn't happy – move. Once in a suitable position, that soldier must scan around, looking at possible firing points, lookout points, people dicking us and suspicious cars. When the pair, or team have moved onto their next position, we get ready to move and try to move unpredictably!

How could we move unpredictable then, if a dicker knows which direction we are going?

From the position the soldier was in, for instance squatting, stand up (predictable so far) and instead of moving forwards, back up two or three steps, then go sideways, then forward, changing direction (about 30') at times as we go. This so we are not walking in a straight line direction.

If a terrorist had a weapon aimed at me, I will be easily shot if walking in straight direction. So change the angle of walk in random times. And hopefully if I am shot at? Will miss me?

Why are we on pins at this part of Craigavon, and not on pins in other suburbs of Craigavon? It's because it is quite predictable that UDR patrols quite frequently go in and out of the Legahory Police Station, perhaps to drop off a Police Officer who had been on patrol with us, picking up a Police Officer for our upcoming patrol. We could be popping in for a quick break, liaison with the station, or to park up our Land Rover's, to start a foot patrol?

The patrol up to the police station is so eerie. Dull lights, no pedestrians, the public bar with very darkened glass (which makes you think, nobody is in there), strange smells such as dust/dirt/pollution. Housing from the early seventies, hidden walkways and paths. When we enter the police station, it feels so lifeless because it is late night, and those still on duty at this station are maybe out on patrol, or doing deskwork. Just one or two police on the front gate, and maybe nobody at the front desk.

We quite often went into the small canteen where there were a few vending machines, three or four tables, and a tv mounted high on the wall (which normally was playing ITV night screen (probably only a certain generation can remember this. It played things like 'Hitman and her', 'The Equalizer' etc).

We waited there for a few minutes until our section commander got in touch with the neighbourhood Police Officer who was to accompany us on our patrol. Quite often we would bring in our flasks from the rovers to have a short break, before heading out again.

Leaving a police station we had to be equally vigilant. A team bursting out of the station (sprinting), Going firm with 'all round defence', the rest of the patrol following. Perhaps leaving the rovers behind. If we did leave the rovers behind - the player/s will know we will have to return for them later! And so! Can prepare and plan to attack on re-entry to the cop-shop, or wait until we leave with the Rovers, and have an ambush awaiting us down the road?

We try to vary our exits. Most times the two teams will 'starburst' out (each soldier sprinting in different directions, to go firm) followed by the Rovers.

One team sprints out going a little further than anticipated, and in two minutes or so, the Land Rovers will leave with the rest of the section on-board.

The two Land Rovers rake out of the station with everyone on-board.

If any one of us came up with a different way of de-bussing from the RUC Station, the team/section commander might give it a go?

We have to be vigilant at all times!

One time when we were on mobile patrol around the Tullygally area, we had a sighting of someone carrying a weapon around the flats area. We quickly got there. Everyone taking all round cover. Stevie and I dismounted the Rover, looking towards the flats and saw someone walking about the second floor. We quickly went into pair fire and manoeuvre drills (without the shooting), quickly making our way up alleyways and stairs to the second floor, where we saw the suspicious man turning the far corner. Was he going into a flat? Or up another floor? Had he seen us, and was now waiting round the corner for us? Stevie and I looked at each other, and ran up to the corner, with me covering round the corner. I remember kneeling down, scared to poke my head around to look, as it could be taken off? Quickly I put my head round and back, too quick for him to shoot. I can't remember what I saw, as I did it too quickly, so quickly that I never got a chance to take in what I have seen. I did it again, only a bit slower. I saw the man still walking, holding something in his left hand. I indicated to Stevie to move. He cleared the corner, went down on one knee, with his SLR pointing at the suspect, and shouted "Army! Stop or I fire!". At this the man stopped and started to turn round. Stevie shouts "Stop" at him again. At this he froze. I made my way over to him, whilst Stevie stayed on his knee, pointing his rifle at him. I approach him saying "Show me your hands". He raised both hands up a little, and it was then, that I saw he was carrying! A tin in one hand, and a paint brush in the other. We both went over to him (not dropping our guard, as we have quite a bit of adrenaline in our systems) and question him on his identity, movements, and purpose, and if he had seen anyone suspicious around here in the last few minutes, or half hour or so? This was quite like, the false alarms we got from time to time. We know that this was a false alarm! But it could be equally a real threat! And false alarms, as like this one. We know there are most probably?

A player, or a few people watching us. To see how fast our response was, and which way we react, thus giving them information, on attacks they may be planning.

Foot patrols being the safest way to patrol through the local Craigavon area, either being overt, being well seen to help with public confidence and safety, or covert, were we can move from estate to estate with ease, speed, and unseen. The players would not know our location, and therefore stop his suspicious movements and activities.

In Craigavon, many housing estates were staunch Loyalist, or staunch Republican. Some estates are derelict (as explained earlier), and some were completed housing estates, but 90% empty.

I remember quite a few times patrolling into the empty housing estates, either by foot or mobile. Stopping in the centre, and having a break there. If it was a hot day, even stripping off our body armour, setting it on the road, whilst sitting on the kerb chatting, and having a quick coffee. Such threats, such risks, but still to do this? Eerie? Too right it is! In the middle of a housing estate, no movement, just the sound from distant traffic, and running water from one or two of the houses.

Running water in houses? In a number of houses the windows were boarded up with metal grills, and behind some, you could hear running water. That house had probably got broken into, and copper pipes taken (thus the running water).

The Craigavon Centre (Rushmere) is now prospering with McD's, M&S and Matalan. It was not like this when we were patrolling there in the late 1980's. The centre was desolate. There were the same raised car parks, but were not in great condition, and the shopping complex (Rushmere) was dark, with very few shops, never mind known franchise shops. As I can remember there was a book makers, off licence, and one or two other shops.

The car park was so empty, that in many documentary programs in the 1980's, when a reporter was interviewing a terrorist in a secret meeting, it would be in that car park. On one or two 'Spotlight' programs I recognised the car park, and knew that we worked in that very spot.

The Craigavon Centre is on man-made raised ground, probably from the earth removed to build the roadways around it.

The roadways were part of the excellent planning of Craigavon. Roadways in cuttings, to reduce noise and pollution, and business/housing developments on higher ground.

I remember one time on foot patrol, walking along the roads near the Rushmere Centre, and seeing a Fox with 4 or 5 cubs walking across a main footbridge towards the Centre. I wish I had got a picture of this, as it was beauty, in such a 1970's concrete urban surrounding.

The threats, attacks, terrorist activity increased in Craigavon. This meant that our Company ('D') was in Craigavon more and more. Almost all our ops became Craigavon Based (foot & mobile). Not as often Lurgan, even though the risk was higher in Lurgan! The more experienced Company ('C' Company) upped their patrols there. They were more skilled in that area. They knew where all the suspects lived, moved, and tactics they used. The roadways/laneways/rat-runs the players will use, if attack is on the menu tonight?

When I gained rank in 1989, I got to know a few of the neighbourhood policemen in Lurgan and Craigavon. We (the UDR) had a great connection with the RUC, in both Lurgan and Craigavon. Together we worked for the safety of the communities and areas. We exchanging information on any new intelligence we had on players, or suspicious activity. Quite a few times we exchanged 'Int' that the other didn't know. In hard area's like Lurgan and Craigavon, we needed one another's help. There was still the threat of attack whether Mk12 Mortar, vehicle Borne IED, CQA (close quarter attack), and still the threat off duty, as in CQA, under vehicle booby trap (UVBT).

On the evening of 13th December 1991 (I wasn't on duty that evening) a coal lorry parked beside Legahory Police Station (about 8pm or so), and it looked suspicious. This raised alarm in the police station. The attack alarm went off (probably triggered from the policeman at the front gate) and everyone took action. Two of the neighbourhood policemen I knew were in the station at this exact time. One was in the small canteen, where he and others got down on the floor, and started to crawl out.

As he was crawling out, keeping close to the wall, the wall above him just vanished. It got blown clean away from about waist height up. It was pure luck, that the blast wall on the outside of the canteen, was of a concrete block construction, and not the newer solid concrete slab walls, as this would just have fallen on top of them. The canteen was a portacabin, and was just blown to pieces.

The other policeman I know was running out the back door when the explosion happened and got helped along quite a few meters with the explosion. Surprisingly, no-one was killed that evening, as most of the personnel had finished their shift that day. But the explosion wrecked the police station. 1,000 lb bomb! It destroyed the station, and quite a bit of St Anthony's Catholic Church that was nearby.

The Birches Police Station which was just over ten miles from Portadown town centre, was destroyed in 1986 by the IRA. In

1987, the IRA attacked and attempted to destroy Loughgall Police Station.

It was the IRA's aim to close/destroy RUC police stations, in or near Republican areas, to control the areas, and have free movement.

Since IRA had removed Craigavon station, the authorities had to think whether or not to establish a new Craigavon station? They did, only this time, making it a lot larger. A greater size increase from the neighbourhood station it once was. There were rumours that either Portadown, or Lurgan station may be closed, and moved to Craigavon. The new station was really well built, with a good roadways, bigger car parks, garages to the rear. The station itself was a lot larger in all ways, with modern electric gates.

We continually got told of the threat of a vehicle born IED targeting the barracks or police station from before the Craigavon explosion, and after.

Foot patrols and covert patrols in Craigavon: When I joined in July 87, I was given shoulder titles, and a black cap badge to accompany the gilt one! black badge? It was to be used in operational roles. If we were rural, or covert patrolling, we wore DPM Trousers, and a black cap badge, so it didn't glint in the night. My first patrol in Craigavon was a mobile patrol (L/Rover), but there were always foot patrols. At the start, the foot patrols were mostly overt, for the public to see, to show our presence, deter the terrorist, but soon it became majority 'covert' foot patrols, where we were all 'cammed-up' (brown/dark green camouflage cream on your full face, neck, hands, and ears). Covert patrols were to stop us getting monitored or watched, and harder to attack!

At times on covert foot patrol, we would start from Legahory RUC Station, where we left the Rovers. Sometimes we doubled the men in each L-Rover, dispersing the extra teams from the Rovers, when at the corner of a car park (hidden) or somewhere obscure. Other times from a CMV (civilianized military vehicle).

I liked doing the covert patrols in Craigavon. Vanish, then appear somewhere, go overt, or do a VCP, then vanishing away again.

From before I joined, through to the Nineties, CLF Jurisdiction No.15 stated that we were not to confront the public with cammed up faces, as it was against the rules of the CLF (commander of land forces), but the Battalion CO (commanding officer) at this time insisted we got cammed-up (a few years before us, he was attached to the SAS Regiment).

The walkways around the estates weren't the best light and when foot patrolling down them, and see someone approaching! We stood with our backs to the hedge, then pushed back into it. It was quite amazing, the number of people dandering by, chatting in depth, talking intimately with close friends. Walking by, closer than 2 feet away, walking past the full team (4 of us staggered about 5 to 10 meters from each other) and never noticing one of us.

We could cover considerable ground quite quickly whilst foot patrolling. We could cut through various places, being seen for about a minute or two, then vanish again. It meant that the active terrorist couldn't be active. On foot patrol we were quite safe, because our locations were unpredictable. If? We were to be taken on, only a single soldier, or perhaps a pair would be hit, whilst in a Rover, the full team could be taken out!

It was patrols like this, in Lurgan/Craigavon that made me feel as one with the men I was patrolling with. We relied, trusted and were confident in each other. Times like that, you know what the phrase 'Band of Brothers' really meant.

When I was team commander I liked having the neighbourhood policeman with me. Raymond chatted about the crime and terrorism in the area, and we also chatted about rock bands! We both liked. For instance, the drummer in each rock band. but most of all, we helped each other on our work/patrol. Often in a VCP, the driver wouldn't give his name or any other details, Raymond would come forward and resolve the situation.

Once when we were doing a VCP, a driver of a car in the checkpoint, was being very awkward, not answering any questions, and shouting at one of my men who is asking the questions! Raymond was attached to us that night, and I asked if he could sort it, he said he'd try. I was very confident he would work it out, as he normally would! The driver got out of the car, and was standing beside the car talking, giving off to Raymond. I couldn't hear what was being said, as I was the team commander, had my radio on (earpiece in), and was standing off, watching the VCP, making sure everything was working ok within the full of the patrol.

When I turned around again, I saw Raymond had the driver by the neck, pushing him backwards over the bonnet of the car, both hands on the man's face, and I think Raymond was pushing, or about to push his thumbs into the man's eyes?. I broke my position, running over to him shouting, "Whoa whoa whoa, what's going on?". Raymond calmed down, let the driver down, and when the frustration dropped, he answered the questions. Just the normal questions! 'Identity, movements and purpose' Nothing came of this situation, but it just shows that not everything runs smoothly, and from time to time, we got very awkward people to contend with!

Some of the estates in Craigavon were quite hostile! We quite regularly had stones thrown at our mobile patrols when passing by or entering some of the housing estates in Craigavon. As I had mentioned, in 1987 we didn't do top-cover, as it was seen as confrontational and perhaps offensive to the public, and our Series 4 Land Rovers didn't always have workable top cover hatches.

In 1992 along came the 'Snatch' Land Rovers. The new Series Land Rover 'Defender' 110 series, that has adopted a semi-armour proof Shell. The shell made the Rover much heavier (about 3½ Tons overall). It had a working slidable top-cover hatch, and as the Troubles had escalated, we were now required to do top-cover in urban areas. By this time, we had our own personal issue body armour (CBA) and helmets

When we got stones thrown at us, it was from the high ground of certain estates (we are on the roadway below, which road is coming up to a notorious roundabout (this roundabout is well known, it is the roundabout that some undercover RUC men shot and killed 3 suspected IRA men, that were travelling through the roundabout in November 1982)).

If the youths throwing the stones were well away from us, that we could see and dodge the stones, rocks or boulders, we stayed up top-cover. But if they were near, we had to drop down, close the hatch. When stones got thrown, the commander of the Rover would pull up the steel grill to cover the windscreen from any damage. The side screen had permanent grills on them.

The windscreen and side screens had thick toughened glass on them, I think of a bullet-proof type, but without that 'green tinge'.

The stones weren't too bad, as we managed (in person) to dodge them, with one or two exceptions of scrapes, or dents in our helmets -but the paint bombs! When there was an escalation in violence (perhaps coming up to the 12th of July, or an anniversary of an attack somewhere) we got many groups of youths stirring trouble, and when we passed by, we got stoned, paint-bombs thrown at us.

Paint bombs - glass bottles filled with paint, so when it strikes the Land Rover it smashes, releasing paint all over the side. But if they were lucky (and we, unlucky!), it hit the bonnet or windscreen, putting paint all over the windscreen, restricting the drivers vision. Stones, paint-bombs! What about petrol-bombs? Funny enough, we got virtually no petrol bombs in Craigavon. It was in Lurgan we had petrol bombs thrown at us.

Over time Craigavon Rushmere flourished, bringing in Debenhams, and it was successful, and brought in Primark, Tesco Superstore, McDonalds, Matalan, and with this, new private housing estates were built. Craigavon redeveloped in so many ways. The Craigavon now, is nothing like the Craigavon I started patrolling in 1987.

5

Annual Camp

Annual camp? To the part-time companies from all the battalions, it's the headline act in the year. To full-time soldiers that go to training exercises throughout the year, it's nothing!

Annual camp is mandatory training in order to receive 'the Bounty' which is a bonus payment, for a full year of dedication and work in part-time.

In order to qualify for the Bounty, each individual has to have completed at least a full 75 duties through the year (April to the end of March). It is not just 75 duties! It has to be at least 50 operational duties. At least 25 training duties. Now remember, if I go in for a night's ops, I will probably get in about 1830hrs, finish my duty at 0130hrs, and that is 7 hours, the next operational night, if I get the same hours, that will be 14 hours (1 & ¾ Duties). On a training night, you would probably have 4 or 5 hours, giving you ½ a training duty.

For the qualifications for a bounty, you also needed at least 4 full range days, pass the rifle APWT (annual personal weapon test), which is to achieve the passing score in a Rupell match, complete a Company Night Shoot, pass the pistol match (APWA) (alternative personal weapon assessment), pass 2 BFT's (basic fitness test), pass one CFT (complete fitness test), pass at least 2 weapon handling tests (within each of the six months), passed all the paper tests – map reading, fieldcraft, first aid, done practical tests – first aid, fieldcraft, attended a number of mandatory lectures – Law of Armed Conflict (LOAC), EOD Lecture (explosive ordinance disposal), and have gone on a camp/course lasting at least 8 days, done 3 weekend mini-camps.

The annual camp fulfilled quite a few of the bounty requirements. Mainly 8 days course, and you would probably get at least 2 range days, Done 1 APWT, a BFT, practical fieldcraft and first aid, so it was quite recommended that you attend the 'Annual Camp'

Most soldiers enjoyed annual camp, as you could let your hair down (to speak). When we finished the working day during camp, we would quickly get changed, and head down to one of the 'water holes' (Bars – either in the training barracks, or in a nearby village just outside camp).

At home most of us can't fully relax, as we are at risk. If we made a habit of going to a Public House, we would be setting a pattern, get targeted, and get fatally attacked.

Over in the mainland Britain, we had very little risk, and when we went out, could chat openly, enjoy the craic. Some men would nearly spend as much in the annual camp, as the bounty gave them at the end of the financial year.

How much do we get for a bonus each year. When I joined in 1987, the first bounty was £200, the second £300, the third and bounty's after that £400

Our (11th Battalion) annual camps were rotated through three main usual training camps in England and Scotland. Barry Buddon near Dundee, WarCop in Cumbria, and The Lydd & Hythe Training Camp in Kent. Each one had a different advantage to training.

WarCop had many ranges, from the FIBA (fighting in built up areas), to long section attack ranges. Cumbria was great for map reading, hiking, TAB's, rock climbing, canoeing, and large and long 24/48 hour exercises.

Barry Buddon, was quite flat, with excellent long ranges, and is close to forest areas where we would do our 24/48 hour exercise.

Lydd and Hythe has a very large 'village' urban training area, with numerous smaller ones as well. The large one was like a small town, and we would do our 24/48 hour exercise there, with movie type explosions, blanks, and normally another full-time company being 'the civvies'. One of the smaller villages, there was live firing at terrorist dummies that popped up in windows.

My first annual camp was in 1988. I had joined the Ulster Defence Regiment in 1987. The 9 days recruitment in 1987 qualified me for my first bounty of £200 (tax free) in April 1988.

My first camp, Warcop, in Cumbria (Lake District) in May 1988. I had been on about 3 mini-camps (weekend Friday evening to Sunday evening) during the past year, but was still quite anxious about going, and didn't know what to expect. Of course, the soldiers that had been going year upon year tried to scare you, giving exaggerated stories of what is going to happen to me, the beastings, long exercises etc. I was still a Sprog (young soldier)(still only 19 years of age, and under 10 stone in weight). A week or so before going, I was given a kit list, of what uniform and personal issued equipment to bring. That was my stuff. The rest of the kit (rifles, ammunition, company store equipment, company papers and documents, was moved to Warcop about Thursday or Friday. There was another company van accompanied the coach in which we were travelling, to carry the last pieces of equipment/ documents.

'Be in Mahon Barracks by 0700Hrs on Saturday, Muster parade 0730hrs, straight onto the coach after muster parade. If you're not there, you will not be going, and might lose next year's bounty. If you're in about 0600-0630hrs, you can get a quick breakfast at the cookhouse, before Muster!'. That was the briefing we got at the later part of the week, and it made me feel on edge, as I, at all costs, couldn't sleep in on Saturday morning.

Friday night/Saturday morning, I hardly slept. I was at the barracks just before 0600. Muster, briefing, and onto the coach. Then the few coaches that were carrying all of us part-timers, set off to the Port of Larne, to head across the water. I bumped into Trev on the ferry, he was with his platoon mates from 'F' Company (full-time) and was surprised at him coming to our camp. He said there were a few teams of full-timers coming across to help in the training (the HQ training company of course). I met Trev when I was coming out of the restaurant, after having some scoff (meal), I was carrying a 'Stena-Line' (Ferry Name) knife, fork and spoon, and Trev asked "What you got those for?", I answered "Cause I forgot to bring my own KFS (knife, fork & spoon) for camp, as the cookhouse's don't supply them, You have to bring your own!". Trev's face had a surprised look, also a look of realism. He said "Fuck Me! I hadn't thought of that". That day, I placed the cutlery into my webbing pouch, for use at camp. I used that very set of Cutlery throughout my entire Army Career. And still have them now!

That annual camp, and a large percentage of our annual camps, we travelled by coach and ferry, but there were a number of years, when travelling by coach was too dangerous, the IRA threat of attack was too great.

In August 1988 a coach carrying thirty two members of the 'Light Infantry' Regiment were travelling from RAF Aldergrove to Omagh. Along the main road from Ballygawley to Omagh, the IRA detonated a 200lb bomb that they had planted in a vehicle along the roadside. It was detonated by command wire, some 300 meters away! The blast left a crater 1.8m deep, hurled the coach 30 meters down the road, and threw the soldiers into the nearby fields and hedgerows. 8 soldiers died, 28 wounded. Subsequently for a few annual camps we travelled by RAF passenger planes, or the C130 Hercules.

Some blokes brought beer in their rucksacks, and were having a few cans, as we travelled to Warcop. Me, a new boy was being good.

Just before turning into Warcop Training Barracks, I saw for the first time, a Golden Eagle, on a telegraph pole. That made my day.

Off the coach, grab your Bergan, put the Bergan in with your platoon's Bergan's, and dress off for Muster Parade, which gave us range/barrack rules, where our accommodation was situated. And 'Yes' it all happened as fast as it reads. Every soldier that has been to camp for a couple of years knows the score. They wanted to claim a bunk or bed quickly (to get the best position in the platoon dormitory), get uniform sorted, shelved, then off to the Naafi or local pub. At least I had got my tooth cut, having been at a few mini-camps, and I ran (with the others) with my kit, to claim a bed, hoping that if I claimed one of the best beds, that a Corporal or senior soldier didn't come along and turf me out of it. The only difference was, I was in no hurry to get to the pub. I didn't want a honker of a hangover on the first training day of camp, especially if it is as terrible as I have been lead to believe?

Warcop has many tank ranges, and it was my first time seeing a working tank. We saw rows of them (Challenger MkII's) at the tank garages just beside the ranges! Purpose made tank ranges.

The training week compromised mainly of range work, section and team attack, fitness as in CFT, BFT, an assault course (of which Warcop has one of the longest), an R&R Day (rest and relaxation) in Blackpool, adventure training day (canoes, hiking and rock climbing).

Strangely in Warcop we didn't normally get the 48 hour exercise, as the 7 Days training was so compacted. Yes, we were away for 9 days, but the first day was travelling, getting to know the barracks, storing personal equipment, and operational equipment like rifles and radio's. The last day was getting the accommodation/barracks cleaned up for hand-over, packing personal and company kit, then travelling back to Portadown.

On Tuesday we went to the FIBA (fighting in built-up areas) range. This range was about 300 meters long. You started the range engaging targets from a window, targets down!, move right and engage targets from the side of a wall, targets down, moving right and engaging targets over or around a short wall, targets down, moving right, engaging targets from a rocky mound. STOP, unload, and reload with a fresh magazine. Breaking cover and foot patrol forward. Targets appeared at various times and places on the range. You would cock the rifle, weave, and get into a place (like a shell hole, or other areas of cover that was set out on the range) of cover, safety catch off, and engage the targets. Targets away, safety catch on, change mag if needed, then break cover. Breaking cover meant not to emerge from the exact position you dropped into, or were firing from, you back crawled, checked pouches are closed, emerged to the left or right of your firing point, carry on patrolling, More targets appear, and you repeated the 'contact'. Once at the end, the range officer unloaded you, made sure your rifle is safe. Then we dress back to the start.

I shot that match really well, in fact so well, that Sgt Lead-Balls asked if I wanted to stay on at the range. The reason being that today, there are many VIP's (Senior Officers in the Brigade, and dignitaries) coming to visit our Battalion training. They would be shown a good shoot, with a good score. Of course I said 'Yes' as I loved that range. Firing and manoeuvring? What wasn't to like? So for most of that day, I was running up and down that range, sometimes getting questioned by the VIP that was there at the time. The normal standard questions, like, 'How long have you been in the army?' 'Do you enjoy it?' 'What job do you do in your working week?'. I even got my picture taken that day. One which I still have a copy of.

We went to Warcop quite a few times over the years (once every three), I enjoyed the ranges and exercises there. It made things a bit more war like, when we saw the tanks working. Around Warcop/ Lake District, we had 'Tornado' Fighter planes contouring over the landscape, just about 8 to 10' off the ground. Sometimes we were looking down on the fighter planes as they passed in the valley's below us, when we were on a TAB, or exercise. It was strange looking down at pilots, as they navigated around the mountains. I sometimes made a joke, that I saw the pilot reading the Daily Mail, whilst flying along. As far as I know, the majority of times, the fighter planes were trying to get as close to the target as possible, without being caught by radar. When they were spotted, the fighter plane pulled up, and went almost vertical in the sky. It was impressive!

One day at Warcop, we had a R & R day where we were driving and walking along Hadrian's Wall. It started well, with short walks, talks from historians about the wall, but when it came lunch time, the company wanted to go to a public house for a nice lunch. The pub we went to was lovely, with lots of historical things around the walls, unfortunately we enjoyed it a little too much. By about half two in the afternoon, we had drunk the place dry. When beer ran out, we went onto shorts, and when they started to run out, we had to leave (and due to time). We didn't know at the time, but it came to our attention later that one of our group had removed a Flint-Lock Pistol from the Wall. (by mistake, as a joke, too much to drink) and when, we found who had lifted it, he returned it the next day, with an apology.

The Year after my first camp at Warcop, we were in Lydd and Hyde, Kent. It is mainly known for it's large (about town size) village, or should I say villages, as there is the very large one for training/exercises/scenarios where there are cameras recording everyone's exact movements. There are training explosives, gun shots and bullet hits, and there is normally another company/ regiment playing 'civvies' in the 'village' whilst any regiment is training. There is a smaller village, where there is live firing and manoeuvring when we come under 'contact'. Another smaller village, where soldiers are in a Sanger overlooking 3 or 4 streets. Small dummies would come in and out of buildings, around corners and down streets. The role there is to shout warning orders, and engage only the dummies that are lawful (under the rules of 'the yellow card') to engage. At this range you have to be very careful (as in real life) to engage the target. Because as you go to engage, you cock your SLR, safety catch off, shout a warning order (if needed) and then engage. However just before you engage another dummy emerges (it may be a woman with baby in arms) in front of the target, and if you fire off a shot, it is very probable that you will hit the woman. Alternatively you could be told across the radio that a terrorist that has just killed someone is moving about, He is wearing a black top with red trousers. You see the terrorist, issue a warning, then take him out, only for another dummy to come out elsewhere looking the same, only to find out that you engaged a dummy with a red top and black trousers. The real Terrorist has come and gone.

I had to take things a bit more serious, as I now had Rank, I was a Lance Corporal, Team Commander, and can work one rank above, and be a Section Commander, but if I was conducting the role of section commander, it is overseen, or I am very trusted with the Job.

We had a 48 hour exercise in the village. Where there was a small barracks inside the village. So we were getting tested on our patrol skills, as well as getting tested on our camp guard and internal security drills. In the exercise (like all of them) we had very few rest periods. We were tested to the limit.

It was very daunting going into the village, but once there, you have no time to reflect. Each patrol you do, whether or not you got into a 'contact' when you came back into the barracks, you went straight to a de-briefing room, where the full section was questioned, critiqued, and shown on film. For instance, taking cover at a corner, and right beside you is a street bin, and because the soldier never checked it, or stood there too long, the bomb (inside the bin) went off. It's all, high octane stuff.

One patrol scenario in which I was the IC (section commander). I was taking a patrol through 'the village'. I had two teams, and we were moving through, using different streets, although we are very close to help each other if anything happens. MADDC (mutual support – all round defence – depth – deception – communication).

As my two teams came into an open square were we are being overlooked by many buildings, we got a 'contact' from the top window of a house (a shooting). We now have the 'immediate contact' period, where we returned fire (blanks), radioed it through, sent my other flank teams in depth, behind the house, where my second team sees the terrorist escaping by car! Now it is onto 'the immediate follow-up'. where we deal with the casualty, establish the 'contact point' , 'firing point' (place from which we were engaged from) secure/cordon them areas, and set up and clear a ICP (incident control point) for agencies like ATO (bomb squad), police, ambulance, to come to. We have to make sure it is safe and secure for us and other agencies to come into, as perhaps the terrorists have set up a follow-up explosion, to take out far more of us than the original contact. And so, the original contact, was just set up to lure us in. The terrorist hopes we will set up a ICP, at the location 'he' has picked. This is like the Warrenpoint Incident in 1979, where the IRA fired an explosion just as the Para's drove past, killing a number of them. But the Para's set up an ICP point in a car park, where there was a secondary device left. When the numbers inside the ICP had grown, a Wessex was just about to Land, the IRA (by radio control) detonated the secondary device, thus taking out more soldiers than the first (a total of 18 killed).

I establish an ICP point, got my team to clear and check it - I have more to do! Is the 'firing point' booby trapped? As in, if we enter the building, will we get hit with a secondary device, that is on a trip wire, or open a door that initiates a device. Also, are there any hostages in the building? The terrorists may have taken over the building by hostile means, and tied up the occupants? If there is are any hostages, perhaps they know if there is anyone still there. Are there any secondary devices? So I near the house, and shout up to the building from the corner of a wall (I don't want to expose myself!) "Is there anyone still in there?". No answer! I shout up again, only this time there is an answer "Yes". I shout up again "How many of you are there?", the answer "only me", I shout up "are you tied up, can you move", "I am not tied up, and I can move" is answered. Things are getting very serious, there is tension all around. I'm getting watched by the training team, and by the rest of my men. Everything is silent except me and the hostage in the top floor of the house. "Can you move about" I shout again. "yes" came the reply. I want to get a face to face with the hostage, to clarify that he is on his own, and not a gunman beside him. I shout, "come over to the window of the landing, and show yourself!" but there was no reply. Everything is silent and intense. I shout up again "come onto the landing, and show yourself, so we can talk". No answer, just silence! Everywhere is silent, everyone looking at me, and the window on the landing. Tension is growing. Then I heard the voice "what's a landing?". At which point everyone (my team, other teams, and even the training and DS staff, me included) stopped, and burst out laughing. It really cut the tension, of the scenario. In Northern Ireland, 'the landing' is the flat hallway at the top of the stairs, where you have all the doors of the bedrooms. the person (soldier) who was playing 'the civvie' came from a region in Britain, that doesn't know 'the landing'.

After that, the seriousness, and concentration never returned in that exercise, and we quickly got an 'end-ex' from the DS.

I have been back to The Lydd & Hyde training camp many times over the years, and you get to learn the layout of the training town. I enjoy the training. It's good to see what mistakes you make, how you have not made certain mistakes.

One year in the late 1990's I was at Lydd & Hyde Training Camp, and was a section commander the full week. The teams I have are good men. Men I work with every day. Men I trust with my life, and men that trust me with their lives. Colin, Eddie, Thomas, Good boy Stephen, John, and my 2IC is Aaron. I have a really great section, and so, wanted to show our potential.

Whenever there was no eyes or cameras on us, I let my teams take it easy, relax, and thus – when I (we) needed action, everyone sprung to it. I thought I'll change my tactics of what the army has set to tactics and response, do it differently, and unexpected.

We are on a rural patrol, of which enemy activity was reported. So going into this area, we can deduce that we will come under 'contact'. I have my own team, and my second team, so I decide to split it a little. My team is now only of 2 men, with another two teams of 3 men, instead of two 4 man teams. I take the centre route along the valley, whilst my other two teams of 3 have moved off a couple of minutes before me. They are flanking out to the left and to the right in the higher ground.

As expected the terrorists are hiding, expose themselves when they start shooting at us, but unknown to them, my two teams are level with them, and return fire upon them from the higher ground left and right of them. Then go in and capture them.

Another rural patrol, we know we are going to get engaged from around 300 meters away. It is to see if I am able to contain, move, engage, give good communications to my men and the other team. But I decided to shake up the army 'by the book' engagement, where each team moves by leap-frog towards the firing point.

The army 'by the book' is where one team goes firm and starts firing, the other team runs about 10 to 20 yards in front, goes down, and engages the firing point, whilst the other team then does likewise. But I thought about this. We are on high ground, overlooking the firing point. So I did it differently. Once we came under contact, my second team went to ground, returning fire, whilst my team Me, Colin, Eddie, and Scottie sprinted the full distance. Such a shock in the terrorist's eyes! As I neared them extremely fast. The terrorists managed to stumble away, escape via the getaway car, but we won the firefight.

In the village, I did similar tactics. Where my second team (when we came under contact) moved forwards in pairs, my team sprinting the full way down the street, weaving as we are running. We caught the terrorists, and were the only team to do so!

That camp! My section was the only section in the battalion (full-time & part-time) to have caught the terrorists in the village and rural scenarios. But I never got any recognition. Probably because I am not a 'Yes' man. Although during that camp another great full Corporal in our company, Dessie (who did not want to go for the rank of Sergeant, and had been asked many times) got 'promoted in the field' by the Battalion CO to the local rank of Sergeant.

Local rank is where you are given a rank, but not paid for it. You only get the pay of rank when you have completed the promotion course. Then you get an acting rank, where you have done the course, given the rank, given the pay, but are under probation, until you become substantive rank. Local and acting rank, you can lose, it gets taken from you by the company OC, but substantive rank, can only get taken from you by the Battalion CO, or above (depending on rank)

Barry Buddon is the third training camp in the trio. It's located in Scotland, near Dundee. It is the camp with the roughest of accommodation, but has the best in pubs and night life. The accommodation is the old Naafi dormitories, where if it's wet, raining, you have to run along duck boards to get to the ablutions. There wasn't much heat in our dormitories, but we got on with the Scottish people so well. In the nearby village of Lucknow there were a few good public houses. If it was at the weekend, then we could (after having a few drinks in one of the local pubs) go into Dundee, where there were a few night clubs, that started near midnight. But if you enjoy the nightlife and social drinking? Then there was a good chance you'll not be getting into bed until about 3 or 4 am, only to be awakened at 6 to 0630hrs, not enjoy the morning! Barry Buddon is quite flat, and has quite a few ranges (I think one ranges out to 800 meters (one of the few in Britain)), and quite a lot of training area.

Often we travelled to a forest Area for our 48 hour exercise.

My first time at that training camp (Warcop), I remember in the training camp, lining up on the Monday evening to use the only public telephone in the camp, which was near the guard room. It was only a small phone (not a phone box) on the corner near the camp entrance. Lining-up, before it was my turn, Eddie was phoning his mum. I overheard him. His mum was asking where he was, as she had made lunch for his work today, but it was still sitting in the kitchen, and your dinner tonight is getting cold! Where are you? When he came off the phone, I was laughing my head off, and when I started to tell the rest of our lads about it, they decided I needed a big pile-on. They pushed me down on the grass, everyone piled on top of me (about 10 or 11 Soldiers), I had to hold my breath because if I let it out, I think my rib cage will cave in?

Annual training camp was hard work, hard training, but it's good to get away from the risks and threats of Northern Ireland, and let your hair down (so to speak, as we all have very short hair) with people that lived in the same wave length.

We had mini-camps about four or five times a year, and they were mainly in Ballykinler training camp in Co. Down, or Magilligan training camp, right beside HMP Magilligan in Co. Londonderry. We didn't get letting our hair down at mini-camps, as we were only there from Friday night to Sunday afternoon.

We don't often have Saturday evening off to enjoy a bit of craic. Sometimes there is an exercise from Saturday to Sunday. Perhaps in the village or Stripwoods of Ballykinler, or around the vast training area of Magilligan.

The difference between Ballykilner and Magilligan, was that Ballykinler had lots of regiments using different areas/ranges. Magilligan! it was only our company had the full training area for the weekend, so we wouldn't be wandering into another regiment/battalion's area by mistake.

Throughout this chapter about annual and mini-camp's, it sounds like I (we) drink a lot. But I only drank when at mini or annual camp, as I had to be vigilant in normal everyday weeks when at home.

As they say "drink in, wit out". If I drank in day-to-day life, I would be setting patterns, could get attacked, and if I was attacked whilst I had drink in me, You can guess who will lose?

Every day, every hour, in my day to day life, I had to be alert!

In Ballykinler training camp, we exercised in 'the village' about 1 in 4 times of going there, sometimes live firing 'fire & manoeuver' through the 'Hollow'. It was quite a long range with training roads, junctions, open flat square space in the valley, and flat gorse land. All of which there were 'fall when hit' targets (steel figure 11 combat targets, on electronics, to pop up from a controller or timer) hidden around, which pop up. Along with live bullets from 'The Gimpie' just above our heads (glad I'm not too tall).

We also used this range to practice contact whilst being in a CMV (Civilianised Military Vehicle).

Beside 'the village' was a newly built hall with the 'FATS' (Fire Arms Training Simulator). We went there to do mandatory training (twice a Year) with the Judgmental Training Team. The F.A.T.S. was an indoor Range, but the firearms (mostly SA80's) did not fire projectiles, but (like a video game) fired lasers. The rifle was powered by compressed air, which gave recoil, the cocking handle went back and forth like the real thing.

The cinema screen/scenario could be set up like an outdoor range, with the reality of wind, stoppages, and mag changes. The computer recorded your shots and hits. You could also have war/conflict scenarios. But in judgmental training, it was just like a foot patrol through an urban area. Four soldiers up, and patrolling, whilst the rest of the platoon watch and take note mentally. In the scenario we are patrolling down an urban street, with the odd kid playing on the bike, other people walking about doing day to day things. Then a terrorist pops out, or maybe two, and an incident (contact) occurs, in which we used lethal force. Once it finished (about 5 minutes or so) we were questioned by the judgmental team, as what had happened, what we did, how many shots did we fire, give descriptions of the terrorists, also the rest of the platoon who were watching, were questioned too.

The team was asked what the mother that was pushing the pram was wearing in the video? Did she have any children with her? How many? Boys or girls? After the open discussion, amongst all of us, we said the woman was wearing a raincoat, and there was red somewhere, one child walking alongside the pram! In fact there was no woman there, and no pram.

In our tunnel vision, where we are concentrating on the incident, anything can be added into our memory.

It all started from an incident in Belfast a number of years ago, where a man wielding a wooden baton, was running at a number of RUC men. As he neared, he drew back the baton, about to hit one of the RUC men in the head. One of the RUC officers, from the corner of his eye, saw this happening. It was happening so quick he didn't have time to warn the officer that the man was about to hit, so the RUC man swung round with the rubber bullet gun, and shot the attacker at point blank, in the chest, which later killed the attacker.

When the policeman was making his statement, he said that a man with a red top was running over to attack, when he saw it, he had to use reactive force, to stop him! But in reality, the attacker was not wearing red! The RUC man was asked to change the statement. He would not! So the investigation team went out to the incident location. To the very spot where the RUC man was standing, which way he turned during the attack, and they saw a large poster on the wall behind, which was predominently red in colour.

This questioned and changed the way of thinking about incidents/statements and witness statements. Everyone sees the same incident, but almost everyone remembers and sees it in a different way.

I enjoyed going to annual and mini-camps. Annual camps were a break away from day to day life, where we could let our hair down (so to speak), didn't have to watch our backs. We trained hard with each other, and enjoyed the craic working, and socialising after working hours.

As for the mini-camps, as I was usually on the training/instructional team, so in addition to joining in, I got to assist and train other soldiers.

6

Lurgan

Lurgan! A different 'kettle of fish' compared to Craigavon. It is much busier than Craigavon, more life around. The Main Street is a busy place, with the big Parish Church at the top of the town and Lurgan Police Station beside it.

Lurgan has some very strong Loyalist and Republican areas, with well-known players. Craigavon has its risks and dangers, but Lurgan is way above that. There have been so many attacks and murders in the Lurgan area. We had to be very careful. The use of ECM (electronic counter measure) in Craigavon was needed, in Lurgan it was essential.

ECM ? Electronic Counter Measure! It all really got started after the two radio controlled bombs in Warrenpoint, Co. Down 1979. When 18 British soldiers got killed. The bombs were initiated from a vantage area, which was in Cooley Peninsular in Co. Louth, Southern Ireland.

The British Army had to move with the times, the same way the IRA was moving with the times, technology, and tactics of attacks. The IRA had mainly used 'command wire' connection to the explosives, but more and more were using remote/radio control to initiate the detonation. Now the British army/security forces needed to stop it. They worked tirelessly to make portable ECM systems. It was so secure, that we (the soldiers) didn't know how it worked, and which frequencies it covered. It was so top secret, that we, under no circumstances, could lose one, or have one taken from us. It was more dangerous to lose one ECM, than loose a 4 tonne army lorry full of rifles and ammunition.

As there were many more people walking about, whilst we were patrolling, and doing foot patrols, I got talking to many of them. They were lovely people, but in the Republican areas, they did not want to be seen talking to us. I remember quite a few times, when on foot patrol, talking to some of the residents, often in places that they could not be seen easily, or when it was quite dark. I walked along beside a resident, and started to chat to them. It wasn't always the easiest to break the ice. But it was nice if I could get chatting to them.

I am a very strong believer in the 'hearts and minds' attitude. When you get chatting, it can be quite surprising what you learn, and sometimes! Unbeknown to the person I'm chatting to, hear about some of the players movements, or that they were seen with so and so.

There were constant threats! And sometimes attacks on the RUC in Lurgan. Quite a few times, when a player heard, or saw a police car coming around from, or to the police car park at the back of the station, they threw an explosive device (like a 'coffee-jar bomb') over the high wall/fence, to try and hit the police car, and possibly a police officer who would be walking along on the inside of the station.

I remember on more than two occasions, when a Mk 12 Horizontal Mortar was seen, on roads near the centre of Lurgan (Aghagallon side) or just into the country about a mile or two from Lurgan centre. By the time of the sighting, information getting passed to forces that can deal with it (Army EOD (explosive ordnance disposal), or even us (UDR)), and reacting, getting safely over to cordon/secure the appropriate area – It was gone.

The IRA knew the Mk12 has been compromised, and did not want to lose it. To lose it, had at least three bad outcomes for the IRA. 1 – It never succeeded, and we succeeded in catching it (one – nil) hence bad propaganda against the IRA, and positive broadcasts for the security Forces. 2 – The MK 12 was difficult to make, and the IRA didn't have an abundance of them, if this task did not succeed, then take it away to use some other time, and we (the security forces) will also be scared, as we knew it was still out there. 3 – If We could get it, then we can take it away to be scrutinized, as in how it worked, how it was made, what it was made with, and perhaps establishing where the parts were obtained. Quite often we knew who had made it, and where it was made, and of course! The forensic evidence obtained from the device. Hopefully leading to a conviction.

After I joined in 1987, the threat of the MK12 kept increasing, especially around the Lurgan/Craigavon Area. In the late eighties, early nineties the IRA has had many successes with them.

My Friend (on a UDR mobile patrol) was seriously injured by one that was planted along Killylea Road, Armagh. March 1991. It struck the Land Rover, killing one soldier, wounding all the rest that were in the Rover, one soldier died from his injuries later, and one soldier lost a leg.

In the Lurgan area, we knew there was at least one Mk12 lurking around somewhere. We had to be ready, as best we could.

The threat of the Mk12 kept growing. threats and risks kept rising! The Mk12 Mortar threats, and attacks on patrols and security forces personnel. Our battalion was one of, if not the biggest battalions of the British Army. And because of the threats and 'players' activities and movements, the battalion set up a 'spotter platoon'! A number of soldiers who were well skilled and fit (full-time & part-time) were taken off normal patrols/ training, to be put in a new (sneaky-beaky) platoon. Patrols to be in the Lurgan/Craigavon Area. Not regular overt patrols, doing VCP's and foot patrols, but to move 'in-depth' and just do lie-up positions, in nearby fields, behind hedges, on top of buildings, and other places no member of the public would be aware of. They just monitored, recorded players movements and activities.

My friend Splodge (full-time Corporal) was the Section-Commander of one squad, and had been doing the spotter-patrol for quite some time, knew all the places to hide, and where the players, and vehicles normally hung out, including times of day.

One morning Splodge commanded a spotter patrol in Lurgan. They had been out on the op a couple of hours (normal patrol would be approximately 8 hours), when the ops room (Zero) radioed him, told him to fold-up his patrol, RTB (return to base) with the trace and de-brief! Splodge asked why? As they had only got out and went firm and had established a good position. Zero told him there was another patrol coming into Lurgan, on overt patrols, and He was to come off the ground in case of a 'Blue on Blue'. Splodge asked who it was, as the area was very dangerous for mobile patrol movements. Zero advised it was a patrol from Armagh, regular soldiers, not R/Irish. Splodge said again that it was dangerous, stupid, as the on-coming patrol knew nothing about the area.

Splodge thought there was something more to it, than he was told. Consequently, when he returned to Mahon Road, de-bombed, changed into civvies, signed out. He then returned back to Lurgan, in his own car, to see for himself. A while later, he was standing at Portadown Road keeping his ears and eyes open!

A mobile patrol was going into Lurgan from the Craigavon direction along Portadown Road. It was the regular army regiment, that was based in Armagh and were heading into Lurgan to start their patrol (as the ops room had indicated). They travelled along the Portadown Road (a very straight road) at a fair speed, where the speed will make the patrol hard to target.

As they approached the first of the traffic light junctions (Old Portadown Road) beside St. Pauls Church, they stopped for a red light. When the lights changed – Red Yellow – Green, the two Land Rovers moved off. Just as the second one was moving off, a Mk12 Horizontal Mortar came to life. Hitting the second Land Rover, killing all occupants in it.

After the initial contact period, a cordon quickly went in, and when a soldier was getting into cover (so he wasn't in an exposed position) in hedgerow, he noticed, in the sunlight, the sun flicking along a bit of spider web? But it looked thicker! It was a bit of fishing line! It was very lucky he saw this, as it was a secondary device/booby trap, set up to kill/mame another soldier or perhaps more. This secondary device was not to be initiated by remote control, it was a self-initiated booby-trap initiated by the pulling or tugging of the fishing line, which is tied onto a peg, and when the peg is pulled free, the connection in the wires comes together, setting off another explosion!

The 'command wire' that set off the Mark 12 ran hidden to, and around the St Pauls church. Perhaps the traffic lights turned red when the mobile patrol was approaching, by a player or sympathizer pressing the crossing button. Then quickly walking away?

Splodge saw the explosion happen, but could not react, as he was in civvies, off-duty, and if he ran in, one of the patrol may shoot at him, in the confusion, and if they didn't, then the Republican Players could see him, then put a face to a name, to future target.

The threat of an attack using a Mk12 didn't vanish, as we knew there were more out there? This threat escalated to the point that we must stop our Land Rovers approaching vulnerable points, like junctions, traffic lights, and other places that the Section Commander (or myself) sees, or gets a sixth sense about it.

We (the commanders) looked out for possible vulnerable points, stop and walk through, taking note of dicking (spotting) points, and possible firing points. We will pass this information on to the ops room & Int cell for other patrols that will be visiting/patrolling the area.

I am concentrating too much on the Mk12. I shouldn't forget about the other devices/ threats? There was still the ongoing imminent threat of a white Toyota Hi-Ace van being loaded with explosives to be used in the towns, or security force strongholds, and a new device (much smaller) was being used – the coffee jar bomb. Like it says on the tin. An empty coffee jar, filled with explosive and shipyard confetti (bits of steel, and bolts). This device was thrown, and when it hit the ground or Land Rover and broke, the fly-off lever was released, which initiates the explosion.

There is still the threat of getting shot at, but it has reduced (at this moment) significantly, as the IED (in its many forms) is reaping so much reward for the terrorist. Off-duty though was different. There was always the threat of getting shot, and when you least expected it!

'C' Company, whose TAOR is Lurgan, were really professional when patrolling the Lurgan area. They knew the ground so well. Knew where the nooks and cranny's where, short-cut lanes, and where there have been attacks/disturbances before. 'C' Company were very committed in stopping the terrorists! Many of the company had personal reasons, as quite a few friends/comrades/family had been killed by terrorist actions. It was hard for terrorists to target 'C' Company whilst they are on ops, as they use the M.A.D.D.C. (mutual support, all round defence, depth, deception, communication) to the fullest extent. Sometimes they would leave the police station with three teams, then split into 4 teams, which gave 2 sections of 2 teams. Quite often with one overt foot patrol, and another section staying hidden – going in depth, hoping to catch the terrorist who would attempt to attack the patrol.

I remember once or twice, being given a rollocking from the 'C' Company CSM, or platoon commander, that my patrolling on a certain night was shit. Piss poor performance! As I had gone places, or done something, or just slack patrolling, that put my section/patrol under so much risk. I learnt from what I was told.

One Saturday, I was on patrol. I was the 2IC (not Section Commander, but still the commander of the second team), where we were patrolling Craigavon in the morning, moving into Lurgan for the afternoon. We did a couple of vehicle check points, overt patrolled for a bit, around by Brownlow House, car parks, streets and around Lurgan Centre.

At 1520hrs, we set up a vehicle checkpoint on the Portadown Road, just outside the centre of town. All was going well. But after around five minutes, the street we were working on was quite empty? My inner alarm started to go off, my sixth sense. Somethings wrong? We normally would be getting a bit of abuse on this street, but we are not! It is a combat indicator! We are going to get attacked! (On Bloody Sunday (1972) the residents of the area, were told to stay away, as there is going to be an attack on the British Army). My inner alarm is going mad! I immediately, told my team to fold/collapse the VCP, and give cover! Then I made my way quickly over to the section commander (a Lieutenant) and said "Pack up NOW, and follow me out". The Lieutenant said we aren't to stop this VCP for another 10 minutes? I was stern, and turned, looked into the Lieutenant's face, once again said "Just fold up, and follow me out – don't question me" and I shouted over to their team "right lads – pack up". With speed I returned to my Rover. We did a 'U' turn, and I made our way out, trying to not use predictable roads or junctions.

When we were patrolling Lurgan, as well as not using predicable routes, or patrols, unlike Craigavon, we needed to be careful with our return to Mahon Road Barracks after our patrolling!

If we were patrolling Craigavon, as risky as it is, there were so many roads between Craigavon and Portadown, it would be very difficult to predict which roads we would use. From Lurgan, there were so many routes home, but we naturally get tunnelled to predictable routes. Let's be human about this. When we have each done a day's work, quickly thrown our dinner down our throats, rushed out to get to Mahon Rd, and out on Ops. Then be alert throughout the patrol. Now that it's time to head back to Mahon Rd, get de-bombed (empty the rifle magazines, hand our rifles into the armoury, get our ppw's, get all patrol/ops kit checked back into the company stores). We/I get slack! We want to get home. I can't do that! I am either a team or section commander, and I still have to think about the safety of my team and section (even if I am only a team commander that night). We have to stay alert/on the ball. The majority of times we headed back to Portadown through Craigavon, and there we were travelling along carriageways that are in cuts, and had foot bridges over them. We had to stay alert.

One other night 'C' Company were returning to Portadown from Lurgan, and driving through the Craigavon area. The lead Land Rover hadn't seen anything, nor did the second Land Rover (my friend 'Honey Monster' was the commander),and something hit the Land Rover bonnet, bouncing off it, falling to the ground. Honey Monster stopped the Rover, radioed ahead for the lead Rover to stop. Honey Monster's team went up the grass banks on each side to see if there was anyone, and to ascertain who it was (nobody seen). Honey Monster then walked back to see what hit the Land Rover (normally we wouldn't do that, as a lot of stones are frequently thrown at us, but this was abnormal as it was after 0100hrs in the morning). It turned out to be a coffee-jar bomb. It never smashed, it bounced off the bonnet, as the bonnet wasn't hard. The bonnet isn't armoured as it wasn't protecting the team. If it had been armoured then the engine couldn't cool.

The threat of the so called 'coffee-jar' bombs didn't last for long, as so many of them didn't smash, and so! Forensics could try to gain evidence.

The 'cry wolf' of the white Toyota Hi-Ace van? We had been told since I joined (and most probably before then) about the imminent attack of a vehicle borne IED.

In the early 90's the IRA found a new recipe for explosives, which could be made very quickly, using icing sugar and fertilizer, ground down, mixed, and just loaded into a van. The van became so heavy, that the IRA had to put wooden wedges into the suspension springs, to keep the van high, and not arouse suspicion.

March 1992, we were on patrol on a weekday evening, and we got a report of a vehicle bomb in Lurgan Centre. We got many hoax threats, and all of them hoaxes! The terrorists were probably just watching how we react, or just to provoke us, and waste our time, bog us down, but this night, we cordoned off the main street (each end) and were awaiting for 'Felix' to arrive (Army Bomb Disposers' (EOD)), when the explosion went off. A very large explosion, then silence, followed by the sound of all the shop alarms going off. 'Tiggy' was standing in front of a large shop window, when the clutch pedal of the van narrowly missed him and shattered the shop window. We had no casualties that evening, but it was a new lesson learnt. It was a 1,000 lb bomb and destroyed most of Lurgan town centre.

In May 1993, on a Saturday morning, Portadown town centre got the same. That Saturday morning, the IRA gave enough warning for the police to clear the main street, but there was a public bar very close to the vehicle bomb, which refused to clear. The RUC had no time to argue, or forcefully clear the bar, so told them to move to the back! When the bomb went off (another 1,000 lb's) nobody in the bar was injured. That was because the premises were long and thin, and the explosion decided not to go that way. A miracle.

After bombs like this, and because they were so easily made, city and town councils around Northern Ireland decided that they needed to secure the centres. So set up barriers around the town centres, that closed in/around 6pm and opened again 8am in the morning. We were tasked with patrolling and checking town centres during our operation times.

The threats kept rising in the Lurgan area. In the 80's Belfast was the most dangerous place to be living/working/patrolling, then in the early 90's it was Newry. Then, in the mid-nineties, Lurgan was the most dangerous place to be living/patrolling

A good friend of mine who was in 'C' Company lived just outside of Lurgan, and worked in Lurgan, and of course patrolled Lurgan. He worked in a factory that had a security fence around the factory car park, and a security gate.

Tommy was very security conscious, varying his routes, checking his car both when leaving home, leaving work, was always ready for an attack on him. Tommy has a .38" revolver, and when leaving work, always had it close to call, was always on his pins, watching for players, or anyone watching him, or following him.

It was a Thursday in May 1993, and a work mate asked Tommy if he would leave him home, after work! But this meant that Tommy would have to drive through the centre of Lurgan. Tommy tried to avoid this as best he could, so not to be seen or dicked, to try not to set a pattern, that might lead to him getting attacked or killed! That evening he had to drive through Lurgan centre!

When leaving work, Tommy acted like everyone else who worked there but stayed ultra-alert. With his workmate in the car, he left work's secure car park, staying aware of anyone who might attack him. On leaving Tommy saw someone watching him, but couldn't work out who it was. He drove his Rover 214 into Lurgan town, and had to stop at the give-way opposite the Lurgan RUC Station.

At that exact same time, a full-time patrol ('F' Company) were finishing their foot-patrol, they were on the Main Street, just about to go through the entrance gates to the police station. Suddenly there was an explosion! The section commander knew his section was under attack! But from where? There must have been a RPG fired at them? But it missed and hit a car!(His thoughts in that split second.)

It was not an RPG, it was a 'Mercury Tilt Switch', and as soon as Tommy pulled off from the junction, the mercury (in the tilt switch) made the connection complete, thus firing the detonator, which ignited the main bomb charge.

The device was an 'under vehicle booby trap' (UVBT) and was directly below the floor of the car, directly under Tommy's seat. The UVBT had been placed under Tommy's car whilst he was nearing finishing work. How did it get placed there, as Tommy parked in the secure car park? The fence had been snipped open, in an unseen area, and the terrorist had an opportunity to place the IED under the car. Most probably with a very strong magnet, on the outside of the box. Then he would quickly adjust the tilt-switch, turn on the 'Parkray timer, to give him a safe time to disappear (so the bomb doesn't go off in his face), then pull out the wooden dowelling pin (it is a safety catch, that stops the connection of the two steel pins, that complete the circuit.)

The UVBT! This is a home-made IED, and is made for just what is written on the tin (a victim operated bomb, made to kill whoever is driving). Its construction is: Semtex. The main explosive, a detonator (looks like a thin tube (about the width of a pen, and about half the length)), one or two batteries (to fire the detonator), a 'parkray' timer (a strong winded timer used mainly in cities like London, where you set the timer to the minutes your car parking timer is set to, so you can look at it, whilst shopping, or in business), and a mercury tilt switch (probably one taken out of home heating thermostats), and a wooden doweling pin which stops the circuit connection (in between the steel pins that are glued onto the parkray timer, and the pin sticking out of the side of the bomb assembly).

The explosive, detonator, batteries are inside a plastic or wooden lunch box (to keep it dry). No shipyard confetti is needed, as steel from the car will improvise this. We are told if we are ever searching someone and come across a wooden doweling pin in his possession! Keep it! As we have been informed, if the person placing the bomb under a car doesn't bring back the pin to the main player, he will most likely be kneecapped. If we find a doweling pin in anyone's possession, as well as keeping it, look around cars that are close to where we are searching the suspect, and inform the ops-room.

The foot patrol soldiers very quickly worked out what has just happened, and instinctively moved in and pulled Tommy out of the car. Another soldier went in, and pulled out left overs of the two legs. Miraculously Tommy hadn't died, but was drifting in and out of consciousness'. He was able to give his name, Ni-Pin and blood group, whilst and during the ambulance arriving and taking him to the Craigavon Hospital.

I (at this moment) was the team commander, doing a static road checkpoint, on Mahon Road, Portadown. I was on the South V.C.P. whilst the other team is doing the North V.C.P.

I heard the immediate 'contact report' coming through the radio, from the full-time section commander in Lurgan, a couple of seconds/minutes after the explosion!

When you hear the word 'CONTACT' through the radio, everything stops. Nobody is to use the airwaves. The priority is to let the contact team get in touch with the ops room, other teams, and other agencies.

I told the rest of my team "Shut-Up! There is a CONTACT coming through!", and quickly got out my notebook to take down relevant information, like the location, 6 or 8 figure grid ref, what has happened, and (hopefully) if we are needed! The immediate contact report came through 'bomb! perhaps a Mk12?' then the section commander found out it was a UVBT and gave 'sit-reps' (situation reports, of what was ongoing, and happening). The section commander started doing what was prohibited on the radio, and curse through it.

Once the bomb had gone off, the soldiers had pulled Tommy from the car, men from a Republican club, that was on the nearby corner, started coming out, shouting abuse at the section, saying things like 'can we come and join the BBQ?'.

I could hear the Republican civilians, and what they were shouting, on the radio. I could hear the section commander shouting 'Get them Fuckers away.'

I knew the location of the explosion, and through sit-reps knew it's a UVBT, but who was in the car? Then the section commander sent the victims Ni-Pin number over the net, and I knew who it was! I nearly dropped on the spot! At about this moment I heard the explosion with my ears. The sound of the explosion had reached Portadown. And about 5 or so minutes later, I could smell the cordite, I could smell the explosion! I thought my mind was getting mixed up, confused? I asked my other team mates if it was my imagination? Or could they too smell the explosion? And they all could.

Tommy went to the Craigavon Hospital, and quite quickly was moved to the Ulster Hospital in Dundonald.

Tommy lost his two legs from about the knees down, and two fingers. The emergency crew (ambulance crew) said that if he hadn't been pulled from the car in the first few seconds, he would have died, and if the ambulance had been a minute later, he would have died with blood loss.

When Tommy was in hospital, he was still under threat. The IRA would like, and would try if they got the chance, to finish off the job they had planned to do – kill Tommy. So our battalion put on 24 hour protection on him. I tried to get down and do the protection duties as often as I could!

The protection duties? As I have said earlier in the book, we were trained in the use and carriage of the Browning Hi-Power 9mm pistol, and this was one of the occasions where we carried it. Ozzie and I volunteered to carry out the protection duties. We couldn't use our ppw's, as it was an active service duty, and we were required to carry service weapons. We both arrived in Mahon Road, Portadown, went to the armoury, signed out two 9mm's with 2 mags for each pistol. 13 rounds in each magazine! Then signed out a civilian type car from the M.T. went to the ops room/int cell finding out the given routes for today to and from the Ulster Hospital, asked if there were any specific threats or/ and terrorist activity.

When we got to the hospital, we parked in the normal car park so not to arise any suspicion, and made our own way to Tommy's private ward (with the pistols concealed on our bodies of course).

A majority of times, we sat outside Tommy's ward, and various times we went in and chatted. Although, often Tommy's wife was with him, if not he was sleeping/resting. There were quite a few times he was alone, but we didn't go in, as he was in a bad way, didn't want to see us. He was still trying to get to grips with what happened.

Tommy was so fit, did a bit of kick-boxing, and so many physical activities. To lose his legs, there was much to think about and work out.

At the incident point (bomb scene), Tommy's MOD90 (Army ID) was found at the side of the road about 30 meters from the car, but his revolver had disappeared/gone, never to be seen again.

One of Tommy's friends was a frequent visitor. John Lyness. John was a Sergeant in 'C' Company, and very close to his comrades in the company. He left the regiment in 1991, after service of over 20 years.

Incidentally: When the incident happened, and the 'F' Company patrol put the 'CONTACT' through on the radio, a Lynx helicopter was on a route nearby. It was the Army Air Corps, and the Lynx was taking an officer to a meeting.

When the pilot heard the contact report, he radioed that he was coming in to casvac the injured man. The officer in the back of the Lynx objected, stating his meeting was very important. The pilot replied saying the injured man is more important than his meeting. The officer further objected, threatening to charge the pilot, if he didn't continue to the meeting. The pilot stated "It's one of us, and I am going in to help!".

The Lynx landed beside the incident point, but the ambulance had already arrived and Tommy was getting moved. It would not have been any quicker to bring Tommy back to the Lynx, as Craigavon Hospital wasn't far away, and there were medical staff in the back of the ambulance. It is good to know, that everyone is trying to help.

In 1989, the IRA had planned to kill a well-known, very senior Judge, who lived in the Ballinderry area. One evening the IRA got an ASU Unit ready to go and kill him. They set off in a transit van. Two in the front, and a few armed men in the back. They had come from the Portadown/Lurgan area, and were a bit early for the planned attack! So the transit pulled into a quite large service station, on the A26, near Moira. They were waiting, to ensure the judge was at his home, getting psyched up for the attack, and making sure everything went according to plan.

Whilst waiting at the service station, a police car was patrolling past, and noticed this lone transit van. The petrol station was now closed! Why was the transit van sitting there, with two men in the front? Suspicious! The police men (2 of) stopped behind the transit, and got out to talk/question to the driver and passenger.

When walking towards it – the rear doors burst open, and the police saw a number of men with long barrelled weapons pointing them at them. The RUC men hit the deck. Just as the police hit the deck, the transit broke away, with some of the men falling out! Not sure exactly what happened after that, but the transit disappeared towards Glenavy, the loose men split-up, running into a field, towards the railway track that was nearby.

Information quickly passed through from the RUC to our Portadown Ops room, which tasked the 'C' Company patrol to cover various locations, that the suspects may use when coming off the railway, whilst on their way back to Republican estates in Lurgan. John Lyness was commanding the patrol that night, and knew the ground well. They went to a spot that overlooked the railway, stayed quiet, observing anything that was moving along the railway, or fields running parallel. John saw a silhouette figure, a man coming up from the railway, and saw he was carrying something. With the int-brief earlier, we knew the terrorists have been seen with long barrelled weapons, so John had a right to open fire, but does not. He challenged the figure, calling him forward. It was a well-known player. He came forward, and had no weapons, just a branch of a tree, like a walking stick/ beating stick whilst going through thick undergrowth. The player hadn't got any footwear on. Anyone who was found coming off the railway that night did not have any forensic evidence on them, and on subsequent searches, no weapons were found. They all got off scott free.

Little did the IRA ASU know. The judge was not at home that evening, but there were some visitors in the judges house, waiting to welcome the IRA Active Service Unit. The visitors were a team from the SAS. They were there to stop the attack and end the terrorists membership of the IRA.

John Lyness left the UDR in 1991 and kept in touch with the comrades of 'C' Company. John visited Tommy in hospital quite a few times. He really looked after his men when he was in the UDR, and was very well respected and liked.

On Thursday 24th of June 1993, John was coming home from work. He was 57 years old, and although he had left the UDR, he still worked.

John got dropped off on Robert Street (near Lurgan Swimming Pool) and was walking a short distance home. It was a regular journey, but there should be no worries, as John had left the UDR two years prior. As he was walking home, he recognised the 'well known' player coming quickly towards him, from the thick hedge, that ran along the left hand wall. The well-known player must have been waiting in the hedge, for John to return home from work. The IRA man (he was no longer a suspect, as he was bearing a weapon to use in murder) pulled a short barrelled weapon (pistol or revolver) from his short jacket, and drew it up to point it at John.

John saw what exactly was happening and had to react. His life depended on this exact moment. John reached inside his clothing and pulled out his privately owned ppw. At that moment the shooting began, but the shots were coming from the IRA man, and not John. He was having problems with his pistol – it wouldn't fire! Had John left the safety catch on? Or had the safety catch moved slightly, which meant the trigger wasn't connecting. Time is short, decisions are reduced! John kneels behind a short wall, trying to clear the pistol, but time has run out. The IRA man has caught up, and is now at point blank range, and again opens up on John, taking his life. At that moment another man who was also in the Royal Irish (the regiment changed in 1991, when the UDR was 21 years old, and got a ROYAL Status) saw what was happening, grabbed his own ppw, quickly coming out of his house to engage the IRA man and help John.

By the time the second man got out of his home, the IRA player, had made his way back to the hedge, grabbed his bike and was now cycling through Lurgan Park, back to the Republican estate, and most probably back to his home, when on his way he would quickly get rid of the firearm (probably another IRA man, waiting to pick up the firearm, and move it on), get into the house and take off all the clothes, and quickly jump into the shower to wash away every piece of forensic evidence, whilst at the same time, his clothes are quickly in the washing machine, in order to get rid of all blood stains, gun powder residue, and any other forensic evidence, which could convict.

John Lyness, aged 57, who was a very loved man was taken from us, nobody ever was convicted, but the off-duty soldier has seen the IRA Player from his house? Yes, but because he was in the Royal Irish, the witness statement could not be used, as it was thought it could be false, and biased due to the witness being in the Royal Irish Regiment.

The impact of that evening's killing was felt throughout the Battalion. Honey Monster was on an instructional course in Ballykinler, and the news got through. Honey Monster was hit for six, but the rest of the people on the course, and the instructors weren't from Mahon Road Barracks, didn't know John Lyness. Full-timers and regular regiments tend not to think too highly of part-timer's and they talk ill of us.

That night one of the instructors said something like 'stupid part-timers! he deserved it!'. Honey Monster! The red mist just came down. Honey Monster pounced over to him, and gubbed him (chinned him, and knocked him flying). Honey Monster wasn't easily angered, and if you ever did, you'd better keep out of his way, as he could smash through walls if he needed! In this case John Lyness was such a close friend and former colleague.

Honey Monster got quickly arrested by the Regimental Police, but they didn't hold him for long once they found out the circumstances!

I heard about the shooting, but didn't know the details, or who it was until the weekend. I took it very personally as well. I knew John Lyness a little, but not much, as he was in a different company. I took it very personally and emotionally, as John was one of us, and also a ppw holder. It was as if I had been shot. I analysed what had happened, what could have gone wrong, what should and should not have happened. Each attack on a Royal Irish soldier and RUC officer, I take personally. And try to learn from it. The attacks were so frequent, and to avoid being the victim, we need to learn what happened. The shooting of Iain Warnock in Portadown (1992), and Colin McCullough 1990, to name just two.

Colin McCullough lived in Lurgan, and was a part-timer in 'C' Company 11 UDR. I just knew him, when on my way to the armoury or the Ops room, or just passing by, as I was in 'D' Company (the portacabin beside C Company). He was always well dressed, very much looked after himself, and was very pleasant. He patrolled and lived in Lurgan. The majority of 'C' Company patrolled and lived in Lurgan, and that was a danger, as the terrorists got to recognise servicemen on patrol, and sight them in Lurgan whilst off-duty, working in their civvie job.

Colin was 22, hardworking, engaged, and looking forward to getting married. It was the 23rd of September 1990, the weather is nice. Colin and his fiancée were enjoying life, and he had this evening free. They were in Lurgan, and fancied getting a takeaway, and enjoying this evening together.

They ordered the takeaway in the centre of Lurgan, but unbeknown to them, Colin was spotted by a suspect IRA man.

Colin, looking forward to the meal, and time with his fiancée, headed out of town, towards a beauty spot beside Lough Neagh. His mind was on the present, future, and didn't realise he was being followed! The IRA watched where he went, and when they saw he had parked, in the Oxford Island car park, they figured he would be here for a while, as he had a meal to eat, and most probably, a bit of time alone with his fiancée? Time enough to get an ASU set up?

Colin and his fiancée had finished the takeaway and were enjoying each other's company. All of a sudden a figure was at the side of the car! A long-barrelled weapon is pointing at him, and shot him many times (13), before Colin had any chance of reacting. Colin's fiancée knew he had a ppw and grabbed it. She pointed it at the terrorist, but couldn't fire a shot, it didn't seem to work? She didn't know how to operate the pistol. Not one defensive shot was returned. The terrorists disappeared.

Threats and terrorist activity escalated in the Lurgan/ Craigavon area, and our company was patrolling more. Our company wasn't patrolling the centre as much as 'C' Company, as they were the experts in the terrorist suspects addresses, vehicles, and the ground, as in roads, short-cuts, vulnerable points, and past incidents.

It was Thursday 20th December 1990, I was taking a patrol out. The threats we heard from int-cell were similar to those we have heard for the last few weeks. Threat of a vehicle born IED coming into town centres or planted near security force bases. Look out for Toyota Hi-Ace vans.

Also, a threat of CQA (close quarter attack) whilst off-duty, keep your routes varied, and don't set up predicable patterns. That's easier said than done! When you have a full-time job, and a home that doesn't move about?

The first of the patrol this evening is to do overt patrolling partially through the outskirts of Craigavon, and through the centre of Lurgan. To give overt patrolling through Lurgan centre is good at this time of evening (just after 8pm) as it is quite a common time for the RUC to change (coming on & going off duty). We keep our eyes open for any suspicious persons or players dicking the station, or around the Lurgan centre. It is also good to pass through Lurgan, whilst 'C' Company is also patrolling Lurgan, it confuses the players, that are trying to see where 'C' Company are patrolling. They might think we are 'C' Coy? And so not know where the Lurgan patrol actually is?

We just do a single travel through Lurgan centre, but our main area to patrol is Waringstown, and on to Donaghcloney, then Gilford. We patrol through Waringstown and set up a VCP on the Banbridge Road.

Just set up the VCP, and just about to check the cars coming through, when I heard a 'contact report' coming through on the radio. I stop everything I am doing and listen. Constable Wethers got shot just as he is parking his car in the drive or garage at the side of his house. I know where he lives, as we had just passed his home on our way here, and on passing his home, we chatted about him and his nice house. I shout to all my men to 'Come on, come on, we're needed'. As the section is running, gathering the 'Stop Sign' I get onto the Ops Room on the radio – "Hello Zero, this is tango two one bravo. Moving now, and moving to Cottage Road, to cut off the terrorist escape route". Cottage Road, is one of the quickest ways to get to the republican estate in Lurgan, and it has been used quite often, as their escape routes. The Ops room return my call "Tango two one bravo, this is zero. 'NO' don't move! Stay at your current location!

At the same time my friend Trev (whom I joined the UDR through, in full-time UDR), had a patrol out in the Moira Area. He told 'zero' that he was moving to the Republican estate in Lurgan, to catch/stop the player from getting home. He was denied his movement also. We sat listening to the net, hoping that maybe some special forces team, were waiting to greet the homeward bound terrorists? Nothing happened? Why were we not allowed to react?

Constable Wilfred Wethers who was a full-time RUC man, had finished his duty at Lurgan Police station, and travelled home in his Mini car. On pulling into the drive/garage, an IRA man stepped around the corner and riddled the car with over 40 shots from a AK47. Wilfred never stood a chance. A lovely man, who had time for everyone. A good man – gone.

As well as the UDR personnel being under threat, so too were the RUC, full-time and part-time reserve.

Just before the shooting of Constable Wethers, a month before, the 10th of November 1990. Four men left to head to Caster-Bay at Lough Neagh, for a wildfowling trip. The four men were David Murphy, an RUC Special Branch Inspector. Thomas Taylor, a part-time RUC Reservist, Norman Kendall, a former 11 UDR soldier, and Keith Dowey, an electrician. When they arrived at Castor Bay, they were ambushed by the IRA. Keith was driving, with Norman being passenger. Keith was shot and killed instantly; Norman put up a struggle but was also killed. Thomas took out his ppw, and shot at the IRA men, but was killed by automatic fire. David struggled, avoiding getting caught, but was also gunned down.

June 16th 1997, two RUC men left the Lurgan Police Station, on a foot patrol. Constable John Graham and Reserve Constable David Johnston. Both had young families. As they walked down Church Walk, just beside the police station, an IRA man who was on a bike, and wearing a long blonde wig to hide himself, shot the two officers at point blank range, then made a quick getaway on the bike.

On the morning of the funerals, the mothers of the police men received a letter. On opening it, it was scene of crimes photos of the two Constables lying dead in Church Walk, with streams of blood!

The IRA had an inside man in the RUC, which passed the photos to them. The two families were constantly taunted thereafter.

Over thirty people had witnessed the attack, and quite a few could identify the IRA man (the known player I was writing about earlier) who was suspected in the shooting of Constable Wethers.

The witnesses made statements, and the suspicious IRA man went to court, but by the time the investigation had made it to court, all but one of the witnesses had withdrawn their statements, because of threats from the IRA.

Whilst the IRA man was in prison, the last witness statement had to be withdrawn, as he was later found to be in the Loyalist Paramilitaries. The player in prison got released, with compensation for unlawful imprisonment.

7

Kilwilkee Man

On a Thursday night Ops, we were sent to Lurgan. Mainly on an overt patrol, to show our presence, and deny the terrorist his movements and activities. It was evening, not night, and was still light. I wasn't the commander of this patrol, just one of the team. We are foot patrolling Kilwilkee, which is mainly a republican area, with quite a few 'players'.

When there was a prison breakout from the Maze high security prison (The 'H' Blocks) in 1983, at least one of the escapees (Sinn Fein Politician Gerry Kelly) stayed for a duration in a safe house in the Kilwilkee estate, until it was safe to leave. He was finally caught after three years on the run, in Amsterdam!

Tonight we are on foot patrol, keeping overt, staying aware. A man in his sixties came over to me, whilst I was standing waiting for the patrol to move on. He came over to me quite close, then spat on my face. I hadn't expected this, and could respond a few different ways! I could arrest him, get the police to caution him, or prosecute for assault, I could accidently (on purpose) hit him gently with my rifle, I could reply with a lot of expletives (as he probably would want), but I am thinking 'hearts and minds'. If I reply with any of the three options, I will make the divide between us wider, and so doing, achieve nothing. So I decided to talk. I turned around to him and asked, "Why did you do that?". He replied "you're a Brit bastard". I lowered my voice and stated, “I’m as Irish as you!”, he tried to corner me with further questions. “you’re in the British Army!”, I said “but I’m in an Irish Regiment!”. “What are you doing here?”, expecting me to reply in a sectarian manner. I replied with “we’re here to protect you”.” From what?” was the next question, “from any burglars, terrorists that may want to harm you, or the community, and just anything that will harm you”. I continued telling him that I care for all the communities, and will give all my time into protecting them. After a little chit chat, he then shook my hand, thanked me, and went on his way.

How amazing!

Republican areas and housing estates. There are many friendly people living here. I have met many lovely people in these (if I can call it that) places. It is just so sad that so few (players) can poison certain areas. When you’re in an open area, nobody will talk to you, for fear that they are being seen. But it is amazing how people chat when no one can see them.

I enjoy occasions where you can show the ‘hearts and minds’.

On one occasion in Craigavon we started to get stoned from a group of boys of school age. Instead of throwing back insults, or running at them, I decided to talk with them! How on earth can I do this in the mist of the hail of stones? I came out from the shadow of the side of the Land Rover and faced them! Pushing my rifle down to my side, muzzle pointing at the ground, raising both my hands and shouted “Woo, Woo, Woo”. They stopped clodding, and I shouted to them “Come over. I want to talk”. They stopped, lowered their arms, letting me approach. I talked to them about how foolish it was, that they were accomplishing nothing, about the dead IRA members, and what they can achieve if they put their minds to it. One of the boys replied “Your Fucking with our heads mister, piss off and go back to your patrol”.

You never know what seed will grow?

Pic 1. Above: Me ad 18Plt - The Hollow.
Pic 2. Bottom left: Loadmaster with GPMG. Pic 3. Bottom right: Me at Sinn Fein Office, The Village

Pic 3. Above: Riot Training
Pic 4. Middle: Heli-Op Patrol with Puma behind. Pic 5. Bottom: Me shooting SLR-Warcop

Pic 6. Above: Company Search-Craigavon
Pic 7. Bottom: Standard Village VCP

Pic 8. Above: Platoon Pose - Village Control Centre
Pic 9. Bottom: Platoon with Flag - Mahon Road Barracks

8

IRA Tactics and the Law

The IRA had the best propaganda around (probably in the world). Anything that happened, such as 'Bloody Sunday' etc. Sinn Fein and the IRA turned the full story around, alleging it to be the fault of the British Government, Army and Security Forces, whilst the Government, Police and Army seldom counter-claimed the accusations.

On one occasion our patrol was conducting a VCP in 'North Street' in Lurgan, about 200 meters away from Lurgan Police Station. John was doing 'stopper' on the road, stopping, questioning some of the drivers of the cars that passed. Whilst we were carrying out our VCP (vehicle check point), a man was walking towards the town centre on the right hand side of the road (same side of road as John). He started shouting at us, shouting abuse and expletives. We ignored him, kept away from him, but John was on the road and had to endure the abuse. The man I think had been drinking, hence his attitude. He didn't like that John ignored him! He wanted retaliation! So he walked onto the road towards John still hurling abuse. John (who wasn't the smallest of guy's, and was in the battalion rugby team) continued to ignore him, at times replied "I know! you're right! we shouldn't be here!", but the man wanted a better reaction, he wanted to make us cross which he wasn't getting. The next minute, he came over to John, then pushed him. John told him to stop, or he would be arrested, but the man pushed John again, only much harder. A few of us went over and arrested him. We placed him into the Land Rover, both teams packed up the VCP kit, mounted the Snatches, returning to the police station.

We got out of the Rovers, then got the arrested man out from the front Land Rover. The man saw John, ran over and punched him in the face. John staggered back, and was going to return the compliment, but as soon as the man punched John, about 4 of the section jumped on top of him, bringing him to the ground, holding him down. Everyone was on him like a 'flash' using reasonable force to contain him (a phrase used in Court), he was then brought into the station and charged.

Everything in this incident was done by the book, but the IRA/Sinn Fein propaganda twisted and changed the story. The Republican propaganda newspaper 'An Phoblacht' ('the Republic' in English) placed an article the following week about the incident. It wrote about a man and his heavily pregnant girlfriend/Fiancé walking into the town, and whilst walking, or trying to walk past an army VCP on North Street, they were ridiculed, sworn at. Members in the patrol were cursing sectarian things to the man and his girlfriend who only wanted to walk hand in hand to the town centre. When neither the man or woman retaliated, they got further abuse. The man asked the soldiers to please leave them alone, to which one of the soldiers came up to them and pushed them back. When the man saw his girlfriend getting pushed, he responded by trying to block the soldier and his girlfriend. To which he was accused of assault to the soldier, was arrested, taken to the police station, then beat-up. The soldiers accused him of assault on the street, and assault in the police station car park. An Phoblacht accused the army of taking the law into their own hands, intimidation on the people in the Catholic housing estates. The 'An Phoblacht' newspaper was delivered around the whole of Ireland, also in the United States of America. It was printed in the USA, as it was great propaganda for the IRA.

In the USA, IRA/Irish supporters sent so much money back to Ireland for the IRA war-machine.

The RUC told the Media of most of what the RUC did, like finding munitions, arrest'. The army seldom gave any information to the Media, of what the army did, or were doing. That is what I mean, when I talk about the two sides of 'The Troubles'. The civilian side, which was quite terrible, like the bombs, shootings, check points. And the Army side, which was everything else that was happening, is not released to the public. These include; the 'contacts' at the Irish border with the IRA and patrolling British soldiers, munitions finds of the army, bombs and shootings that are stopped.

In the early days of the troubles, quite a number of terrorists were brought and convicted through the courts, some things happened that were to turn around what the government was trying to do (stop the troubles) and promote recruitment in the membership of the terrorist organizations, such as 'Internment' in the early 1970's.

Since I joined the army, the courts changed greatly. A jury could no longer be used, as the terrorist organizations threatened to harm them and their families.

Bad propaganda by the terrorists and their organizations, claimed that the British courts were convicting innocent people. When I joined, we had 'the Diplock Court'. Introduced in 1973 by Lord Diplock for terrorist related serious crimes.

'Diplock' Court is where there is no jury, but three judges. When I joined the army in 1987, the verdict could not be given as 'beyond reasonable doubt', but 'without any doubt', it had to be 100%.

The IRA then went on to play on this '100% Sure'. For instance. A contact, where the patrol was fired upon. A firefight took place, the IRA man drops his weapon and runs away, to which the army team chases, flanks around and stops the man. To make sure there is no cross-contamination, the suspect is told to go down on his knees, with hands on head, fingers locked into each other. Whilst the soldier gets out his evidence bag, puts on the blue-gloves. Gets out the white body suit (which is in a sealed plastic bag), goes forward placing the body suit onto the suspect, thus holding any forensic evidence inside the suit, and any cross contamination outside. A perfect arrest. But in court, the defence states that his client was out for a walk along the road with his dog, then ran away when the firefight started. Prosecution "but there is gunpowder residue on the suspects clothing, which proves that he was there, and the body suit shows that there was no contamination!", to which the defence asked, "Is there any possibility that gunpowder residue was airborne during the firefight, and landed on my client, whilst he was out walking?". There may have been less than 1% chance of this happening. but as there is that chance, the suspect gets off, then will probably push for a claim on unlawful arrest and unlawful detaining by the British institution. In light of this (100%) there were very little convictions. So few that I can never remember during my time in the army, any convictions of IRA suspects in the Lurgan/Craigavon Area.

In the court, we had to be very careful how we phrased, and talked about, description of cars, items, people and munitions for instance, if a terrorist was shooting at us, and was arrested. When we went to court, and I stated that 'We were being shot with an M16 Assault Rifle'. If the rifle is a different rifle than I stated, like an 'AR18 Armalite', the case may get thrown out of court, as the suspect was not carrying a 'M16' defence would state. We were briefed that we should state 'We were being shot at with a long barrelled weapon'. A pistol or revolver was referred to by 'a short barrelled weapon'.

It was usual at court for the defence to fire in quick succession question upon question so quickly we had little time to think, so an answer we gave may trip us up. So, I was briefed that if this happened, deliberately stick in a pause "Can you repeat the question please?", and so, knock the defence off the stream.

If in any incident we had to return fire, then using our rifle or pistol had to be justified, justified to the conditions upon 'the yellow card'. Basically in the up to date yellow card, we could only return fire / use 'lethal force' if your own life or anyone else's life was in danger, and there was absolutely no other way of stopping him/her.

Talking about force! When we had to arrest/restrain a suspect, when it went to court, we needed to phrase everything correctly. To say we had to use 'force' to retain him, was subjective, and defence would say we used excess force. Minimum force was also a subjective term, to which defence could say, prove by theory that we didn't use minimum force. Minimum force might be just to ask the suspect to 'stop', or arrest, or to wait until the incident had passed. We used the term 'reasonable' force, or necessary' force, the defence had to prove that we didn't.

Other difficulties in court are that we couldn't use any of the suspects' previous convictions to show their MO or character. The defence would try on most occasions to prove that we were victimising the client, and had been victimising him for quite some time, then would read out incidents in the past where we had stopped, searched him and his vehicle, we abused him verbally and physically.

We did watch, stop and search this suspect, as he was a known player (member of a terrorist organization), but not to victimise him, but to check if he was carrying illegal munitions/transmitters or stolen goods, and so to protect the public (and the security forces).

The IRA's intelligence and attacks were very underestimated in the 1960's and 70's. The British Army/intelligence needed to have undercover information of movements and future attacks and so, The MRF (military reaction force) was conceived. Deployed in Belfast 1970, which never had a great success, and was easily compromised as the British Army had overestimated their covertness, accents, blending in, knowledge of the IRA's active service units (ASU).

The MRF came to a finish in 1974. After that with lessons learned, the British MOD deployed undercover SAS, 14 Intelligence Company (the Det), and other units, along with the RUC's 'E4A'. The agencies got plentiful information, but never enough.

The tout's, informers, and infiltrating the IRA gained so much information, that each IRA Brigade did not trust each other.

We knew during Ops that there were undercover ops/tailings done by the special forces and the RUC's E4A, when we were given 'no-go' areas on our operational/patrol ground, before going out on Ops.

Sometimes the 'no-go area' would be because the int-cell knew there was an attack/bomb planned for that particular area, or there was an undercover Op/surveillance going on. Sometimes when we were doing a VCP, when a car was coming into our VCP area. I could see it was a 'player' I knew of, but when I put a car check through to the ops-room, the ops-room radioed back "DON'T STOP".

When we radioed in a VRN (vehicle registration number) we also followed with vehicle description, location (bio-diagram), direction of travel, and number of occupants on board. Then after the ops room fed it into the computer, they gave us a feedback, such as "ok", "family trace", "stop and search", or sometimes (like now) a "don't stop". If a 'don't stop' came back, we knew that either there was a watch on his house or known locations, or he was being followed by a car containing 'special agencies'.

The well-known IRA 'player' I talk about through this book evaded prison for so many high-profile murders, that the IRA Belfast Battalion, wanted nothing to do with him. They thought it is most probable that he was a tout/MI5 agent'. In my own view, I think that the Belfast IRA Battalion distrusted the 'player' in Lurgan so much that they wanted to eliminate him.

On the 15th of March 1999 Rosemary Nelson (a solicitor who worked with the IRA (a Human Rights lawyer)) lost her life when a UVBT (under vehicle booby trap) detonated whilst she was driving her Silver BMW. I believe that the bomb was meant for the 'player'. Reasons for this - Rosemary was on holiday and wasn't due home for another day or so. It was usual for the 'player' to use her car, because it was harder for the intelligence services to keep a tab on his movements. The loyalist 'Red Hand Defenders' claimed responsibility for this murder!

Internment (Operation Demetrius (1971)), mass arrests by the British Government, gained much intelligence through questioning, causing the IRA Commanders to have to think up means by which someone who is arrested does not divulge information on individuals involved in attacks, or information on future attacks. The first way is to 'SAY NOTHING'. There were no 'No-Comment' statements (Americanism on the 'Fifth' Amendment in the United States Constitution). All IRA volunteers were told not to open their mouths, because if you said anything, even their name, "I know nothing" will be like opening up a crack in the door, after which the door could be prised open! Some IRA men could sit in the interrogation room, look at everyone else in the room and stay silent. Some would pick a spot in the room and stare at it. Others who thought they couldn't hold out, would curl up underneath the table, 'say nothing'. After 48 hours or whatever the arrest length was in that year, the suspect would get released, most likely 'without charge'. The RUC would try to combat this by moving the clock time. In Gough Barracks, Armagh, the terrorist was held and interviewed in rooms that had no natural light, so when the suspect (Loyalist and Republican) went to his/her cell and fell asleep, the guard would come in and wind forward the clock and watches that everyone is wearing. The suspect was wakened after just a couple of hours sleep. The suspect thought it was more! The questioning continued. The suspect watched the clocks/watches, checking the time. Eventually the suspect would state that "My time is up!, You must release me now!", to which the interrogators would show them the real time, and tell them that there were still many hours to go. This tactic would break some, but others didn't sway.

The IRA commanders (many would say that it was Gerry Adams idea) came up with the 'cell' structure, in which each person did just one of the tasks in an organised attack. The operation started with a terrorist or member of the public informing a person in the IRA of a potential target. Let's say for example a member of the security forces didn't check his car before going to work or town! The sympathizer went to a member of the IRA and spoke of the security force member not checking his car, he knew it was a security force member, as he has seen police/army clothing on the clothesline outside the back of their house. This information is passed onto an IRA commander, who had the security force person watched, on at least three occasions. The worst-case scenario for the IRA, is that he checks underneath the car and discovers the IED which would compromise the attack, and forensics might get picked up. After three or four times watching, the commander might give the thumbs up to planting a UVBT (under vehicle booby trap). The attack is Go! The bomb maker will leave the device in a transit hide somewhere on a specific day/time. The next person will collect it at another specific time and move it to the next transit hide. He would not know who had left it there, or who will collect it. The next in line will lift it and place it under the target's car, adjust the mercury tilt switch, turn the timer (for safe, get out period of time) then remove the doweling pin (wooden pin which stops the electric connection to compete the circuit), giving it to another IRA man, to show he has done the job successfully! If he did not give the IRA man the doweling pin, he might be knee-capped as the attack might fail.

The 'cell' structure meant that if anyone was caught/arrested during their role, they don't know and can't know where/who it came from, or where it is going to and who, and had no knowledge of the target or who it is.

The same was in a shooting, or CQA as we call it (close quarter assassination (or attack)). Target is identified! Watched, then given the go-ahead! The IRA Quartermaster in charge of the big main hide, would lift a weapon based on the attack, then place it in a minor hide (perhaps for days/weeks or months), where, when the attack is imminent, it would be moved to a transit hide, perhaps another one or two. The last hide is perhaps under a hedge near the attack area. The attack happened! And the weapon left back to a small hide, and in turn, days/weeks returns to the IRA main hide. Each person in the chain cannot tell to whom or where it is going. If the terrorist is caught he will be prosecuted for any / all the deaths/attacks that this weapon was used for. This Law was brought in in the 1990's. Before that, the person holding the weapon could only be prosecuted for the very attack of that moment, or for possession of an illegal firearm.

With the Diplock Courts, difficulty in securing a conviction, we had to adapt, become stringent and professional in how we dealt with firing-points, contact-points, cars and suspects to gain evidence.

We had a good idea of who was involved, and in that moment our priority was to capture that 'player'. He may have left the scene, but we knew there was a good chance that he was making his way back home. Once he reached home, he would strip off, clothes in a washing machine, then jump in the shower. That way he would destroy forensic evidence on him, also his clothes. If we arrived at his home after he has de-clothed, has had a shower, we would go straight to the washing machine, and turn it off at the mains, to stop it's cycle, so the water remained in the machine. The forensic squad should be able to recover forensic evidence that has not been lost.

Each year the terrorists became more sophisticated at what they were doing, and we, the security forces had to up our game too.

9

Army, God and Me

God has always been a big part of my life, even though I didn't think it.

I became a Christian in 1980, and was going to church, bible reading through my school years. After I left school I slowly stopped going to church. I still knew that I was a Christian, but stopped reading my bible, attending church, wanted to enjoy the world, and lie in on Sunday mornings!

One of my first patrols, I was in the back of a Land Rover, when Davy (our team commander) turned around and asked me if I was a Christian. I don't know how he guessed? But I denied it and asked "What gave you that idea?". That denial played on my mind no end! I felt like Peter, denying Jesus. I felt like Peter for a few days. The next time I was on patrol (three days later) I was in exactly the same team. We loaded our rifles, and when driving out of the barracks, I spoke up. "Davy!", and everyone (including the driver) turned around and looked at me. All eyeballs on me! I continued "Remember I said on Monday that I wasn't a Christian?", Davy said "Yes", "Well, I lied! I am a Christian and have been since in school!". Davy replied "We thought so!", and everyone turned back to what they were doing, and it wasn't mentioned again. I thought that I was going to be taunted throughout that entire Patrol. This gave me courage in future times to talk about Jesus, God and faith, whether on patrol, training, or otherwise.

When I was promoted to Lance Jack, I had been in the regiment for almost 2 years. I never tried to stop the bad language, in fact since I joined, the F's and Blinds were in my speech too. I couldn't stop the troops swearing as it was a release valve. There were some men who couldn't put a sentence together without F's in each sentence. There was one soldier with a speech impediment, and if there were no curse words in his sentences, then he couldn't talk, couldn't string together a full sentence, there would be too many stoppages.

I did however try to stop anyone taking the Lord God's name in vain. I used to say to them "I don't mind the 'Fucks' and the 'Bastards', but please, especially when you are near me, don't take the Lord God's name in vain". Most soldiers, no matter what their rank DID! With the exception of those who wanted to annoy me, and try to wind me up!

I sometimes prayed that on the next operational patrol I could get a chance to talk to a particular person about God and Christianity, and every time I asked, the Lord let me have the perfect opportunity to do so.

There was a Sergeant who was a self-confessed Atheist. He felt so strongly about it, that he refused the set of 'Dog Tags' that were issued to him, as they had church or religion on it. He did eventually get the 'Dog Tags' with 'Atheist' on it. We had great debates in the L/Rovers whilst driving to and around our TAOR whilst on operational duty.

When I was completing my first promotion course I didn't pray to God about it, and got through it ok. The second promotion course (to be a full Corporal) which is one of the toughest in the Army – I failed.

We had a very tough training Commander on that course, who failed over 50% of those on the course. If you failed in two exercises, YOU FAILED. I was good at map reading, and when on night exercise, you had to go to 6 grid references and get your card stamped (like orienteering) then return to base. I was so confident, but I never found one of the six grid points and dwelled too long trying to find it, instead of moving onto the next. I found out that the soldier that was at that grid point, did not like part-timers, and never called you in, or shone a light when you were within about 10 meters. I also failed one of my command tasks in the village (36-hour exercise).

A year or so later I got onto the full-screw (Corporal) course once again. I went well prepared, and this time I prayed about it so much, asked the Lord to guide and help me through it. This course was in Ballymena and was a fortnight long course. I prayed as I was going through the course and I can safely say that as the course was progressing, I was the top of the class. I was so confident, and had much more patrolling command Ops than many others on the course.

The last of the course was the 46-hour exercise in 'the village' in 'Ballykinler Training Barracks, and I was really good at command and control in the villages. It was my 'Forte'. So when we went to the village, I was standing just outside its entrance, looking at it, smiling, looking forward to it, and I prayed to the Lord "Thank you so much Lord for looking after me throughout the course, guiding and carrying me, but I am really good at command and control in the exercise areas, and I don't need you now. I can do this 'no-problem!'. I FAILED the course, due to everything coming apart in the village. This taught me a very important lesson. I do have skill at command and control, and am skilled in many other subject areas, but they are ALL God given skills. God gives each and every one of us skills in one form or another, and that is what makes us. However, it is given by God, and as the village exercise shows, he can just take it away, and let you do it, or should I say 'try it' on your own.

Over the years, I got to discuss Jesus and Christianity in so many different places and so many different ways. Surprisingly there are so many soldiers, whom I found to be Christians too.

Like me, at the beginning of their service, they too didn't want anyone to know.

The Lord has saved me so many times. Some situations even my fellow soldiers were asking "How did you get out of that? you should have been a goner? I can't understand how you got out of that!". It happened to me in different circumstances so many times. Once when I was on Ops in Lurgan we were on a high building and had to make our way onto another high building, so we decided to jump across from the building we were on, to the next one. It saved climbing down, and back up, which would take time and energy, and we may be seen (we were on covert operation). One at a time we jumped across, and I was about the middle person to jump. I had a radio and backpack on, and when I jumped, I just wasn't quite making it to the other building (we were 2 floors up). I was going to fall two floors onto concrete ground. I wouldn't survive this! I was going to die! Well? If so, then I wanted to enjoy it. The last few seconds of my life! I would enjoy it - instead of panicking . Before I know or think about it, I will be bouncing off the concrete. Just as I was turning around to face down, I felt a hand on my thigh, and I got pushed up, pushed up enough to grab the hand from my mucker who pulled me up onto the building. I looked behind me to see who had pushed me up, as I definitely felt a hand pushing me up, and I saw no-one, in fact no-one could be there, there were no steps or ladder to hold anyone.

I never went on another 'full screw' course, but for most of my operational duties, and training duties I was a 'full screw' but without the extra stripe or extra pay. I treated my fellow soldiers well, I got so much respect, and I gave back so much respect.

10

Portadown

Portadown & Mahon Road

Our barracks (Mahon Road) was on the outskirts of Portadown on the Armagh side.

Mahon Road Barracks was opened in 1974. It was the UDR 11th Battalion Headquarters. 'B' Company (Portadown part-time company) were also based there. 'C' Company (Lurgan part-time company) moved into Mahon Road from Kitchen Hill, Lurgan in 1980. In 1982 'D' Company (Banbridge Part time Company) moved to Mahon Road from Scava Road, Banbridge. 'A' Company (full-time) started in 1983 in Mahon Road. 'B' Company (Lisburn Company) were in 9 UDR, and became 11 UDR in 1984. They remained in Thiepval Barracks, Lisburn, but were under 11 UDR command. Portadown Company became 'E' Company. 'F' Company (full-time) was formed in 1984, and 'G' Company (full-time) was formed in 1989. This Battalion (11 UDR) was the largest battalion in the British Army.

Even though 'D' Company's TAOR was Banbridge, Dromore, Dromara, Annahilt, we patrolled Portadown frequently and we became familiar with the area. Whilst on a camp guard weekend, in addition to guarding the barracks, we did the occasional patrol around the barracks and Portadown. These patrols were called 'doing the GDA's' (ground defence area). Short patrols around the nearby roads were undertaken to check for anything suspicious, then we also checked around the police station, and town centre. Additionally, we patrolled around Portadown when we were on QRF duty (quick reaction force). During QRF we mainly stayed within the barracks, or the immediate Portadown Area, as we were awaiting a call from either the Police or another Army patrol, who might be asking to assist them, should an incident occur. The QRF duties were usually at weekends, and during the graveyard shift, with Ops commencing at 2359hrs through to 0900hrs.

Portadown! A regular patrol area for us, as it was where our barracks was placed. Within the town there were some areas predominantly either Loyalist or Republican. Neither were quite as staunch as Craigavon or Lurgan, but still very strong.

Although the security forces didn't feel quite as under threat in the Portadown Area, there were still many incidents/troubles. Patrolling Portadown felt very easy, and very safe. The Loyalists (UVF & LVF) from the Portadown area have committed many murders in the Mid-Ulster triangle. It is estimated that at least 100 Catholics and numerous Protestants were killed by the Mid-Ulster UVF.

The year I joined 11 UDR Portadown in 1987, there were still ripples from July 1985, where 52 Police Officers, and 28 Rioters were injured in Obins Street (the 'tunnel'), where the 'Orange Order' were demanding for their rights to march.

We patrolled all areas, Loyalist and Republican, with little trouble. Just the odd heckling! Although we never felt welcome in the Republican areas, and of course we were still careful when patrolling there!

I enjoyed patrolling the Portadown area, as it was so vast. It had so much history, with many interesting places. And to our delight, countless places to 'sit-up' (park the patrol Land-Rovers somewhere off road, that nobody knows) to take a break.

In May 1989, we were looking forward to going to our annual Training Camp (8 days training, in a training camp in England). The threats, and threat of an attack on security force bases were very high. Every hour, or sometimes half hour, Our Ops room asked for a patrol of the GDA's (ground defence areas). They were numbered 1 to 5. If it was GDA No.5 then there were areas A to D, which could only be done by foot. They were the ground between Mahon Rd Barracks and Tandragee Road.

Mostly it would be GDA No.1 and No.2, and they were the private housing developments beside our barracks. Perhaps the timing was quite predictable? If you watched, saw a couple Land Rovers checking an estate, you could be sure it will not be checked for another half an hour or so.

The part-time companies in Mahon Road, at this date, were preparing for the annual training week, gathering the equipment needed for the following week, literature, training pamphlets, all administration to be done. Some personnel and gear were already away, as an advanced party was sent before the rest of the troops followed. It was a Friday, and we travelled the following day. Some in escort Land-Rovers (armed and on duty the full way across), some in the Army 4 tonners (kit and weapons), some in company vans (kit that our company needed, for company detail). The majority of us were travelling on one of the coaches the next morning. Black-Adder was in that day as he wasn't on permanent employment at this time and could come in on 'dole patrol'. Black-Adder helped to get all the company kit sorted for the trip. Just after 1200hrs he was returning to our company lines from 'E' Company ('E' company was just across the parade square, and its TAOR is Portadown and the Birches). He was ¾ of the way across the parade square, suddenly there was an almighty explosion! Then silence, pieces of shrapnel falling all around him! He then sprinted over to the company lines and attempted to get into shelter from the falling debris. The mortar alarm of the barracks started, and everyone tried to establish what had happened. No one could leave where they had sought shelter - "was it a mortar attack? How many have been fired? How many have landed inside the barracks? How many have not yet exploded?" The IRA mortars were unreliable, and may not have exploded, or perhaps they were on timers, to go off in five minutes or so, when soldiers and personnel had come out from the cover positions. It was half an hour before everyone began moving again. No one had been killed or injured in Mahon Road, as no mortars had hit inside the barracks. What had happened? It was quickly established that the mortar lorry was in Brook Road, opposite the barracks.

When the IRA launched a mortar attack, the lorry had a number of tubes fixed onto the back, angled in such a way that the driver was told where to park, and which way to face the van (perhaps facing a prominent building), in order for the mortars to hit the designated target site.

When the lorry was parked, the driver set two timers. One to launch the mortars, the second to detonate the explosives that were left on the lorry in order to destroy all forensics. I thought that the driver had set the two times in the wrong order? The mortar that Friday had the most tubes of any IRA mortar before that, and perhaps after that date. It was a Mk10 mortar with 16 tubes. What had happened? The timers WERE set correctly, but the first mortar that launched, malfunctioned and exploded before exiting the tube, thus, blowing up the rest of the mortars. The explosion completely destroyed one house (it was a new build, a new estate), and damaged the roofs, and walls of approximately four or five other newly built houses. No-one was killed or injured in the attack. A no-warning attack! Soon after this attack (the threat did not lessen) Our battalion set up permanent VCP's, both North & South on Mahon Road, to stop any suspicious vehicle getting anywhere near our barracks.

Strange! As these days, if that explosion happened in 2025, the incident site would be closed for a number of days, and there would be much news coverage, but in 1989, life just carried on. The explosion may have made the local news (not British news, and certainly not international news!) on Friday evening, but everyday life carried on. On Friday afternoon, the barracks continued as normal.

On Saturday morning (when I found out about the explosion) we arrived at 0700hrs, changed, and boarded the coaches for Warcop Training Camp in Cumbria.

28th March 1991 the UVF (under 'Billy Wright') entered a 'mobile shop' in Drumbeg, Craigavon, which was owned by a known IRA suspect, and shot dead three Catholic civilians. They were innocent civilians, and by irony, the owner of the mobile shop was not there.

On operational patrol in Portadown June 1992. When I was in a team, not commanding. We were on mobile in Corcrain and Garvaghy Road Areas. It was a normal patrol, overt patrolling to show our presence, support, with a few VCP's on the main roads, mobile through the housing estates at slow speeds to observe if there was anything amiss, or anything suspicious!

We then were conducting a VCP on the bottom of the Garvaghy Road just before joining the town. After this VCP, we were to take our evening break, and planned to park behind Irwin's Bakery factory, where it was quiet, with no traffic. There wouldn't be anyone coming into the factory at that time. There would probably be a squad in the factory and doing their baking.

The VCP was quite easy, not busy. Just before we wrapped up, we stopped a car with a well-known IRA player driving. In fact it was Aidan Starrs, one of the IRA commanders of The Portadown IRA. We scribed him (took down details of time stopped, location, car details, movement details) and a couple of the patrol members searched his car. I was doing cover, and when I saw who was stopped, I came over and asked to do the body search on him (I was very confident and thorough when searching). The section commander gave me the go-ahead! I took Aiden to the side, to the side of the road beside his car, and told Aiden I was going to search him, 'For illegal munitions or transmitters that could be used against us.' He said "ok", and I asked him to take the contents out of his pockets, which he did. I looked through them - nothing out of the ordinary. This felt strange! As I wasn't feeling any hatred from him? Usually, if it was a known IRA personality, or even a civilian with republican views, you would feel the hatred. I couldn't feel any from Aiden. I set the contents of his pockets on the wing of the Land Rover and continued the body search. I felt around his collar, the top of his shoulders, with my two hands; felt under his arm while the other hand felt along the top of his arm, and felt along it, covering the full round of his arm. Then did the same on the other. He didn't speak. I was then standing behind him, as I wanted to search his body, and it was better to stand behind, as that way he couldn't spit on me, thump me, or as I moved down his body knee me in the face. I felt and searched his torso with my two hands, then his sides, then his back. I am now going to search around his rear and genital area, and said to him "I am now going to search you around your private areas!", and still no hatred or aggressive talk, movement or looks. He said that's ok, and I searched around his bum, then when my hand moved to the front I squeezed his balls, but he never jumped, said or shouted any expletives back at me. I searched on, down his legs and around his shoes. Then I'd finished, and told him I had finished, and he could go back to the car (the car search had finished). He then said "ok", and went back to his car, and drove off into the town. We wrapped up the VCP, grabbed the 'Stop – Vehicle Check Point' sign, threw it into the back of the Land Rover, and we all mounted up. I got in the back, and before I went up to do 'top-cover' I said that it was so very strange searching him. I couldn't feel any hatred from him. I've never experienced that before! Searching a well-known IRA man and getting no hatred or quotations out of him. There was something not right about him. Why was there no hatred from him, what was different?

The following week John Dignam, Gregory Burns, and Aidan Starrs went missing! All were known to be in the IRA. Messages and information were circulating around the security forces (Police, neighbourhood Police, Int cell, and the Army) that these three hadn't been seen for the last few days. Was there going to be an IRA attack anytime soon? Were they away training, or at meetings with other IRA commanders, what was going on?

The three bodies of these men were found on 1st July. All had been shot dead by the IRA. They had been taken away, tortured and shot. The IRA stated they were informers for MI5 and MI6!

The threat of an attack on Mahon Road Barracks, and Portadown Police Station rose year upon year. That was on top of the rising threat in Craigavon and Lurgan towns, and police stations. We also had our own T.A.O.R. to cover (tactical area of responsibility) which for our company was Banbridge, Dromore, Dromara and Annahilt. Quite important Ops were the V.C.P.'s on the 'A1', an A class dual carriageway between Lisburn and Dundalk.

Whilst working camp-guard in Mahon Road, we also had to patrol around the areas of Mahon Road Barracks, and Portadown RUC Station. As well as patrolling these areas, we had to 'think like the terrorist' and look around roads within the surrounding industrial estates, small hidden tracks, roads and streets where a bomb laden van may be waiting.

Like that which occurred in 1989 (mortar attack on our barracks), the occupants of the van may have been waiting for us to drive past and then thought we would not be patrolling along that street for at least another hour. When I commanded the patrol, I would sometimes revisit the same roads again after a ten-minute period had elapsed. Be unpredictable!

Whilst we were on guard duty in Mahon Road, the G.D.A. (ground defence area) patrols could be done by one team (one Land Rover) as we didn't set up full VCP's or foot patrols with depth. With one team we could cover greater areas much faster, and with unpredictability.

The weekend from Friday 21st May 1993 to Sunday 23rd, our company was on camp guard. One evening 16 Platoon section commander went down to the guard-room, checked the complex for damages, made sure it was all clean, checked that all items on the equipment list were present and correct, asked if there were any incidents, or anything happening in the barracks, anything we should have been aware of. The hand-over time was 2000hrs, but we always tried to hand over the complex before 2000hrs, often by 1930hrs. The reason? We were taking over from a full-time company, and if we didn't take over before 2000hrs, it came back ten-fold when we handed back on Monday morning 0001hrs. They wouldn't be early, and if the commander saw any dirty marks they then might say, "I'll be back in half an hour – get it cleaned!"

My platoon took over at 0100hrs Saturday morning until 0900hrs. I was the guard commander for that 8 hour period. Everything went fine, no incidents, and no threat-risk of an attack from int-cell. At 0900hrs, I handed over the guard complex to the next guard commander (18 Platoon), for his duty to 1700hrs. I handed my SA80 into the armoury, got my ppw, went up to the company lines, changed into civvies, back down to the guard room to sign out, and then home!

That morning as I drove through Portadown town centre, it was quite a nice morning, all was quiet. Little did I know, less than 10 minutes after I left Portadown, a 1,000 lb bomb would explode in the centre, and destroy the majority of buildings and businesses.

1995 Drumcree and Garvaghy Road

One patrol in Portadown. Our patrol area tonight was North of Portadown, out as far as the Birches. But we got a re-task from the ops room, telling us to come back into Portadown, patrol north side of the Garvaghy Road. We had to patrol and protect the streets south side of 'St. John the Baptist Catholic Church'. The int cell told us that a special undercover team (army or police) was following a Ford Transit van, full of explosives. In fact, the van had a 1,000 lb bomb on board, destined to be planted in a town centre, or beside one of our security force buildings. Whilst it was in transit, the occupants noticed that they were being followed and decided to abandon! They were travelling along the A4, and turned onto the Garvaghy Road, then right again into a housing street, where they parked up, and abandoned the van. There must have been another car with them, either in front or behind. Perhaps it was that car which sussed out the under-cover vehicle. We had to patrol around this 6-figure grid reference quite closely, one or two streets away. I was the patrol commander, and followed instruction, but we wanted to get an "eye's on" to the van, to confirm it was there, and hadn't moved. We saw the van on a side street from Garvaghy Road, but I wanted a closer look, so I instructed my second team to drive around the roads and meet us at the far side, whilst I drove along that very street.

Before we moved, I asked a few of my team to transfer into the second L/Rover, to avoid endangering their lives. I moved into the back of my L/Rover. Then Keith my driver, drove the Snatch past the suspicious van. I also wanted to see if anyone was watching us, or who may have been the person from the van. We drove past reasonably slowly. I saw all the springs in the wheels had wooden wedges hammered into them, to keep the van in a raised position. If a van was loaded, then the body of the van would get squeezed down, and there would be very little gap between the tyres and body, and so suspicion arose that the van could be loaded full of explosives.

There was 1,000 lb of home-made explosives in the back, mainly finely ground down and mixed 'sugar and fertilizer' mix, with a timer or remote-control Box, an explosive detonator, and a small batch of high explosive like the plastic explosive 'C4' which was provided to the IRA by Colonel Gaddafi in the 1980's.

Upon driving past I could tell it was a full load in the back. Luckily enough we had the Electronic Counter Measure to stop the bomb exploding if it was operated by remote control. If however it had been set on a timer, Keith and I would not have gone home after this patrol. It was the closest I ever was to such a major explosive. I was standing out the top of the Snatch

L/Rover with most of my body exposed (although with such a massive bomb, I don't think it would have mattered whether I was inside or outside the L/Rover). I was 3 feet away from the van, as we drove past, with Keith laughing his head off, as to how mad we were!

11

Camp Guard

Mahon Road Camp Guard

Mahon Road Barracks, and most of the UDR/Royal Irish Barracks, were secured and protected by its own Battalion, rather than an outside agency or police.

The full-time companies protected the barracks during the week, and at the weekends (Friday 2000hrs to Monday 0001hrs) The part-time companies had responsibility. This rotated between B , C, D (ours), and E Company.

The shifts were shared between the three platoons in our Company, in 8 hour session - Friday 2000hrs to Saturday 0100hrs, Saturday 0900, Saturday 1700, Sunday 0100, Sunday 0900, Sunday 1700, with hand back Monday 0001hrs. While the shift was eight hours, we must report to the barracks one hour before duty, as we had to change into combats, sign out our rifles, and perhaps have a clothing and kit check by the platoon sergeant before going onto guard.

We completed our eight hours, and once the next platoon took over, we signed our rifles back in (ppw's out), got changed into civvies, returned home for a rest, before coming in again later. In total, we were in the barracks for nearly ten hours per duty.

It was usual for me to be the Guard Commander, as most of my platoon liked me to, as I was really fair in both the duties I allocated and timings.

I always arrived more than an hour before taking over, to avoid rushing, and took time getting changed, signing out my rifle and spoke the armourer about what had been happening around the barracks and companies, before heading down to the guard room.

Once in the guardroom, I received an update from the Guard Commander after which I checked and signed for the kit and rooms. My next task was to find out all the stags we were to cover. This rarely changed, but sometimes when there was a high threat or incident, we needed to provide for it. For instance, if the SAS were on an operation, arriving by helicopter, it needed to be under guard so that no-one entered the Puma whist unoccupied.

Stags normally required were: front gate (1 soldier), front sanger (1 soldier), cctv's in the guard room (1 soldier), front office (me or my 2IC), and perhaps another. sanger (1 soldier).

I confirmed all the stags needed, how many soldiers I had in for the coming guard. I then calculated to the minute how long each soldier had on each stag. Quite often it worked out at 5 hours and 20 minutes per soldier, with 2 hours and 40 minutes rest. Stag times work out to be 1 hour 20 per stag, and sometimes I broke that in half with 40 minute timings (perhaps if the stag timings overlapped meal timings). I knew my men well and worked to all their personal attributes. Some needed their sleep; some were football fanatics (if there was football on tv during our shift). If it was through the night, some wanted to do a double stag, and that suited, for those that slept. I worked out the timings to the very minute, then went around my soldiers, and confirmed they were happy with the plans I had arranged. Sometimes another person from my platoon would turn up just before the guard duty, and I didn't know that he was coming in for duty, so I had to sit down again, and rework the timings. There were almost always rest periods for my soldiers during guard time, but I never wanted to sleep, I wanted to run the guard to its best, and be aware of all that was going on. I (the guard commander) wasn't on stag during the guard duty. My time was taken up managing the guard, answering phone calls, passing information, and papers back and forth from the Int-Cell and ops room, writing reports, and drinking coffee (lots of).

Quite often with 3 or 4 on rest, they would have a card school going, especially during the night. I only took part at the start of the night, when the bets were only 5 or 10p raises, during the night a large amount of money was on the table. Throughout the night it wasn't the same soldiers in the game. Those coming off stag joined in, and similarly those going onto stag left the table. After a few months of watching this, I didn't like seeing my friends lose more money than they intended. I bought gambling chips, and let each soldier buy into the table for £5, and at the end of the guard duty, the one who had the most chips, took the 'pot'.

I wasn't keen on card games, and after another couple of months, I brought in different board games from home, and it truly was a hit. The guys loved the different board games. I introduced them to 'Yatzee' the dice game, where it was so easy to start, stop and finish games. I ran hundreds of score sheets from the copier at work, and we had a plentiful supply of score sheets.

Frequently when working a guard duty from 1700 to 0100 we would get a take-away. Whoever was on rest period, would get changed, and go downtown to collect our order. Sometimes I'd ask the ops room if they wanted one. We often chose Indian (especially a vindaloo).

Mark Roberts (who was in the Royal Signals, before coming to Northern Ireland, and joining the UDR) introduced me to the vindaloo. The Indian in Portadown had such a hot vindaloo, if you asked for a hotter one (a tindaloo) and they didn't know you, they said they know nothing about it. There were a few soldiers who loved the hot spices, like Terrance, who one time ate the full vindaloo without a drink. And after finishing, said "Oh! I forgot about the rice". I remember one time leaving the guard room with my vindaloo, going down to the front gate, letting Steve take a forkful of my vindaloo, which burnt the mouth off him, and he asked for a drink. I told him I'd have a drink ready for him after he finishes his stag. He begged me to get someone to come down with a drink for him? But I told him that everybody was too busy. LOL. Love is?

One time Brian was down doing his stag in the front sanger (beside the entrance to the barracks), he was getting bored. About half an hour after going into the sanger, the ops room phoned me at the guard room. "What the **** is going on?" I was asked. An alarm had gone off in the ops room, to say that there was a known vehicle of a well-known terrorist suspect coming into our barracks, and not only that, but there was a convoy of terrorist vehicles coming in. The first alarm went off in our ops room, but when Loyalist and Republican top terrorists were entering our Barracks ! Alarms all over the other barracks in Northern Ireland were going off, saying that our barracks was being attacked by the Loyalists and Republican terrorist organizations. Or where they all coming in for a get-together, a party?

Brian in his boredom started to key all the registration numbers of all the terrorists car's into the computer at the front sanger. The computer was used to gather information as to vehicles coming and going, and also to check them, in the event of a suspicious vehicle.

The ops room went MAD! It was province-wide catastrophe (or should I say embarrassment) that this happened, and in our battalion! Brian was surely in for an 'official charge'. Upon investigation, there was no warning notice in the sanger stating 'Don't put registrations into the computer, which have not approached the front gate'. He got off with it, not even a warning! The next week, a sign had been made, and put up in the sanger!

On a serious note! Whilst on camp guard we had to be ready for any attack on the barracks or married quarters. Drive by shootings, where the IRA would drive past the front gate/sanger and fire a fully automatic weapon at the sanger/front gate/or front office. Fortunately the entrance to our barracks was off the main road, and on a length of road which stopped about 50m beyond front entrance.

Mortar attack, where a van/lorry would have all the mortar tubes on the back, park in an area close to the barracks (In line) (perhaps in one of the housing developments). We combatted that attack with cctv cameras around the perimeter of the barracks and sent out GDA (ground defence area) patrols at irregular timings to check the areas, and gave an overt presence.

One attack we dreaded was 'the proxy bomb' attack, Before the proxy bomb, the IRA would try to get a van into the barracks loaded with explosives (VBIED(vehicle borne improvised explosive device)) On a timer, leave the barracks, and wait. Our SOP's (standard operational procedure) was to check in the back of all load bearing vehicles, and the boot of cars if we had a sixth sense. Sometimes when the risk rose we checked ALL car boots. We checked everyone's, and I mean everyone's ID.

Once! I was on the front gate duty one dark weekday evening, and a Land Rover with a horse box came through the front entrance and approached me. Two men were in the front, and when I asked for ID, the two of them showed me. Why a horse box, I thought. I wanted to see what was in the back? Horses, or maybe a sofa. When I went round the back of the horse box and looked inside, I saw over 8 sets of eyes staring at me, not one bit of noise! It was a section of SAS or some other special-force team returning from an Op. I waved them on and said nothing back to the guard office.

Although the IRA managed to get two VBIED's into Thiepval Barracks in Lisburn on Monday the 7th October 1996, which killed one soldier, and injured 31 people. How did they get them in? Thiepval Barracks is a very busy barracks, and at the time there was some construction going on inside the barracks. The IRA gained access using either a forged 'contractor' pass, or a forged army ID. They drove in and left two 800lb car bombs.

One went off at just after 3:30 in the afternoon beside a travel arrangement centre, the second (secondary device designed to kill or injure those helping or attending the first incident) 12 minutes later. Warrant Officer James Bradwell died four days later of multiple wounds.

'The proxy bomb'! In the early hours of 24th October 1990, proximity 0345hrs the IRA carried out a series of proxy-bomb attacks. Two border checkpoints and Lisanelly Camp in Omagh. The IRA wanted to put vehicle borne explosives in the middle of a border checkpoint, or at the entry buildings at a Barracks, but we were well protected! We had ECM in our Snatch Land Rover's and around the entrances to security force bases. To get a radio controlled explosive near the target is too hard. A command wire to the explosive on a vehicle was even harder, so the IRA used another way, the proxy bomb. Where a person was strapped or chained into the driver's seat of the vehicle which had the explosives in the back. They were forced to drive into the military targets, where the driver (unknown to him) initiated detonation, or the timer ran out and the bomb exploded.

Three synchronised attacks were planned. All three planned for 24th October 1990

The first was at Coshquin Border crossing checkpoint in Co. Londonderry. A catholic, Patrick Gillespie whose family was held at gunpoint, was forced to drive a van containing 1,000 lb of explosives to the border checkpoint. When he reached the checkpoint at 0355hrs, Patrick tried to get out, but the bomb detonated when he opened the door. The IRA had installed a detonation device linked to the van's courtesy light, but as a safeguard, there was also a timing device linked to ensure the explosives went off. Patrick and five soldiers were killed

The second (in tandem) was at another border checkpoint 'Cloghoge'. Another catholic family were held at gunpoint, it was James McAvoy's family. James was strapped into a van packed with 1 tonne of explosives and ordered to drive it to Cloghoge border checkpoint. When James stopped at the checkpoint, he climbed out of the window. A soldier started shouting at him to move the van, moments later the timer detonated the bomb.

One soldier was killed, 13 injured. James McAvoy escaped with a broken leg.

The third simultaneously was at Omagh Lisanelly Barracks, it was a 1,500 lb van bomb. A third man was strapped in, but the explosion only partially exploded, due to a faulty detonator.

Within a very short time all security force bases heard about what happened!

How do we safeguard against this new form of attack?

Knowledge of the devices filtered through. Family held under duress, driver strapped into van, with instructions, and if he didn't carry them out his family would be murdered. Self-initiated detonation, or the timer will connect. No command wire! Not radio controlled! And with the size of the explosives (1,000lb) it would eradicate the guard complex, and all those in it.

There was little time to devise an action plan if a 'proxy bomb' landed at your front gate. The rash action was to get heavy duty 'bolt cutters' and leave a set at the front gate posting. We were instructed that if a proxy-bomb came in, under no circumstances were we to open one of the doors. We were to utilise the heavy bolt cutter to smash the side window, and tell the driver to cut himself free, climb out a window. As soon as we did that, or sooner, if possible, hit the 'mortar attack' button, and shout to the guard room 'PROXY BOMB, PROXY BOMB' and run. Once the guard room heard the alert, they were to drop everything and run out the back. This threat sat with us for a year or so. There were later proxy-bombs. 22nd November 1990 Newtownbutler, Co, Fermanagh. February 1991 a UDR base in Magherafelt, 8th April 1991 Belleek.

About a year or so after the first attack, security forces calculated how to stop it. Have an outer gate near the front sanger (about 100 meters away from the front Gate). When a vehicle approached this outer gate, the soldier in the sanger (or by cctv camera) could check the VRN via computer, and have good visual on the incoming vehicle. If it looked ok the gate could be lifted, and the vehicle let in through the front gate.

Mahon Road got a mortar attack, but hadn't to this date, had a VBIED or proxy-bomb attack.

On our weekend orbit rota for the part-time companies, the weekend after the barracks camp guard, is Bacombra Guard. Bacombra - a housing development – cul-de-sac on the Craigavon side of Portadown. It had approx. 20-25 houses, it was the married quarters for officers. When I joined in 1987, there was little threat to the houses, but within a short space of time int cell got information, that it may get attacked by a VBIED, as other housing developments had been attacked because there were many of security force members living there (Clover Braes, Donaghcloney in June 1991 (600lb)). There was a sanger and gate built at the entrance to the cul-de-sac, and the second detached house on the left, was occupied by the section that was doing guard duties.

We occupied the downstairs only, as the upstairs was where hi-grade bodyguards/drivers stayed and slept. They normally slipped in and out without us seeing or talking to them, but through time I got to know one of them (only on a small chit-chat way), and he let me see, feel, and strip down some of the weaponry they carried. I loved the Heckler & Koch MP5k. It was a very small 9mm sub-machine gun, that fired single shot, fully automatic, or bursts of 3. It was so small and compact, it had a hook below the front, to stop you putting your forefinger in front of the barrel and getting your finger shot off. They were hi-grade body guards, and never told us who they were guarding, or where they were going.

Bocombra Guard. No more than one section were to be there (sometimes we snook another 1 or 2 there). We were to cover the front sanger/gate (2 soldiers), back sanger at the bottom of the cul-de-sac (1 soldier), and when I was the IC, I asked one of our soldiers (normally Timmy) to be the cook. That way we didn't have the full section tramping in and out of the kitchen, making things filthy, putting boot marks all over the lino floor, which meant less a clean-up operation before handing over to the next section.

I enjoyed my coffee, and when Timmy brought me a coffee, I sometimes complained that it is only half full (it was in fact about 80 or 90% full, but that was an ongoing joke), and a couple of times Tim filled the mug up so much, it was actually bubbled above the rim. He told me to come and collect it from the kitchen, and if I spilled it, I would have to personally clean the floor at the end of the duty (another joke, but I would have done it). Each time I managed to carry, without spillages, from the kitchen, to my desk that was at the corner of the living room.

Once again, I always worked out the stag duties to suit everyone. This meant everyone was happy.

We started doing the Bacombra Guard in 1991, and soon for the camp guard and Bocombra Guard the duty rota changed. It changed because most soldiers liked it the new way!

The army working day began at 0800hrs through to 0800hrs the next day, so if we went on duty before 0000hrs, and stayed on duty to 1700hrs, we would get 2 full duties. This meant that you didn't have to go home, have a little rest while at home, and back again for another duty. Therefore - 16 Platoon took over at 2000hrs Friday, to 0100hrs Saturday, 17 Platoon 0100-1700hrs Saturday, 18 Platoon 1700-0100hrs Sunday, 16 Platoon 0100-1700hrs Sunday, and 17 Platoon 1700-0100hrs Monday, and handed on to a full-time company.

One time I was Bacombra Guard IC on the Sunday 1700-0100hrs Duty. It was a rainy night. 'London's Burning' was on TV at 9pm, I had completed all my reports, just got a new mug of coffee, and leant back on my chair watching TV. About five to ten minutes later the Mahon Road ops room phoned me, and asked if we were under attack. They had not heard anything over the radio, but the mortar-attack panic button has been pressed, but it wasn't on now. I told them everything was fine, however I would check the two sangers, to see if anything was amiss. I checked out the sangers, everything was fine! I filled in the occurrence book, and phoned the ops room back, to tell them everything was fine. After that, I leant back on my chair and continued to watch 'London's Burning'. The ops room phoned again, saying the alarm was going off again, but had just stopped. 'Is anyone being a smart arse?' I was being asked. It was at that point that I noticed! When I leant back on my chair, it was pushing the mortar-attack which was on the wall behind me! We couldn't hear it, as it relayed to the ops room (silent alarm). I phoned the ops room back after a couple of minutes and told them that I checked all the sangers, and nothing was wrong. "It must be the rain" I told them. It must have short circuited somewhere along the wires.

I got off with that one! But it could have got me into trouble (bullshit baffles brains, as they say!)

Bocombra Guard only lasted just over a year, as Mahon Road Barracks was enlarged giving it married quarters for regular troops, and officers.

12

Cenotaph

Cenotaph

Our Company ('D') had the privilege of doing the Cenotaph each November in Donacloney and Banbridge. Donacloney at 11am, and Banbridge at 3pm. I joined the Army in July 1987, and 11th November, six men from my Company were on Cenotaph duties (the six men were composed of four doing rifle drill on Cenotaph, the Colour Sergeant or Sergeant Major taking and commanding the Cenotaph, and an extra man who had been in the training, and was a 'reserve') We were on patrol around the two areas of the Cenotaph parades, when they were taking place.

It sounds as if we (D Coy) only did the Cenotaph. The other two part-time (C & E Coy) also did Cenotaph duties. 'C' Company in Lurgan, and 'E' Coy in Portadown (both towns were within their area of responsibility (TAOR)). Both Companies carried out the tasking as we did.

It was Sunday 8th November 1987, and we had the privilege of patrolling, helping secure our two Cenotaph areas.

All that was the ops that morning, was to have clean combats, look smart, and be in Mahon Road before 0800hrs. I was in before 0730hrs to have a breakfast at the cookhouse, to set me up for the day ahead!

Our patrol (1 section (2 teams)) left Mahon Road in Land Rovers just after 0900hrs, and our patrol orders were to check, clear, and ensure safety of the Donacloney Cenotaph that morning, and Banbridge in the afternoon, quite an easy day's Ops

We went straight to the Donacloney Royal Legion hall, checked the car park, around the nearby area such as gardens, hedges, behind short walls, we also checked around the hall (bins, parked cars). After which we went into the Royal Legion, showed our presence, formed a good attachment with the parade officials, and of course – got a mug of coffee and a bit of cake.

Afterwards we left the Royal Legion and made our way by foot patrol along the route to the Cenotaph (land rovers following), checking everything on the route, as this was the route that the parade was taking. One of the main areas of interest was around the village centre, where the road was a little wider, with cars parked, public litter bins and suchlike. Most cars were fine, with people coming and going into the local shop that was open, but any suspicious looking vehicles were checked through our Ops room (VRN and car details) by radio.

Once Andy (our patrol commander) was satisfied that all was clear, we proceeded into the church hall at the back of the Cenotaph and touched base with the soldiers who are manning the Cenotaph. They were still practicing the rifle drills, and 'Lower on Your arms – reverse' for the perfect timing. When we arrived, they paused the practice (but still checking their boots were 'bulled', medals were in high shine and the attachment (pin) was still good (the last thing you wanted, was for your medals to fall off when on the way, or at the Cenotaph), and there was no fluff or dirt on the No.2 Dress). We chatted with them, breaking the stressful tension of what they were about to do, then left again for mobile patrol around and through the village.

The Cenotaph team marched out to the Cenotaph at approximately 1040hrs, the parade from the Royal Legion was due about 1050hrs. Our patrol was positioned one team at each side of the village, stopping cars from entering the village, until the service ended.

Just as the parade was breaking away (finishing), and had almost returned to the Legion, word was coming over the radio of a 'contact' in Enniskillen. A large bomb had exploded beside the Cenotaph when the UDR section of the parade was approaching, there had been many injuries and some fatalities!

During the afternoon we heard there had been 11 people murdered, one of whom was a police officer, and over 60 people injured, some badly. That same afternoon the IRA admitted planting the bomb, but declared the bomb had been set off prematurely by the army's electronic counter measure equipment, and that the army was responsible for the deaths of the innocent people. That incident was bad propaganda for the IRA.

Once the bomb, which was behind a wall, exploded, everyone in the parade (including the UDR Section) or people watching, rushed over to remove the bricks and rubble to rescue anyone who was beneath.

When we heard the news of the bomb in Enniskillen, it upped our game. The IRA would normally conduct a number of attacks simultaneously, so we were caught unaware.

The next Remembrance Parade we had was to be at 1500hrs Banbridge. We had to make sure we conducted a thorough search to ensure the same thing wasn't replicated here. Our section commander Andy had to find out through the ops room, details about the Enniskillen bomb, to make sure we searched places similar to the incident area in Enniskillen, for instance, was it a car bomb, a bomb left in a wheelie bin, an unattended bag by the time (1330hrs) we were moving over to the Banbridge area we still were unaware of the type of device used in Enniskillen. We had to be very stringent in our searches along the parade route, and around the Cenotaph which was located at the top of the town.

The patrol was not as easy-going, as it had been and felt earlier!

The IRA placed another bomb that morning. It was about 20 miles away in Tullyhommon village. The IRA had planted a 150lb bomb beside the Cenotaph area. Boys' and Girls' Brigades had gathered. The IRA said it attempted to trigger the device when UDR soldiers and RUC were standing beside it, but it failed to explode. Later the army EOD defused the device.

The Enniskillen bomb was triggered by a timer, and not by remote control as was said by the IRA. The timing of the explosion was perfect, but the parade just was delayed a little. Had it gone according to plan, then the UDR section of the parade would have taken the full force of the blast.

The following year (1988) as our Cenotaph team were beginning to prepare and train for the task, I asked if I could join and train with the team. It was a very proud thing to do, and I wanted to join the team and take part. I was granted permission, and that year I was on reserve, ready to take part if one of the team couldn't make it, or was ill.

The standard parade commands were ok, and easy to remember. 'Squad! By the left quick march", "SQUAD! Halt" etc. But then we had to become proficient with rifle commands, such as slope arms, shoulder arms, change arms. We had to be well versed in all the commands. The main reason was something you would never think of, but which is obvious. The four men on the Cenotaph are facing away from each other, and can't see one another. So, there would be nothing more embarrassing than hearing a command, but carrying out the incorrect drill, and not being aware of it. One of the most important drills, and with the most respect, is the 'lower your arms in reverse!'. This is where we bring the SLR's up and slowly drop it until the muzzle is on the ground, then drop the head down. Anyone could do this drill in a reasonably slow time, but we had to practice it, in a very slow movement, to show great respect for the fallen comrades, and those soldiers that have fallen before us in the previous years. From the Command 'SQUAD! Presssent Arms", then comes "SQUAD! Lower your Arms In REVERSE". From that 'REVERSE' we lifted the SLR up, - from that point – to when we dropped our heads, we wanted it to last as near 30 seconds as we can, and most importantly – drop all our heads all at the same time – the same second! To learn we all faced each other, like the four points of the cenotaph all facing inward. The commands clicked together ok, but it was just the timing in lowering the Rifles. We started by counting out aloud "One elephant, two elephant - - - twelve elephant, down". The elephant! It is hard to speed that word up, and so the timings came together. Then we worked on the drill, silent – counting in our heads. Then completed drill facing away. This sounds like it was only a one-night training. But it was training at least twice a week, for three or four weeks, as well as getting our boots bulled.

I was a reserve to the Cenotaph team 1988 and 89, it was 1990 before I was in the Cenotaph team, and the main reason for that was that we changed our rifles to the new SA80 edition, which changed where the rifle was, on Slope-Arms, Present-Arms, and on 'lower your Arms in Reverse'. I was so proud to be in the Cenotaph team, and did so for another 12 years. There was nothing as daunting as standing at attention with your rifle in Slope or Shoulder Arms, and starting to daydream, as we stood in the town centre for quite some time. But what was most daunting when your mind wandered was coming back to reality! Did I miss a command? Am I the odd one out? Did we change Arms? As much as my mind panicked, I daren't turn. I Can't Turn. I had to believe that I was in the correct position.

Sometimes over the years, the Sergeant Major, or whoever was leading the Cenotaph, gave the wrong command, however we had practiced so much, that we performed the next drill on the list as per our rehearsals.

13

Childhood

I was born in 1968, a year before 'The Troubles' began, even though the troubles had started in the 1900's, and came to head in 1916 (Easter uprising)

I never knew life before the troubles, and to me, and my peers, the troubles were normal life. I never knew life before bombs, army checkpoints, police and army patrols, security in city centres, and shops checking mum's handbags.

I grew up in a council estate near Lisburn, and for as long as I can remember, I always saw the army patrolling in green Landrovers, some with hard tops, others with the canvas soft tops. I remember the soldiers patrolling through Lisburn, with their SLR's, backpack radios, with the last soldier of the foot patrol looking backwards and moving about more than the others. I remember the police walking along in pairs, body armour on, both hands slung inside (in the large arm gaps) to keep them warm, every policeman (R.U.C.) had a side arm. I think mostly revolvers (Ruger Speed Six), and sometimes with a rifle. Not like the British Army SLR, I think a Ruger M14. The police cars were unmarked (mostly Ford Cortina's and Granada's), most were heavily armoured, with bullet proof windscreens, and side windows.

Growing up in the early seventies, there were many cowboy films and army films on, eg. 'The Good, the Bad and the Ugly',

'The Great Escape', 'The Guns of Navarone', and many similar type tv series. I watched 'The Sweeney', 'Starsky & Hutch', 'The Six Million Dollar Man'. War, Police, troubles – they were normal life.

As for tv in the seventies, when we came home from school, we watched, children's tv (on from about 3:30 to 5:50) It wasn't uncommon to be interrupted by a newsflash, either with the newscaster, or just the tv channel logo, saying there was a bomb, or a bomb alert on a certain street, asking for the keyholders to return to their premises. The news was mainly headlined by shootings, bombings, and what was happening in the province.

In Lisburn, we could go through Thiepval Barracks, which was on the north side of Lisburn, but it slowly got closed-off to the public travelling through. Firstly it was closed in the evening (after the rush hour) and opened before work hours the next morning. It then closed the through-road permanently, and the fortification around it got more intense, with tall steel fences, sangars and barriers at the entrances.

When growing up, my best friend Drew and I played 'Army' with sticks for machine guns, and had 'Action Man' toys (He had an Action Man tank, which I was jealous of). We watched all the army/police based series on tv. We dreamed of being 'Commandos' but I never thought it was in the realms of reality, that I would one day be a soldier. Throughout my schooling and within family life, it was never suggested to me to follow my wants and dreams, and become a soldier. It must have been too dangerous, due the troubles, to suggest it. The closest thing I thought I could get, was the Boys' Brigade where we would do marching, drills and stuff.

My family moved out of Milltown, Derriaghy in the summer of 1978, to Ballinderry, where my dad built us a new house. Ballinderry was a completely different place from Milltown, it was as though the troubles didn't exist. There were no army patrols around, and no sectarian views in the country people.

I met my friends Trev and John in school there, and Trevor was the first friend who cycled over to my house. John & I cycled over to his house, and we had a good connection, as John liked army stuff and Action Man too.

In the summer of 1979, I remember cycling up to his house and playing with Action Man.

It was 27th August, and that day news spread to everyone, that there was a serious Bomb which killed over a dozen British soldiers, earlier in the day a bomb had killed Lord Mountbatten in his small boat. I remember vividly that day/evening, as the street in Upper Ballinderry where John lived was so quiet, everybody was so concerned. I think it was at that point, that the realities of the troubles first became reality to me.

14

Helicopters

Helicopters! heli-ops, as we called it. Ops at the border, South Armagh, Crossmaglen rely on heli-ops, as it was so dangerous to travel by road. In Portadown, there were variations in the numbers of heli-ops required. It was decided by the amount and types of threats at the time.

Each battalion was allocated a certain number of flying hours, depending on threat levels. In Mahon Road (Portadown) many flying hours were taken up with full-time patrols, which reduced the amount of flying hours allocated to the part-time patrols. The helicopter we usually used was the Wessex (Capacity – 16 Soldiers (2 Sections)), flown by the RAF or Army Air Corps. There were other helicopters used in Northern Ireland, but we, at Mahon Road (here in 1987) seldom saw any other. The others were 'the Puma' mostly used by Special Forces (capacity – 16 soldiers (2 sections)) which was newer, faster, and more manoeuvrable. The Gazelle which was a small helicopter and usually used in cities for observation. In the 1980's you would normally see one above Belfast – moving about – hovering, and generally there so often, that you'd think it was a permanent fixture. We would very rarely have seen a Gazelle in Portadown. The Lynx helicopter was quite a recent helicopter in the Army/RAF, it was substantially smaller than the Puma and Wessex, and only held one section (8 soldiers). It hedge-hopped (stayed very low to the ground, jumping over hedges, and so couldn't be heard, and spotted until it was close you). It was normally used at the border ops, for dropping soldiers in and extraction. We didn't see them often in Portadown, in 1987/8. The SeaKing, which was the only helicopter in which I was warm inside (no wonder it was used for mountain/sea rescue). It holds 24 (2 multiples). Then there was the big one: the Chinook Helicopter, that held over 50 soldiers.

The usual one we saw and used, was the Wessex. But as far as we knew, we (Northern Ireland) got the cast offs, the ones that were coming to the end of their life. In Northern Ireland helicopters only completed short runs, compared to other theatre's like Germany etc.

The first time I was up in a helicopter/Wessex was Late July 1987, on a weekday evening. It wasn't an ops night, it was a training night, and the three part-time companies were taking part. The training was concerning how to enter, sit, exit, signal for it to come in to collect us, re-enter, and to experience it, so that when we were on heli-ops (eagle V.C.P.'s) we knew what to do. Were we going to get more heli-ops? Perhaps the threat on the ground meant we had to (like battalions near the border)? We weren't told!

That training night: There was a section of us in our company (those who were on training duty that evening, and not the designated ops platoon for that evening) who got changed into combats for ops, got our rifles and radios for going out on ops, but we were on training tonight. Because we were going out on the ground (ops areas), we had to be 'contact' prepared.

We marched down to the loading bay, got our SLR's loaded, and continued towards the heli-pad, and when we were nearly at the heli-pad, we saw the other 2 companies' sections there. The other two companies (C & E) had more than one section each. They had 2 sections each, and we only come with one Section. I think our company thought there was only one required. Each of the companies, had to gather round, listen to the briefing given by one of the full-time training team (many of soldiers already knew the heli drills). We were wearing berets, and were instructed to remove head dress before entering, keep rifles low, remove or secure down any aerials. The Section Commander approached the helicopter first, but didn't enter. He stood by the door counting his troops as they got into the copter. Once all his section got in, he also got entered and told the loadmaster "Last man in!", then it quickly lifted off.

Our company wasn't the first to lift off (it was 'C' Coy), and when the Wessex came, I could not believe the size of it. It was so BIG! How on earth could such small rotors lift such a big mass of metal? Such noise, such a feeling of the rumbling power. When the Wessex was landing, we all had to drop to one knee, put our heads down to avoid getting hit in the face with debris which was thrown up, and hold our berets on, making sure everything is secure. That was another thing! We had to ensure all pockets were fastened closed, and we had no loose slings etc, as it could have been blown about and hit your face!

When the first of the lifts took off, Andy (our section commander) started winding us up, as there were a few of us not long off the recruit's course. Although I was anxious and a bit apprehensive, at the same time I was really looking forward to it and joined in the banter. Andy said that the back quarter panel looked loose. I said that I saw that, and if the rear rotor gave a few revs, it might detach and fly round and hit the main body. Each time the Wessex came in to pick up the next section, the banter got worse. We'd say it was serviced on a Friday. And you know what the lads are like on a Friday? They don't give a toss, just want to finish the working day, and get home for the weekend. The banter continued. But Bod (who was on my recruitment course, and was the Best Recruit) became silent, and if I remember correctly, he started to go quite pale. When the Wessex came to pick up our section (8 men) he didn't want to go, he was scared. So when given the go ahead to get into the heli, Andy and myself grabbed Bod's webbing at the shoulders, and pulled him in. It was the RAF, and they were being 'Good Boys' tonight. Lifting off and landing quite easily. When we got on, Andy got in, sat beside the loadmaster (man at the door, and was the man that operated the GPMG at the door), and put on the headset, to talk to the co-pilot. The loadmaster pushed the arm, that the Gimpie was on, back to the door. Sometimes you don't know you're a real soldier in a real conflict, until you see this happening. It wasn't just a Gimpie, but had the full link-box attached (at least 200 rounds), with the lead round in the chain already fed into the gun.

This was only a training evening, so we weren't going too far. We flew out towards Loughgall Road, Portadown. When we got into the heli, we filled the seats (loose canvas type hammock seating) from the back (seating is around the helicopter, not in rows). Once we were seated, we then placed the SLR upright between our knees, to avoid it knocking against anyone else boarding. If anyone felt sick, the procedure was to pull your jacket forward, put your nose and mouth into it, boke onto your chest, and close the jacket.

Landing in a field. Well, it wasn't as easy as landing, the Wessex when it got to the landing area circled it, banked over so that the loadmaster is hung out the door (which was always open) looking for dangers, such as telegraph or electric wires that would take us down. Once he'd circled, he would come down and land. As soon as we touched down, and it was safe, the loadmaster gave us permission to dis-embark (thumbs up). We jumped out, ran about 25/30 yards, went down on one knee, rifle in our shoulder, looking outward, observing and protecting the Wessex. After the last man left the heli, it revved up and took off again, barely touching the ground. I don't think there was any weight of the helicopter on the ground, when we were getting out. Once the heli lifted, we ran over to the roadway, jumped, climbed, or rolled (sometimes the best way) over the hedge, onto the road. We did a quick VCP, stopping cars in both directions, taking notes (just like a usual VCP), and when Andy heard on the radio, that the Wessex was returning, we clambered back into the field, faced outward from the landing site, and waited for the go-ahead to get back on. I Loved it.

We didn't get another heli-op for quite a few months. Sometimes they came thick and fast. It depended on the area we were patrolling, and the threat levels on mobile patrols. Doing heli-ops / eagle VCP's we could cover vast areas in a short space of time. The area from our barracks, and the area between each VCP location.

The RAF and Army Air Corps would pilot the helicopters. The Army Air Corps were sometimes 'Mad Bastards' and I am sure that if any of them were reading this, they would probably laugh, as I know they liked to be thought of as 'Mad Bastards'. Quite soon into the heli-ops, the Army Air Corps took us up. When we boarded, our section commander would quite often tell the co-pilot that there were a few 'new flyers' on board! We were flying quite low over the fields, and I saw an electric pylon in the near distance - Were we going to fly below it? We got closer. Bloody hell, we were going to fly below it! And there wasn't much space! What a mad pilot. But then! The Wessex banked up, and we sank into our seats. How the f*** were we going to clear this? As soon as we cleared the highest wires, he did a nose dive back down. None of us expected this, and lifted off our seats, with our heads almost touching the roof. Then when we came down, straightened. we all fell back onto the floor. Most of us missed the seating when coming down. The loadmaster laughed. There were so many mad moments like that. You got to know, and when you realised something was about to happen, you kept one hand between your knees holding onto the metal front bar of the seating to avoid lifting off the seat, and you watched (whilst laughing) the others who did not expect it, floating from their seats.

One ops we were flying, the pilot was sneaky, he gently took us higher and higher, without us realising it, then just dropped the Wessex, and for quite some time! All of us had lifted to the roof, and when it went level, we all clapped down like a pile of shit. It was really funny, as the section commander was our O.C. (our company commander), and he was definitely not amused.

Believe it or not, there were a few times with the Army Air Corps and RAF when we'd been flying along, and all of a sudden, the Wessex would pull-up, but so viciously that you could hear the rotors straining, the engine noise went low, as the rotors strained more, then the noise stopped, Wessex would stall. That's right! Engine stopped! The pilot turned the helicopter round and nose-dived it. This meant that the rotors didn't stop. It was called circular rotation. The engine was then switched back on, and the flight levelled. The Army Air Corps and RAF practiced this quite often, but I'm sure they weren't supposed to do it with us on board, even though we loved it!

One of the Army Air Corps pilots was nicknamed 'Airwolf', and some say he had it written on his helmet? Now he was a mad pilot. One heli-op ('F' full-time company) they were flying along the route of the M1 motorway, the road was clear in front, and he flew below one of the road bridges that crossed the motorway.

Strange but true - most of the helicopters in Northern Ireland, found their way about, by following roads. You would quite often see the helicopters flying along high above a main transit route!

I quickly learned that the best position to be sitting in the Puma or Wessex was the seat opposite the main door (always open) (always open, as the loadmaster had the gimpie set – looking out, with the full belt of link ammo loaded). Unless I was the IC (section commander) of the patrol, in which case, I was sitting beside the loadmaster, with the headset on, talking to the co-pilot. When I was the IC, the first time I got in, on this patrol, I gave him a map, of all the HLS's (helicopter landing sites) marked. Anyway! Back to my seating position opposite the door! Most soldiers didn't like being in that seat, as they were first off (I loved that, loved the adrenaline), it was the scariest position, as when the heli was banking round looking at the HLS, I was looking straight down at the ground, On the sweep, I was nearly sitting at 90' to the ground. Sometimes the heli didn't quite land, and as soon as the loadmaster gave the 'GO', I bolted out the door, quite often jumping, as the heli was still lowering the last few feet. My main aim was to get straight onto the road, whilst the rest of the section was giving all round defence for the heli – till it lifted (about 2 seconds, after 'last man out'). Why did I want to get onto the road? To stop the car. Quick, surprising, hoping that word got to Mr Terrorist, that there was no getting away. Remember! Once we had the VCP going for about 5 or ten minutes, word had probably got through to the bad guys, that we were there, and thus, they knew not to come that way.

One occasion we were collected by a Puma near Portadown, and whilst lifting off, there was a train passing by at a decent speed. The pilot brought the Puma alongside the train and was running at the same speed. We were waving at the passengers, and they at us. It probably lasted about 5 to 10 seconds, then our Puma turned away; as the Puma was turning, the loadmaster pretended to be firing his Gimpie at the train. We all burst out laughing.

I was in Ballymena Barracks on a promotion course, and during the course our cadre had to go down to Ballykinler barracks, to 'the village'. We were waiting at the heli-pad, when a Chinook came along. We were delighted, because they are fast, and we would be transported to Ballykinler in no time.

Along the way, the loadmaster went to the back and lowered the back ramp! Strange? Why was he doing that? He walked to the end of the ramp (he was harnessed), and sat down on it, looking out. Then he got up, turned to us, shouted, and waved for one of us to go to him. I Immediately stuck up my hand, and jumped up, everyone started to laugh. He waved me down to him and put on another harness onto me. Then took me to the very back, onto the ramp, to the end of the ramp, And I sat on the end, with my legs dangling off. Like sitting on a table, with your legs dangling down. My left hand was holding onto the frame of the main helicopter, whist the loadmaster was sitting on the opposite side. I was looking all around, and down (whilst my left hand is tight – like a vice, holding the frame). Then I felt the frame of the helicopter raise, and it kept raising! I looked around to see the loadmaster, and he was no longer there. My left hand was still going up, I lost the grip of it. Then I noticed! The frame of the helicopter wasn't going up, the ramp I am sitting on was getting lowered down, it was getting so steep, that I was having trouble shuffling back. I couldn't slip and fall out, as I had the harness on. I looked around when I was trying to shuffle back, and saw the loadmaster smiling at me, with the ramp switch in his hand. I shuffled back ok. Everyone in the aircraft was laughing their heads off at me. I was more than happy to make their day.

Drumcree! Disturbances were now occurring, many regular regiment troops were stationed in Mahon Barracks, patrolling, and keeping the peace at the riot fronts. We (R/Irish) wanted to continue our patrols, VCP's, but wanted to move about covertly, quickly, and cover as much ground as possible. Heli-ops were the answer.

Since Drumcree was going on, our battalion, were given many more flying hours. One Saturday afternoon, we were tasked with Eagle VCP's around the roads between Portadown and Lurgan, Craigavon. We wanted to make sure we kept the terrorists in check, watching any movement, restricting the movement of weapons, and collating evidence and Int. We were dropped into a field alongside a main road. As usual, I was sitting opposite the main door (always open), so as soon as it touched down (I sometimes jump out before it has touched down) – I was OUT. As we were circulating, checking the HLS (helicopter landing site) for wires, level ground for landing, I saw a van pulling into the side of the road, with about three people clambering out. It was 'UTV' news crew, they started filming us landing, and dispersing. I jumped straight out, and was running towards the general direction of the camera crew, but kept my head/helmet tilted, so the camera can't catch my face/ID. We didn't bother them, and they soon left.

That footage was shown in clips during the Drumcree standoff, for quite some time, showing myself and my team disembarking from the Puma.

The Wessex's were an aging helicopter, and during the 90's vanished, with the Puma's doing all the work Wessex's did. When we were in the Wessex, we would see more and more fix-its. Like lagging around pipes and other bits n pieces tied in. On one heli-op around Craigavon, my team got dropped off to complete an Eagle VCP, whilst Frankie's team was dropped off at another road/route. The Wessex came back and collected my team, then straight back up, then over to collect Frankie's team. We circled around, ready to land, and all of a sudden, the Wessex started to fly off, lifting higher slowly. I could see Frankie's face when we started to fly off – disbelief. When we were gently gaining height, whilst flying out of the Craigavon Area, the loadmaster stood in the middle of the Wessex looking at us, and gave the indication, to fasten our lap seat belts. He gave the sign, just as a flight steward would show you, on a plane, without the pretend belt of course! He then told us to tighten them and went around each one of us checking we had done according to his instruction. One of my team hadn't bothered putting on the belt, and the loadmaster was absolutely furious.

We flew into RAF Aldergrove, and the Wessex landed like an airplane would. Flying along straight, dropping height, until we touched down. (it's less stressful to the helicopter to land this way) We then taxied over to one of the hangars, where we disembarked, went and sat in a room near the operational room. We had to wait for ages until another craft was available to us to fly us straight back to Mahon Road.

Frankie had contacted the ops room, to get in touch with our own company, which sent out a CMV (civilianized military vehicle) for his team.

15

Humorous Times

I have been writing about the threats, risks, and enemy attacks, but we also had an enormous amount of light-hearted humorous times, and I know it was all these times that made us all so close to each other.

When I joined there was always banter, jokes, and when we were driving to our operational area, Dicky and Alex would be having a singsong in the back of the L/Rover. Songs like 'I am a music man, and I can play'.

We made fun of what each other was eating during our short break times 'Out on the ground'. Once I brought a can of rice pudding out on patrol, and as I was talking about it, Good Boy Stephen asked "Is that a 400 gram tin, or a 275 gram tin ?" Good Boy Stephen worked in the supermarket trade, we all fell silent then burst out laughing, as Stephen was so serious.

The banter was normally good in the back of a Land-Rover. One summer Friday evening on ops, on our way to Banbridge for a series of VCP's, whilst on a 'A' type road, making our way through Seapatrick, I decided to act the clown and entertain. It was 1988, and the film 'Teen Wolf' starring Michael J.Fox had been out for a few years, I had always wanted to go surfing on top of the L/Rover. So tonight, why not? I opened the top cover hatch and climbed out onto the roof. We were the 2nd team (rear L/Rover), and the front L/Rover saw me doing this. We were travelling about 40mph, and I stood up, as if to be surfing, with everyone laughing their heads off. Then I heard a shout from the rear of my L/Rover "Get down – the cops are behind us!". I looked back, and sure enough there was a police car behind. So I dropped onto my belly on the roof of the L/Rover, hoping the police did not see me, waiting for them to overtake our patrol, but they didn't, they hung behind us, and stayed behind us, for what seemed like an eternity. Eventually they passed, but I think they too were laughing! After that episode, I wanted to do it again, only better. The thought came to me again a few years later, when we were to travel to Ballykinler, the route was via the M1 to one of the Lisburn junctions. We were in the Defender 'Snatches' which were much faster than the old Series 4/5. I was the 2IC (commander of the second team), and instructed the section commander to ensure they were driving at over 70mph, and make sure it's over 70! On the M1, at the right time. I climbed out of my front seat into the back, out the top hatch crouching, and over onto the bonnet. Then my Snatch caught up and closed in on the front snatch, where I jumped from the front bumper – into the back of the lead vehicle. I then sat behind the commander, to which he replied, "Your Fucking mad, you know that?". After sitting for about a minute, I made my way back. My snatch caught up with us, and I jumped back onto the front, and made my way back.

The threat of an attack in Craigavon and Lurgan Police Stations was getting very high.' Imminent threat' as the Int-Cell would put it, but now there were attacks on the Orange-Order halls across the province. We had to have overt patrolling around the halls in our TAOR, whilst still having overt patrolling in the Lurgan/Craigavon areas to deter the terrorist. Our battalion chatted with other battalions and the police, to establish which orange halls were at risk, and should be patrolled. In our case, with our main TAOR in Craigavon, we also had to patrol the Orange halls as far as Moira, Ballinderry and Glenavy. Glenavy was actually in Lisburn Battalion's TOAR, but it was easier and quicker for us to cover that area.

The peculiar thing was that my parents' house which was in the country, was near Ballinderry. I used this opportunity to have our tea break, or coffee break (if you're like me) at my parents' house. The first time we did this, I phoned in advance. At around about 2200hrs our two Snatches (Land Rovers) pulled into the drive, then round to the rear of the house. We all piled into the living room (leaving 2 men at the Snatches to watch them) set our loaded rifles in the centre of the carpet, helmets and body armour off, whilst mum was running in and out with tea n buns, and my dad 'yarned' (chatted) away with everyone. My dad loved it, and it was great for the morale of the section and platoon. We did this a few times, and sometimes we had a multiple, which is 3 teams (12 soldiers and 1 police man). One night we thought we would be in Craigavon the full night, and the ops room re-tasked us to cover the Orange halls, so being in the area, and close to my mum n dad's, I decided to have a break there. But as we (multiple – 3 teams) approached my parents' home I noticed quite a few cars parked in the drive, and round the back of the house. I wondered what was happening, and instructed the Snatches to stay put on the road, whilst I investigated. I went in the back door, and I saw nobody in the kitchen or dining area, then I went through to the living room door, opened it and walked in. I had my full combats on, webbing, helmet on, my face was all cammed up, loaded SA80 rifle diagonally across my chest, army radio on my back with mic on my shoulder, and I walked straight into the living room. There were over a dozen people there. It was a prayer meeting!

Due to the troubles it was not well-known that I was in the army. Maybe only one or two at the most knew that I was in the Royal Irish. Imagine the look of shock? In a quiet country house, a fully operational soldier came into the living room! Nobody in the prayer meeting stayed for a cup of tea after, but they had brought sandwiches, cake and buns. Between the ten of us (and policeman) in the living room, with a pile of SA80's in the centre, we managed to demolish all those sandwiches and buns, Once again dad was yarning away, having great craic with all of my patrol. He was talking of things he had done in the past, and sometimes I had to interrupt "DAD! there's a police officer here!". My patrol mates were laughing their heads off, enjoying the evening (and the cakes), as did the police officer we had with us (he was from Craigavon Station. We collected him earlier). Despite the tough times, such evenings brought our platoon/company closer together.

After I got promotion, I was leading teams, or patrols (either 2IC, or IC of the operation), either way, I was normally the one who composed the 'flap-sheet' detailing those in each team, and their role. E.g. Ozzie section commander, with Steve driving, Colin and Paul in the back along with Alison our Greenfinch, together with any specialist equipment we were carrying, My team, with Keith driving, and Timmy and Terrence in the back. The majority of the time we had similar teams, as the same people reported for duties. We all knew each other inside out, as when you were on patrol you learnt each other's hobbies, gripes, groans, problems with family and family life, personal problems.

Morale wasn't always high, and I tried to maintain it within my patrols. Sometimes at the start of the patrol, Timmy would say "Let's have a Nuclear patrol?" in which we all pretended to 'Fall-Out' (thus the term nuclear patrol). It was full night, where it would probably start, with me slamming the door of the Land Rover after getting in from the loading bay, where I have loaded-up the team (each team member comes over to the loading bay, with me there, check the rifle is in a safe condition by cocking back the action and hooking it open whilst I look inside making sure there are no live rounds in the chamber of the rifle, and no magazine attached. Then let the cocking handle go forward making sure the rifle muzzle is pointing at the sand, and squeeze the trigger. Rifle is safe! Now show me the new magazine, in which I looked to check there was a round at the top of the magazine and that is a 'tracer' round, then put the magazine into the rifle, Now I knew that the rifle (or SA80) was loaded with a full magazine, but there was no round in the chamber (loaded, but not ready).

Anyway, I may get into the Rover and slam the door and turn around to the team members and YELL (with obscenities) about their loading drills, and how I'd been waiting too long for them to arrive! 'Fucking shite', to which Timmy in the back would shout back about how bad I was at commanding, and they should have a decent commander (once again, with obscenities). There was nothing wrong with anything, it was all just made-up fantasy. Further into the patrol one in the back might shout "When the Fuck are we having a break, we've been on the ground for 7 hours, and we haven't had a break yet, just a shite patrol" and I shout back "We'll have a break when 'I' decide, not fucking you! your lives are a break!" and the full night will be filled with expletives, and banter. It does sound strange? But it was brilliant for morale, and letting off steam.

Other nights when we were working in 'The Sticks' (countryside, rural areas where we patrolled smaller roads, that linked towns, or border crossings), I might declare that we'll have a 'Democratic Patrol', and that was where we conducted the patrol to the set of orders, but when it came to having stops, and VCP's, I'd ask who would like to do it? "Who wanted to be stopper?", "who wanted to sit and keep warm in the Rover".

We got the work done, just not as hard core. In the sticks it would be virtually impossible for the terrorist to know where we were, or where we were going, so we could lower our guard slightly. It was nice to look after the soldiers and team members. I tried to look after my teams as much as possible, as I knew that I couldn't be a good commander, without a team that looked after me. It was a two way thing.

Sometimes, when I knew what we were doing throughout the weekend, I'd pop into a famous butcher in Moira village on Friday, after work, and buy speciality sausages, and maple-cured bacon, and bring that with eggs and soda farl's on patrol, either on Saturday or Sunday morning. When we set up a section VCP, which would be in place for about 20 minutes or so, Ozzie would cook the fry's on my 'Trangia' stove (with gas conversion for speed), and I would go around the section of soldiers, giving each one a 'filled soda', which is two halves of the soda (like a sandwich, filled with 2 sausages, a couple of rashers of bacon, and fried egg. Sometimes when I did this, I had someone different on my patrol, and I was so happy, when I walked down to that soldier, that might be in a 'cover position' (at the outside of the VCP, behind the hedge, watching for anyone bursting through the VCP, or any danger) and handed the soldier a filled-soda. They were so surprised. 1, that there was some food made! And 2, that I was sharing with them. Some soldiers who were not familiar with me, asked "How much do I owe you?".

Quite a number came on duty in the morning, and hadn't had brekkie, or may have been in the tail end of a hang-over. I loved to show my appreciation for my teams, and they me. Ozzie would normally cook, and I washed out my Trangia set when I got back into barracks.

We were in Land Rovers (Snatches) so much in our operations, and it could be quite monotonous at the best of times. Each team had their own way of dealing with the quiet times whilst moving from one location to the next. Of course there was chat, but that dried up from time to time. As I've written before, we sometimes sang when travelling along. One time we all heard the song 'Lovely Day' by Bill Withers (1977). Towards the end of the song Bill Withers gives a very very long 'Dayyyyyyyyyyyyyyyyy' and in our Rover (later to be joined the other team) each of us tried to give the longest 'Dayyy', but we made the competition to include "A Lovely Dayyyyyyyyyyy", whilst in the background the rest of the team is singing "Lovely Day, lovely day, lovely day, lovely day..........". and we timed each soldier in the full section (2 teams) to see who could hold the note for the longest. Each of us thought we were going to trump the competition, but it turned out that Kippy did the best a few times with a time of about 25 seconds. Kippy was given that nick name, as he often fell asleep. He fell asleep having breakfast and his head went into the fry on his plate, fell asleep on top-cover, fell asleep whilst driving home after duty, and many other times. Kippy was quite short, and not very loud, so we were all amazed when he could hold this Dayyyy for so long.

In my Snatch, to break the monotony and lift morale I bought a small 'ghettoblaster' (powered by army batteries), and it sat in the seat behind the driver. I know I would have gotten into trouble if we were found with a regular radio in the back, but the morale it brought was far above the risk of getting caught. Also in my Snatch, I used an improvised air-conditioner, which was an old vacuum cleaner flexible tube. What was this? In the winter, the only heating in the Snatch, came from the blower in the dashboard that blew out and up for the windscreen. The driver and I were getting cooked in the front, whilst the soldiers in the back were still freezing, and often wet, so we worked out a way to pipe the heat into the back. By coincidence the tube that came from below the dashboard to the top, was the same size as a hoover tube, so disconnect the Snatch one, and push in the 'improvised air-conditioning' whilst the other end went out into the back. Problem solved; Morale good.

One Saturday afternoon, about July/August, after we'd been in for lunch, the ops room told us to go and patrol GDA (ground defence area) 6, which was the area between Mahon Road barracks and the main Armagh Road (A3). It was a rural area of fields, ditches and streams. Our two teams split up, and headed out. I was in charge of the second team, and we were to meet up with the first team, just beyond the roundabout at the start of the A3. I was leading, patrolling through a field, with long grass or crops, and when I got to the edge of the field, I looked for somewhere to cross the short hedge. Not an obvious place, but an easy place for my team to follow. As I neared the hedge, all of a sudden, I felt a thump going up my arm to my shoulder, " ouch", "What's that?". My SA80 barrel hit an electric fence, and I got a thump of 12 or 24 volts! My team closed in on me, and we were daring each other to touch and hold it. Billy said no problem, and held it. He got a thump of voltage through him, saying it was no problem? And we were wooses! I said "No way! It's quite sore". Billy said it was nothing, and that he could pee on it! After a bit of debating, Billy said he would do it, and did! When the thump of electricity went through him, he doubled up in pain, and the rest of us doubled up in laughter. He said it was no problem, and continued on with our foot patrol. Although I thought he was walking with a bit of a limp. Hope his population rod still works?

In winter time the Land Rover Series 4 and 5 were very cold, as the MT garage disabled the heater, so we wouldn't sit in the Rovers too much, but when we got the new Defender Snatch Land Rovers, we had heating, and sometimes in the middle of winter, so cold outside, some soldiers would fall asleep in the back. One night on ops, we went down to the guard room, I got out to get in touch with someone, and when I got back to my Rover, two of the three men in the back (Eddie & Colin), had buried their heads in their jackets while sitting (it's easy to get a wee rest this way. You're not lying down or being slack, you just bury your head into the jacket, still with rifle in your hands, and catch a wee bit of shut eye) and the two had fallen asleep. I could have wakened them, but I decided to let them sleep until we get to the first VCP location. We were patrolling quiet roads tonight, and when we got to the VCP, I decided to let them continue to sleep; the three of us were well able to run the checkpoint at our end. We got out and into the Land Rover quietly, so not to disturb.

We wondered how long they would sleep, and continued to do VCP's whilst they slept. Coming back into the barracks at the end of the night, about 0100hrs I woke them, telling Eddie and Colin to get out. They both asked "Why? sure we'll get out at the next VCP!", and I told them that the patrol was finishing, and we were back in camp. The three of us laughed at how confused they were.

The next night I asked Eddie and Colin if they got any sleep when they got home, as they had been asleep the full of the Patrol, and surely it messed up the sleep pattern? Both said that as soon as they got home and into bed they slept again like babies.

Eddie and Paul quite regularly came out on my Patrol, as they liked how they were treated, and knew that I had their backs, and if the shit hit the fan, I wouldn't crumble. But they were both from a different platoon, 18 Platoon. Like myself, Eddie and Paul liked coming in for operation duties. We got plenty in our own platoons, but we came in to help other platoons out. If anyone came from a different platoon to help me, I tried my hardest to look after them. For instance if I had a full patrol (one section (two teams)), I gave anyone who came in as an extra the option, to either go out on patrol with me; or stay in the company lines and take it easy. Clean your rifles, clean the company lines, most of the night drink coffee and watch the telly. An easy task, with a full nights pay!

Tommy (of my platoon) complained to me, that I looked after the 'helpers' more than my own men! But I explained that I didn't, I just gave them the choice if it was there. If I didn't treat them well, they would stop coming in for me, and we may be short staffed. Tommy felt it was unfair, and that he and Good-Boy Stephen wanted an easy night. A few weeks later, I was in the same predicament! Too many men for the patrol (counting Eddie and Colin), so I thought 'this is the night to give Tommy and Stephen an easy night'. I produced the 'flap-sheet' (name and service numbers of soldiers going out on patrol) leaving out Tommy and Good-Boy Stephen. Left the flap-sheet up in the ops-room and came back down to the company lines. With a smile, I went to Tommy and told him he was staying in that night. An easy night! Tommy thought about it for a few seconds and replied "I'm not sitting here all fucking night - all night sitting about here! I'm going home!".

Whinging? We UDR/Royal Irish had degrees in whinging, and Tommy came tops, he was brilliant at whinging. No matter what happened, Tommy whinged!

16

CMV Patrols

CMV – Civilianized Military Vehicles

Not all patrols were overt patrols, where we wanted to be seen by the public. Overt patrolling was to show our presence and show the different areas that we were there protecting them, and at the same time showing the terrorist that we were there to stop them, deny their movements and activities. Of course, that meant the terrorist would know our locations and movements.

To stop the terrorist, we also wanted to have covert (undercover/hidden) operations, were the full op (patrol) is done without anyone seeing us, or an op where we pop out onto the road or street, do a VCP, then vanish away again, to our next grid reference. In that patrol, the terrorist can never record or know where we are, or what we are doing. Patrols like this could still be done by Land Rover, but we must still get into the area, such as the Craigavon or Lurgan Police Station and from there, go by foot, but there was still an element of knowledge that we were in the area, as we may have been 'dicked' either entering, or leaving the Station on foot patrol.

To add another level of covert, we quite often used a transit sized van, that looked like a normal everyday work van. Not the cleanest, perhaps a paper or coffee cup on the passenger side dashboard, but in the back, a section (8-11 people) of us, combat ready, and ready for the upcoming Op. The back of the van was empty, no seats or anything.

In the perfect CMV there should be a rubber, or carpet flooring, to reduce noise when we were entering or departing from it, but seldom did we ever have that. There also should have been an intercom between the front cab and the back, but usually it was the CMV Commander shouting through to us!

CMV Ops! Different threats, risks, word on the ground concerning Int-Cell, and different operational objectives, were to determine how much CMV work we were doing. Quite often if we had a heli-op planned and the helicopter was cancelled for whatever reason, then we would conduct the task by CMV, or just get collected from a heli-op, as the helicopter was unable to collect us.

We would start our CMV patrol night, the usual way we would start an Ops night. Arrive at Mahon Rd, get changed into combats, get our rifles and ammo, get our kit, only this time the equipment will be less. Only equipment needed for the task, which may include a lightweight fold away 'STOP, HEADLIGHTS OFF' sign. We would have our Ops order and Int-Cell update, as well as Int-Cell asking for which information to collate! Then we were ready make our way down to the loading bay, load rifles, check kit was working, and file into the CMV. Depending on which areas we were going into dictated which sitting arrangements we took, the threat risk would determine the seating arrangements. When the threat was great, or we were going into the Lurgan/Craigavon Area (a short distance away) we would take up the 'Herringbone' position, in which we all sat down the middle, in staggered formation, facing outwards (if you were on the right-hand side of the middle – you faced to the left. The soldier behind you sat slightly in front of you pointing right, and the same as you moved to the back.) It was set that way, so that if we came into a contact situation we could cock our rifles, and when the CMV Commander said we were going to drive through, we would make ready our rifles, and shoot directly out the side of the van, whilst the van drove through.

Some years later, whilst talking to a soldier from the Marines, whilst at a shooting competition in Bisley, he openly spoke about one such event. Years previously on tour in Londonderry he told of a time they were doing a rural CMV Op, and on route back to base, they unexpectedly came across an illegal VCP set up by the IRA. The van slowed down when approaching the VCP, like a normal work van might do, but the soldiers in the back were being informed of what was coming up, and all cocked their SLR's, CMV commander still talking of what was seen, which was another good reason for slowing up. When they came close to the illegal VCP! The CMV commander gave the SHOUT. The CMV then raked as fast as it could through, whilst in the back the Marines were shooting out both sides.

After they had passed through, they informed their ops room of what happened, after which a Land Rover patrol returned to the illegal VCP area. No bodies or vehicles were there, but lots of blood was found on the ground.

The Marine that spoke about it, says he has PTSD and nightmares about that day – to the present day. The noise of 8 SLR's going off in the back of the van for 100 to 200 meters, not seeing outside the van to know what was happening, the unknown if they would get out of the killing zone without any casualties or dead?

When we left the barracks in the CMV, there was little talking as we all tried to concentrate into what was going on, and where we were. The cmv commander kept us updated, as we drove along. When we approached the area into which we were to be dropped, the cmv commander told us what the ground was like. E.G. high hedges to the left, low hedges to the right, no streetlights, but a light from a farmhouse 100m ahead. The cmv driver made sure that no car had been following us, and if there was, he would drive around, or pick another location close the planned one.

After the CMV Stopped. All lights off! ….we waited for a few seconds, with the driver and cmv commander looking around for any signs of life, and their eyes adapting to the darkness. Then the cmv commander got out and walked around the van looking for any life or threat. Once he was satisfied, he opened the side or rear door, where (silently) we would disembark, going into the hedges for cover and all-round defence. The cmv commander then shut the doors as quietly as possible, got into the passenger seat, and the van drove away, turning on the headlights about 20 yards or so away. We stayed still for about 20 seconds or so, then got back into our teams, continuing with the Op.

When we needed collected or wanted something dropped off for us (dead letterbox) we would keep in touch with the CMV by radio, and the patrol section commander would set out a 'marker' on the road. The 'marker' was an everyday object that nobody would look twice at, but the cmv driver or commander would spot it. For instance, a can of Coke sitting out onto the road about 2 feet. I personally had a 'Cats Eye' that I had taken (long-term borrowing) from motorway roadworks. It's a vice-versa way of dropping us off. The van would pass the 'marker' and pull in. Headlights off. Once the cmv commander felt it was safe, he would get out, walk around the van and open the door/s, but we did not move until he went over and lifted the 'marker'. Then we silently climbed back on board the CMV.

What was the ops/patrols by CMV? We may have a foot patrol around some smaller villages/hamlets, where the roads going through could be a transit route that was off the main motorways, dual carriageways, or A type roads, we got dropped off near a hamlet, in which we mainly stayed off the roads (foot patrol through the roadside fields), just coming onto the roads to do VCP's, which made us unpredictable.

We were dropped off close to a town eg. Banbridge, and did an overt foot patrol along a main 'B' road, either a 'rolling' VCP, or set/planned VCP's on the route.

On one occasion I was 2IC on a cmv foot patrol which began just outside Banbridge, moving towards Rathfriland, along the B10. We had two policemen with us to assist us, however instead of assisting us, they decided to check the tax discs, insurance and tyres on each car that came into the checkpoint! I didn't like this, as they weren't assisting us, but coming down on the motorists that came into us. This didn't portray us in a good light. I favoured the 'hearts & minds' on the public that we chat/talk with, to get them to like and help us, thus closing the gap between communities, and not pushing them away.

We had set VCP grid locations tonight, but after our second VCP, where the police were trying to catch people out with tax/insurance checks, I went up to Derek who was the patrol IC, and asked him not to complete the set stops, but to break into a TAB (TAB stands for 'tactical advance to battle'. A yomp forward carrying full army kit with speed). Derek agreed, so we turned that evening's set VCP points into a rolling VCP, where we continued moving, and if we saw a car approaching, waved it down with the red torch, checked it, and let it move on, and the police didn't get a chance to check the road tax and tyres. We were moving rightly along the road, and a car was travelling very quickly towards Rathfriland. I stood out on the road, giving the full circle red light wave down (mag torch with a tall red filter, which you waved around in a windmill circle with your arm straight), but the car drove straight through my team, and was going to get away clear if the lead team didn't stop it. So, I shouted towards team 1 "STOP THAT CAR".

The vehicle was driving through the lead team, when it slammed on its brakes, locked up, and slid to a stand-still. The driver was rigid straight pushing himself back into the driver's seat, the policeman in the lead team was in front of the vehicle had his sub machine gun cocked and pointed towards the car. The driver thought he heard me shout "SHOOT THAT CAR", and surprisingly, so did the policeman! The driver was just speeding along the road, and when coming around the last corner, only saw us at the last minute (or so he said?) We just asked the normal questions 'Name, ID, where are you travelling from, and where are you going?' then let him carry on.

There was a period of about a year, when we were doing quite a few CMV ops. Perhaps due to the threat on army land rover patrols, or to the change in ops and orders? Int-cell wanted us to carry out quite a few ops, where we gathered, or should I say 'collated' information. They were called 'lie-up patrols' where we would be dropped in on the ground about half a mile or so away, and would covertly move into our 'lie-up' position, and watch/ collate info.

We would be dropped off and have two teams (1 section). All of us would be cammed-up, full combats, body armour, rifles, one night sight per team, ECM equipment per team, radio per team, and everyone carried something to drink and eat (for the short break).

Before we left the barracks, everyone was checked (perhaps by jumping up and down) to ensure nothing rattled amongst personal kit.

If it was a household we were to watch, we most probably had seen/observed a set of photos that has been taken for this op, showing 'dead-ground', high-ground, light sources, carparks, entrances etc. When we neared the target, the two teams split. One going into lie-up position, the other team would satellite around or go to high ground to dominate the area. The team that went into the lie-up had to remain quiet, minimum movement, and collate the information required, such as vehicles and VRN's, description of persons seen, and stay in that position for the task length. Perhaps as little as ¾ of an hour, perhaps 2 hours. When I knew that I was going into lie-up position, I liked to bring a flask of coffee, and a paper bag of chocolate-covered raisins. Chocolate covered raisins? They were a great source of energy, and they got you through the long wait. Eat some one by one, suck the chocolate off them, munch a mouthful. Something to pass the time, without getting restless. The lie-up positions also included public-house carparks, where we knew 'players' frequented. There we would get all the VRN's of cars coming and going, and cars already parked there.

Ambush positions! I'd been involved in very few of these, and we normally got placed into them by CMV. The usual order! Full combats, fully cammed up, full team kit, but perhaps more ammunition carried? We would have at least two teams inserted around the 'area of interest', being careful not to have each team's arc of fire that may overlap each other (so we didn't shoot each other) if we came under 'contact'. It was a time of sitting still, watching, listening, listening to the radio for sit-reps of other teams, and any Int update. There was probably another section, just outside this area, in Land Rovers, to either come and assist us, or come onto the roads and block them so that if the players have left this area of interest, they can still be intercepted. Usually there would be one Land Rover on each road that was leading out of the 'area of interest' and they were normally parked in some small laneway, somewhere that they were not seen from the roads

CMV's were also used in other ways. For instance, if we had been on the ground for quite some time, we may need new batteries for the radio, or other equipment including meals, and we would set up what is called the 'dead-letterbox'. I would be in touch with our company by radio, ask for specific equipment needed, and give them a 6-figure grid-ref of where I wanted it left, where I would collect it. The company (or CMV, as it has a radio) gave us a time for the drop off. I set a 'marker' on the side of the road which confirmed my dead-letterbox (as we are human, and I may have got the grid-ref wrong), and the CMV parked beside it, and dropped off the kit. It was usual for the cmv commander and I to see each other, as a further confirmation it was the correct spot.

Another quite common use of the CMV was to collect us from an Eagle VCP heli-op, where the helicopter couldn't or wouldn't for some reason come and collect us when were out on the ground.

We always had a back-up CMV just in case. On one heli-op night, we were dropped off near Crossmaglen. The op was not going well as our radios had the wrong decryption in them (for this TAOR), and we couldn't contact our ops room, so we just had to wait for another 30 minutes until our next lift, for the Puma to come back in to collect us. It came as timed and collected one team, but not the other (the team I was in!) It flew off (probably back to Mahon Road, Portadown?). We were only 4 soldiers (1 team) stuck in the infamous South Armagh. It was the early 1990's.

I was carrying something that I shouldn't be carrying (during this time). It was a Nokia mobile phone. Not a smart phone (many years later). I was in the company's OC team, and after the Puma had left us, I told him what I had! He turned to me and said "Corporal CARDY! You know that you should not have it out on Ops? But thank goodness you did" The OC phoned the ops room, explained what happened (an MFU), then contacted our company to explain the area and 6-figure grid for pick-up with the CMV.

Not a nice situation, as it was a weekday night, the daylight has dropped (dusk, getting dark), and we didn't have good observation on the fields/roads around us: PLUS, the Puma has come down and away again. The IRA ASU may think that a team of soldiers have just been dropped off. The danger level had just raised ten-fold, almost to a level that we make-ready our rifles, for an upcoming 'contact'. Thankfully it never hit that bell, we just went into 'all round cover', stayed still and silent, waiting for our CMV to arrive!

Another time we were conducting Eagle VCP's near South Armagh, and had the company OC with us. I was commanding the second team. Normally when we returned to barracks, I had the team/s to do a 'silent' unload, where we quietly clicked our magazines off the SA80 – checked that the top round was a tracer round (if so, as it was the top round in our magazines – the chamber was empty – without checking). However that night I got my team to come to the loading bay with me to go through a proper unload, as the Company OC was on ops with us, and if he saw my team just slipping off their mag's? Walking from the heli-pad towards the loading bay, one of my team (Alan) told me he didn't have a magazine on his SA80. I told him it was ok, just slip the mag back onto the rifle so we can go through a proper unload, as 'Snooker' was with us. Alan again said to me "I don't have a magazine on my SA80", I say again, a little louder "I know, you've already said! Just slip it back on". We reached the loading bay, Alan beside me, and I say for him to point the rifle at the loading bay, and he again says "I have no magazine on my SA80". "Stop Fucking around Alan, just go through the motions". "I've lost my magazine!". It was only then that I'd figured out that the magazine had dropped off his rifle whilst doing the heli-op, the Eagle VCP's.

We completed about 5 or 6 that night, and they were quite widely spread out across the area. I told the OC (not amused), and a team of us (my team) got into a CMV, which drove back to the area (not close) we were working in. We didn't think we'd find it - a needle in a haystack! What if someone else had found it? We would never see it again! 1 magazine, 25 rounds of ammunition – result – Alan would be charged, or maybe worse? At the first heli-drop location, we stopped the van, a few of us got out, went into the field and beyond any expectations, or logic? The magazine was there. It was sitting upright in the middle of the field, just where Alan would have jumped out of the helicopter. It must have just dropped straight down when Alan thumped down out of it. Lucky or what? I don't believe in Luck, but this time?

17

Banbridge

Earlier chapters I have written about areas, such as Lurgan, and Craigavon, but I have not written in depth of my own company's TAOR (tactical area of responsibility).

'D' Company had their company lines/barracks on Scarva Road, Banbridge, before moving to Mahon Road, Portadown in 1982.

The company's TAOR remained the same. Banbridge being the centre, with surrounding areas such as Dromore, Dromara, Annahilt, Loughbrickland, Gilford, Donaghcloney, and other hamlet villages. These were not the most troublesome or dangerous areas, but they were still very important, as some of the main transit routes went through them such as the A1 that travels from Dundalk (Southern Ireland (N1)), through Newry, to Lisburn, where you could join the M1 onto Belfast.

'D' Company having come from Banbridge, most soldiers in the company lived in and around Banbridge and Dromore, and quite a majority still do. A majority of personnel in 18 Platoon lived in Banbridge, 17 Platoon Dromore, and 16 a mixture of Gilford, Portadown and Tandragee. Although numbers had dropped from 'D' Company, and 'D' Company had 'reprobates' or 'blow-ins' as the older members liked to call us, joining the company from the Lisburn area (as Lisburn 'B' Company was fully manned)

When I joined in 1987 most of our ops/patrols were in Banbridge. My company knew the area and roads so well. Each patrol period would normally have one or two VCP's on the main A1 road that flows through our TAOR.

'C' Company's forte and skills lay in the hard patrolling in Lurgan, 'E' Company in Portadown/Birches, whilst our forte was VCP's on the A1 dual carriageway. We could deal with the heavy amount of vehicles (other companies got large tailbacks, and became overwhelmed). We knew the best places to set up VCP's, perhaps giving each vehicle no chance of changing direction or avoiding us, or places where the vehicles saw a side road or two, and could turn off in order to avoid us, but little did they know, that they were turning off into a 'rat-trap' where a team, or only a pair of soldiers would be awaiting them.

On an A1 VCP, when the Section Commander decided to set up a VCP, his Land Rover would put on the hazard lights, and pull onto the hard shoulder. We'd drop off the two 'STOP-checkpoint' signs (one from each L/Rover) and one soldier (cover position), then take the two L-Rovers around 2 to 300 meters down the road, dropping off the 'stopper' soldier (with torch at night-time) to wave down and stop the traffic. First Land Rover going onto the, and blocking the right hand lane, the second staying on the, and blocking the left-hand lane behind the first Land Rover, giving enough space for any vehicle to zig-zag around, when driving out of the checkpoint. A double chicane, so that any car who tried to drive through, couldn't do easily, and if it did? Then there was another soldier doing cover, who also had hold of a rope, that would pull across the road (call trap) a length of hollow spikes that would instantly flatten all of the tyres.

Roles in the VCP: The 'stopper' will stop the traffic, tell them to "Put your headlights onto sidelights, and continue into the checkpoint – thank you". We had one or two soldiers (the chatter) in the checkpoint questioning each driver, quickly establishing whether to question further, or let them drive-on. Section commander watching everything that is going on, assisting in different ways. Greenfinch, patrol 2IC and any remaining soldiers, were on the hard shoulder beside the back L-Rover interviewing and perhaps searching and logging vehicles. As with all VCP's we had to work fast and slick when setting up and taking down such VCP's, giving little time for the public to know we are setting up a VCP, and little knowledge that we took it down, disappearing again. As with any VCP, when we took it down, we had to beware if the IRA had set up an ambush whilst we are doing a VCP, for us to run into.

One evening we were conducting a checkpoint on the southbound (Newry bound) dual carriageway between Dromore and Banbridge. Everything was going well, and as I was moving around checking everything in the VCP was running smoothly, I noticed the 'chatter' in the checkpoint was having problems with the driver of the car he was talking to. I walked over, my Radio was on my back, I have full webbing on, rifle in right hand, mag-Light torch in the bracket on my webbing belt, I noticed that the driver had an speech impediment. Steve was asking where he was heading to, and the driver was replying "Nnnnn Nnnnn Nnnnnn Nnnnn", so I thought I'll try to help out. Steve was saying "Newry? perhaps?". I go over beside Steve, and try to guess a few other places, like "Meigh?", the reply "No, No, No! Nnnnnn Nnnnnn Nnnnn". I got out the map from my trouser leg pocket, opened it and mention other locations that started with 'N' or 'M'. The other commander came over, and joined in, trying to guess where he was going. Each one mentioning different locations, with the reply being "No, No, No! Nnnnnn Nnnnnn Nnnnn". Then the 'cover man' came from the hedgerow and joined in. After about another 30 seconds, the driver managed to complete the sentence. "Nnnnnn Nnnnnnn RATHFRILAND !", as soon as he said this – All of us were in fits of laughter. We could hardy speak. Steve (the chatter) gave the driver back his driving licence (in between laughing) and said, "Go on ahead!", whilst we were heading back to our positions still laughing away, trying to see clearly through the tears. The last thing I wanted was to laugh. I went over to give my support and help the man!

In 1988, I was in around a year or so, and was starting to think of promotion prospects, we were on a standard Op patrol around Banbridge. Just after a short coffee break in the Banbridge Police Station we were on the A1 Northbound (Lisburn/Belfast direction), we set up a checkpoint, I was a chatter that night. A coach/bus came into the checkpoint, and it was about ½ to ¾ full. The passenger door opened, and I stepped onboard, I was wearing the canvas 58 pattern webbing, and carrying my SLR, with rifle sling around my wrist.

The driver told me where he was coming from, and the location of where he was going. I thought I'd be smart, and walk down to the back of the bus, and back again, to see if I could identify any 'players', suspicious people, or get a sixth sense of anyone, or anything! Everything and everyone looked fine, I got back off the coach, letting it continue on its way. The checkpoint lasted another 5 minutes or so, then we packed up.

Sitting in the back of the Land-Rover as we drove off, I noticed that my SLR was minus a magazine. A magazine of 15 rounds! The colour suddenly drained from my head down. Panic? Someone on the coach must have clipped off my magazine. They have it! It's on the coach heading towards Belfast! This means that I'll have to tell my team commander, who will stop and tell our section commander, who will have to radio the ops room, to get in touch with Thiepval barracks, who in turn will have to send out, or divert a section 'out on the ground' to the A1, to intercept the coach. 'Goodbye any thoughts of getting a promotion'. Before I spilled the beans! I checked that I still had my second magazine to load onto my SLR. Checking my left-hand front pouch, I felt it was still fastened, I knew I still had my secondary mag! When I pulled it open, to reach in for my second magazine, I found there were two magazines in my pouch. I had forgotten to slip No.1 magazine back onto the SLR, when leaving the cop shop. Most times when we went into a police Station, or barracks, instead of stopping at the 'loading bay' and going through unloading drills, we just 'clipped off' the magazine, looked at the top round (checking it's a tracer round), and then put it the magazine pouch on the webbing. vice-versa on leaving. It was the fastest and safest way to 'unload' or 'load'. You hadn't cocked back the breech block, and so it was impossible for a round to move into the chamber without the breech block being carried back. I still felt a right fool, with carrying an SLR out on patrol, but forgetting to load it, but it was much better than losing a mag (or getting it stolen). I quietly slipped one of the magazines onto my SLR. In that moment – I think I lost a couple of years off my lifespan!

In our TAOR, Banbridge, Dromore etc, we were always quite close (in minutes) to HMP Maze. Why do I mention that? It's not like we could bypass arrest, conviction, court and sentencing, and put a player straight to prison! (the Maze was for political prisoners).

On the Maze grounds, there was an Independent Search Cell (ISC). Not too sure of its full role, but it was a place where the regiment based there was trained and skilled in searching vehicles. If ever we stopped a vehicle that weren't happy that our search at the checkpoint was thorough enough, we could request through the ops room, that we it be taken to the MAZE ISC to have it searched.

It was a separate hangar that was purposely available for searching. When we delivered the vehicle, it was parked in a designated area. We watched the 'search-team' come in, and each member of the team was openly searched by another, to show he wasn't carrying anything into the search area, to 'frame' or 'contaminate' the car they are searching. They went right through the car, taking panels off the inside of the doors doing swabs as they go. The search took between 45 minutes and maybe a hour and half, depending on the vehicle. Meanwhile the driver (who also got searched) sat in a rest room awaiting the finish, and we (the patrol who brought the car in) went to the NAFFI and got our break for the night. I liked to try and stay and watch the search team, to improve my own search techniques but seldom were we permitted to stay and watch. Afterwards we released the vehicle, and guided it back to the Sprucefield roundabout along the Blaris Road (where the A1 ends), and is a junction (8) onto the M1, or into Lisburn centre.

Of course, we patrolled and conducted ops in Banbridge town. The threat was not as great as Craigavon or Lurgan, but it was still there. We always had the threat of the Vehicle Borne IED (VBIED), as in the notorious white Toyota Hi-Ace van. In Banbridge we not only had the threat from the Lurgan IRA attacking us, or planting a bomb in the town centre, but we also had threats from the Newry IRA.

From the 70's and early to mid-80's the most dangerous location for deaths of security forces personnel was Belfast. In the late 80's early 90's the location changed. Now Newry IRA has taken that gauntlet. The Newry IRA was ahead of the other IRA Battalions, as they had thought of different ways of initiating/detonating IED's. They had managed to figure out how our specialist ECM (Electronic Counter Measure) systems worked, and which frequencies they worked on and jammed. One of our ECM systems was just a constant jammer, and the newest one we had, was a reactive system, which stayed in sleep mode until the remote-controller was pressed, and before the signal reached the bomb, our ECM reactivated, and scrambled the signal, and in doing this, the system gave out an audible sound into the carriers earpiece . The IRA twigged onto this, and fired out lots of false alarms, which had the ops teams (regular regiments, and the UDR) running about like headless chickens, trying to establish where the IED was, where the 'firing-point' was, where to go, and where to cordon? The army remedied this by removing all the earpieces in this bit of ECM in the Province. Newry IRA knew that they could not use radio-controlled, as we had Electronic Counter Measure to stop it. So, they thought up different ingenious ways to initiate the devices. One way which was successful, was the use of 'Flash-light Slave Units'. When you are in a photography studio, and the photographer takes a picture there are quite a few flashlights go off simultaneously around the studio, but they are not connected. The IRA used this technology in Newry.

One such incident was 28th March 1992, at Newry's Merchants' Quay, where a blue Toyota Corolla was parked, in the boot was a Mk12 Mortar, and elsewhere in the car was a flash-light slave unit wired to the initiation of the mortar. On the other side of the canal was an IRA man/men waiting with a hand-held flashgun. When they saw an unmarked police car driving past the blue Toyota, the flashgun sent off a flash, which was received by the slave-unit which initiated the Mk12. Constable Colleen McMurray aged 34, and Constable Paul Slaine were in the car. Paul lost his legs, and Colleen lost her life the following day. Newry IRA had also thought of another form of initiating a 'device' which also gets round radio waves being blocked by our ECM. This was by using 2 x thin copper panels, put together, with only a very thin sheet of plastic separating them. This panel could be glued/fixed to the side of a regular van, then sprayed the same colour, or more probable a company-logo, whereby no one will notice the join. The initiation of the 'device' inside the van, being a Mk12 or a large IED, is initiated by shooting into the side of the van, shooting through the double copper plate sheet. This would connect the two plates, thus completing the circuit for device initiation.

When word of these new threats came through to us via the int-cell, we then had to be on the lookout for such devices. The flashgun initiation didn't have to be from the one flash-gun, but could be a series of flashes (like dominos). We had to be wary of 'open' areas, for the 'copper plates' and be aware of vans with overlooking firing-points. These new threats added to our risks, making it harder to do our job. We wanted to give the public so much attention, and show them how we were helping/protecting them, but now our attention was fixated on possible IED's and firing-points. We wanted to protect the public, but also had to protect ourselves. To lose one soldier in an attack was bad luck, but to lose a team of four soldiers in a IED or mortar attack was bad patrolling. If I lost more than one soldier on my watch? How could I ever forgive myself?

Sinn Fein (Republican political party) held their annual conference (Ard Fheis) in Dublin, and sometimes, by coincidence, we had some VCP's on the Northbound A1 dual carriageway after the conference was over. It was amazing who within the Republican political party, and suspects of the Republican paramilitaries came across our VCP. One evening we were conducting a vehicle checkpoint; I was the 'chatter', and a 4 door saloon car came into the checkpoint. I asked the driver his name, and where he was going? He told me his name, and said the destination was 51 Falls Road – Belfast! I wanted the car further checked, so I told the driver "Pull in on the left-hand side, just behind the Land Rover, thanks!". I heard a voice from the back seat, behind the passenger seat. It was the only passenger in the car, and had a newspaper up, reading it? I couldn't see his face, and didn't hear what he had said, so I said "Pardon?", to which he lowered the newspaper, and said "what's the problem? we are in a rush back to Belfast!". "It's just a routine checkpoint, I would like you to pull-in, to further check out your vehicle!", "I'm Gerry Adams, what's the problem", "Pardon" I said again, as I didn't hear him clearly, and I thought he said, 'I'm Gerry Adams', "I'm Gerry Adams, we need to get to Belfast !". Just then, I realised that it IS Gerry Adams, widely suspected of being one of the 'IRA Army Council' (the 'IRA Army Council' is made up of 7 or so senior IRA members, which made decisions regarding tactics, attacks, and who to murder). I had to watch what I said and did, as he knew his stuff, and would probably put in a complaint of harassment, or a claim of unfair conduct. I reached my right hand through the open passenger window (behind driver) and said "Mr Adams, pleased to meet you", as I was thinking 'I don't care who you are, I know the Law inside the VCP, from when you pass the 'Stop – Headlights Off' sign until you pass the last Land Rover of the section, YOU are in my land' and I didn't want to sound flustered and confused, and his name and who he was would not get him a 'Get-Out-Of-Jail card'. Gerry never shook my hand, and said "I'm Gerry Adams!", to which I pushed my hand and arm further into the car for a forced handshake and said "Mr Adams! pleased to meet you", and he shook my hand. Gerry then said, "We're in a hurry here, why are you stopping us?", "We are just doing a routine checkpoint, and we stop and check one in three or five cars, depending on how busy we are!" I was thinking on my feet, not letting him gain the upper hand. "If you just pull over to the side and let us search and check the vehicle, you'll be on your way in no time". I knew he couldn't do me for harassment, as I didn't see his face, until he lowered the newspaper and started talking. I could (if it came to a harassment point) say that I was stopping and checking the one in three ratio.

Gerry then upped his authority and voice and asked "Who is in charge here? ", I wasn't flustered, as he was on my ground, my rules! "Pull into the side, over there! (pointing in behind the Land Rover) and if you want to chat with the commander? that's him over beside the Land Rover!" pointing to Major Paul (our company OC). The car pulled over to the side, and as soon as it stopped, the back passenger door opened, and Gerry got out. I broke away from my position, and shouted over to others "take my place! I need to go over here".

My intention was to carry out the search, person & car. Major Paul was hit for six (as we all would be) when he saw Gerry Adams getting out of the car, moving quickly towards him, and to make matters worse? I came over faster, to make sure Gerry didn't get away without a search. I wasn't sure if Gerry Adams could be personally searched as he was a British MP, but damn sure the car and driver could be searched. I pulled Major Paul away from Gerry whilst in the middle of Gerry Adams trying to push his (as if?) authority; and stated to Major Paul, that I wanted the car and driver searched, we had every right to do so, and 'I' wanted to search. Major Paul was now computing what was going on, and said to me "That's ok Corporal Cardy, we'll get it searched, go back to your position". "but I want to search the car or the driver, or both?", "No Mark – we'll get it searched, go back to the road", which I did. I had just realised 'Gerry could be a distraction, perhaps there was another major player coming through, or weapons, or bombs?', as the IRA would do that.

They may have a well-known player about five cars in front of a car carrying weapons or pyrotechnics, and once the 'player' comes into the checkpoint, the patrol are round him like 'flies on shite', and the soldier on the road was so chuffed with himself, he would wave on the next few cars! So, on to my 'chatter' point again, now I was really switched-on, and I shouted over to the other 'chatter' to be stringent, concentrate, and be on the look-out for weapons, that might come through. I was switching on my sixth sense as each car came through. If I got an inkling, that car would be stopped, searched, and taken to the ISC, if needed.

We never got that 'Golden Catch'. Most likely there was no other. It was probably just Gerry coming back from the 'Ard Fheis'. We tried our best, but will probably never know of the weapons that we never caught?

We also concentrated on other main transit routes that were of importance though our area like the main roads from Banbridge to other towns. The Lurgan Road (A26), Castlewellan Road (A50), Rathfriland Road (B10), and other minor roads that ran alongside the A1 which could be used to transport illegal items without going along the main roads where there were more frequent checkpoints, either by the army or RUC, or perhaps customs.

One weekend our company was on Ops (operational weekend, where we could be called to any area, mainly in our own TAOR). The operational task was to patrol on foot and mobile, an area between Banbridge and Rathfriland. That day I was not a section or team commander; we were in a multiple (3 teams) operation! We stopped to set up a VCP. But in addition to the VCP, the other teams could patrol/move in-depth to see any movement or suspicious activity. I was in the VCP team (for this VCP). I was not the stopper or chatter but was to provide 'cover'. I climbed over the low fence/hedge into the field. I was going to go to slightly higher ground to overlook the VCP and see further down the given road both ways. I climbed over the fence onto rough ground that may be used by sheep (too rough for cows or crops), and whilst walking along the back of the hedge I spotted a piece of brown plastic sticking out from the ground. It didn't blend into the surroundings of an old farm field, and was only poking above the ground a couple of inches. It would have been so easily missed. I got down to have a better look at it, and I recognised it as a bit of sewer pipe, with an end (to make it waterproof) on it. I knew what this was! I had been taught about these since before my recruits' cadre and had always been looking for them! A TRANSIT HIDE! Should I alert the team and commanders to my find? No! there is 'OP-SAFE'

OP-SAFE, is where if we came across a hide or perhaps even a culvert-bomb, the individual soldier, and perhaps the team commander keeps it a secret (if safe to do so and will not threaten lives). Either go onto another radio frequency (which is also connected to our ops-room) to report it, or wait until the patrol is over, then go up to the ops-room/int-cell and report it. The rest of the patrol teams or other individuals should not know of this. Knowledge cannot spread of the OP-CLEAN. Upon reporting to the ops/int-cell, we give them a description of the find, 8-figure grid ref, and other info such as nearby buildings, land lay out, high ground, any person/people seen at the time. Ops/int-cell would then pass this on to the Special Forces, perhaps the army special forces or the police (E4A). The special forces/E4A would make note of the find, perhaps overwatching it with the intent of gathering more information, or an ambush situation.

If it was a culvert bomb? Then make that road/area 'out of bounds' to other patrols, until the ambush had played-out, or the EOD had disposed it, SOCO gathering forensics!

I could have just taken the 8-figure and moved on? But I was too inquisitive, carefully opening the top to see if there were any munitions inside. A stupid move as it could be booby-trapped; but using common sense, I didn't think it would be. I slowly eased off the top (keeping my face turned away), and when the top was removed, looked inside. Nothing! I shone a torch inside the length of the pipe, and saw it was long enough to hide a rifle. I quickly closed it again and moved on, continuing the task of 'cover position'.

When the patrol RTB (returned to base), left our rifles into the armoury, unloaded kit, and before I got changed! I went up to the ops room, asked to talk to the watch-keeper (Sgt/Commander of the ops room today) in private. I passed him all the information of the op-clean and went on my way.

I never ever heard anything further about that 'hide' and spoke very little about it.

Over the years 1987 – 2007 the areas have changed. Banbridge has got considerably larger, Dromore has grown (some say that Dromore should have 'City' status as it has a Cathedral), and Dromara. But we have lost the police stations in Dromore, Dromara and Gilford, but the Banbridge Police Station got much bigger. Banbridge Old Police Station came into being in Victorian times (around 1860), and due to the threat on the building from IRA bombs, and being small for the number of officers, a new Police Station was built on the Castlewellan Road, (which was formerly a Glass Bottle Factory (Crystal M.W. Co.) in1988. We had only gone into the old police station in Banbridge two or three times, as it was quite cramped, and wasn't always open for us to use as a tea break point. We used the new station quite regularly, but I never felt welcome in it. Perhaps because Banbridge was a quiet area, unlike Lurgan and Craigavon. The police building was substantially bigger, and the parking area was big, and could accommodate so many police vehicles, police personnel private cars coming on/off duty, and of course army vehicles. This larger station came into operation before the closure of the village stations that I mentioned. Most likely due to better roads and better cars. it was better to have a bigger central station?

18

Tuckshop

When I joined, I was in 16 Platoon, and Drew, our Platoon Sergeant bought us condensed milk, coffee, teabags, sugar, and packets of army biscuits with the platoon allowance each month, to have on breaks whilst out on patrol.

After getting promotion, I moved to 17 Platoon, where we got the same supplies each month, but also had a 'Tuck-Shop' which sold crisps, chocolate and coke tins. After a year or so, it phased out, as the platoon soldier that ran it had left the army, A few months after that, with soldiers complaining about the boring army bickies. Ozzie and I started it back up. Ozzie had a card for the 'Cash & Carry' trade supermarket, so he bought the supplies. I bought a small notebook, so that anyone who wanted something from the tuck shop, but had no cash, could write an 'IOU', at the end of the month, tally it up, for them to pay. The book also was used for credit. I threw in let's say £10, so each time I lifted something out of the tuck shop, I'd write in the item, cost, and take it off my credit. I thought of the credit/debit system, as we had no cash to start it, and that way when I threw in £10, Ozzie threw in £10, we had a little cash to stock it up. Ozzie and I provided a far wider variety of snacks and drinks than it had ever had, hence those from the other two platoons bought from it as well.

Snacks from the tuck shop made your night Ops a little more pleasant.

The items in the tuck shop were cheaper than the main street, as we only added about 5 or 10p on to the cost price of each item - just enough to keep the tuck shop going! The tuck shop became very popular within the company, and despite only a small mark up, because we sold so much, there was a large accumulation of money throughout the year. What should be done with the money made? I didn't want to use it for myself, as it was money spent by the platoon, and others in my company? So I decided to have a night out, a dinner in one of the Banbridge hotels (that was quite central to where most of our platoon lived). The money from the tuck shop might not pay for the full dinner, but it gave each member of the platoon a cheaper meal, and a night out.

The following year/s things changed a little. Sometimes after a training night, or training weekend, the men asked for a beer. Not a Coke or Fanta, but a beer to quench thirst. So I decided to purchase a few cans of Lager, to sell after training. Ozzie couldn't get Lager or beer from the cash n carry, so I just bought a few of the common brands from the off-licence, and as with the other supplies, just added 10p to the purchase price per can. I searched for deals when buying, and sometimes they turned out cheaper. I imposed rules onto the purchase of alcoholic drinks, to ensure no-one was drinking whilst out on Ops, and ensure also, that nobody drank more than 1 if driving. However, the success of adding a greater variety of confectionery to the tuck shop. It paid for a full platoon meal (with a little left over perhaps for one round of drink) for the following couple of years.

The tuck shop came to a natural end, when our operational and training duties were getting reduced due to the 'ceasefire' appeasement by our Government and Sinn Fein.

I enjoyed running the tuck shop, it was easy. Being a chocoholic – supplying various choccy bars and other confectionery items that I thought of or was asked to get by other soldiers.

It was mostly an honesty box. I couldn't be there all the time, as I had Ops and training to prepare for, teams to sort out, equipment to collate.

As I still had to fulfil normal duties, I relied on other platoon members honesty to pay for their goodies. In fact, sometimes the tuck shop would be open, with no-one about, and the cash box unattended. I think everybody respected me and what the tuck shop meant, that I never had an incident of stealing or plundering from the cash box.

I had said to the platoon when I took over the running of the shop that if at the end of the month, there was less cash in the pot, than could pay for a new consignment from the cash n carry, then the tuck shop would shut. I stated that I couldn't abide dishonesty, and that there would need to be mutual trust.

If members of another platoon came to buy anything from the tuck shop, I liked myself, Ozzie or one of our platoon to be there, to ensure everything was honest – so to speak! If nobody was there on each duty/training night. At the end of the month, if the balance in the cash-box was to not add up, I needed to be able to establish where the discrepancy had occurred.

On saying that, I also have to say that all the soldiers from the other platoons respected me, as I did them, and never tried to thieve from the tuck-shop.

Off the subject of tuck-shop, but staying with the honesty! One year at annual camp, 18 Platoon had brought a flat or two of beers. Perhaps to use after a training day when we didn't have time to go out? A new lad had joined the regiment a few months prior, and was at camp with us. One evening when our company returned from training, we cleaned our rifles, and were going into our accommodation, when myself and Colin (from 18 Platoon) saw this lad lifting a six-pack of beers from the flat of beer. Colin stopped him and demanded "What the fuck are you doing?", and the thief said "Nothing!". Colin followed "You're taking some of our beer, without asking! I can see you are! Who gave you permission?". The thief replied, "I'm not taking anything!", Colin "I can fucking see you are lifting it! I can see with my own eyes" "Psycho? What did you see?". I answered, "I saw you lifting the beer, I saw it with my own eyes!". Colin continued, "We saw you lifting it! Just admit it?", the thief stuck to his story "I never took anything!", Colin "What is in your hands then? not only did we see you taking it, but the box of beers is missing 1 six-pack!". "I never took anything!". "Just admit it! we saw you". "I didn't take anything!". Colin was getting wound up, and went over to him face to face "Just Fucking admit it, and we'll take it from there. Just Fucking admit it!". "I didn't take anything". "What the Fuck is in your hand then?" "Just fucking admit it. Just fucking admit it, and I'll talk to the rest of the platoon?"

Colin stood back a little, and asked him again and again, but with no admission of guilt. Then as quick as a flash, Colin floored him with as quick a punch as I've ever seen.

The thief was now nicknamed Fingers and was 'sent to Coventry' (Mr no-mates, where nobody talked or stood with him). Any pictures of that camp from then onwards, you will see a lone figure standing behind the men, with a black eye. Fingers never stayed in the regiment for much longer, as no one was mates with him. Honesty and integrity were so important in our platoon, company and regiment. It's most probably the fact that we must trust each other so much, and our attachment to each other is so deep.

In all honesty, I think the beer aspect of the tuck-shop made the most profit. I only added 10p per can, but it became so popular, that I had quite a few different types of beer, lager and stout, and all platoons came to buy, as we were the only tuck-shop in the company that sold beer. Sometimes a Sergeant/Platoon Officer from another platoon, would come and buy a flat of lager for his platoon, perhaps when the platoon had an accomplished day training, competition, or long Ops, and he wanted to thank his soldiers.

I hope everyone has fond memories of our tuck shop. I certainly do and was so glad to provide sweet treats to make their Ops night a little better.

19

PPW

PPW – Personal Protection Weapon

When I joined the UDR, you weren't automatically offered a Personal Protection Weapon, if you wanted one, or felt you needed one, you had to ask! You then had to complete forms detailing the reasons for your request. HQ would then look into whether or not you were eligible to receive one, due to threat, personal life, personal profile, family dynamics, and your social activities.

I was informed then, that on the streets (1988) one in 6 men at any given time, would have been be carrying a ppw. In the Lurgan Company ('C') quite a number of guys carried ppw's, whilst in my Company ('D') less carried them, as many of my company didn't live in quite so high risk areas.

When 'C' Company were patrolling, their faces got known, often to the IRA. Subsequently the 'C' Company personnel were targeted much more.

There were still quite a few in my company who carried ppw's, but not to the same extent as 'C' Company.

Once you had been authorised to carry a ppw, you were issued with one. Most usually a Walther PP, in .22" calibre, whereas if you held rank, or were at risk, you were issued a Browning 9mm Hi-Power. Having been issued with a firearm, if you wished, you could apply to purchase your own weapon, perhaps a pistol of your choosing, or one you could shoot or operate well.

In 1988, I felt the need to get a ppw, as threats were increasing, and I was so often on duty, the odds of me being targeted were becoming far greater. I applied, and was issued with a Walther PP. A few months later, I wanted to purchase my own, as I felt the .22" calibre was quite feeble, should I ever need to use it, so I applied for a Firearms Licence, with the licence of a firearm for my own personal protection.

A ppw doesn't always save your life! Roy Montgomery of 'C' Company had his own ppw (a .38" Revolver) and was quite prolific in both carrying and using it. He worked in a petrol station.

One day a man came in to the counter, and asked Roy for a pack of 20 cigarettes, when Roy turned around to get the cigarettes from the shelves behind him, the man drew a pistol, shot Roy in the back of the head, then went around the counter, to fire another shot into his head. This incident happened in 1986, in a petrol station near Moira, Co. Armagh

Having a ppw doesn't mean that life and risk is easy going! Quite the opposite! Having a personal protection pistol, there were now so many other things I needed to think of. For instance, where should I carry it? I couldn't leave it in an office drawer, whilst working, or in a car glove compartment, when going shopping. It had to be with me, and on me at all times. There was the legal side, that I was not allowed to leave it in the car, but also – if someone was going to be taking my life, I didn't know where, or when this would happen, I was at risk 24 hours a day, so the pistol had to be on me but, where does one place it?

Perhaps a shoulder holster or a belt holster, on the outside of the belt, or an inside waistband holster, that is inside your waistband (you need trousers one size bigger in the waist). If using a shoulder holster, there were many different types, and they changed placement of the firearm, and how it was drawn from the holster. Like a thumb snap release. You had to wear a jacket for a shoulder holster. A belt holster? Where on the waistband should you carry it? Front (appendix), on the right-hand side where the pistol is angled to the rear, for ease of draw, on the left (cross draw), or the small of the back?

Wherever you carried it, it had to be concealed, but easy enough to draw, because if you had to use it, your life was under threat, you only had split seconds to draw, use it. Wherever it was carried, you had to get on with normal life, continue as though you were a shade of grey, not standing out from the crowd.

When we were off-duty, perhaps at home, we needed to practice the draw, and use of the pistol (not using live ammunition of course)

One of the practices, was to stand as in any normal day, and drop a ping pong ball behind your shoulder. When the ping pong ball hit the ground, draw, and dry fire (without ammo). If the ping pong ball had hit the ground again before you had fired the shot – you were too slow! Try again, because if that happened for real! You may be dead!!!

In the army, we all chatted to each other about gun carriage, where to place it, how to carry it, such as loaded with no round in the chamber, loaded with a round in the chamber, with safety catch on; what pistols could be carried loaded and one in the chamber with safety catch off, or if there was no safety catch. How was this safe? Should we carry a secondary magazine, and where was it carried – a separate mag holster? In your pocket? In the car where should you carry it? All these questions, and no definite answer!

We regularly practiced with our personal protection weapons, and we learnt a little from each other, however about six months after I'd got my ppw, I got onto a 'P.P.W. user course' which was split over two weekends.

We learnt a great deal during those two weekends, including where best to carry, and conceal the ppw.

Where it should be carried when in a car? Many on the course said they would keep it below their thigh, or somewhere else in the car that was easily go to!

It should always be carried on the body. If carried under your thigh, and an attack happened, you would have to brake suddenly – the weapon would probably launch onto the floor, where it would be hard to locate in those vital few seconds and the panic of the moment. If you had a crash – not attack related, the same would happen to the ppw, only you may be rendered unconscious, and if someone came along to help, and they saw the ppw, they could stop helping, take the weapon and disappear.

So where on your body should you carry a ppw, whilst driving? We were taught a few places on which to carry it, being wary of getting at it, drawing and using it in the car, not only to draw and use it, but to be able to draw without showing you were doing so. For instance, if you had the weapon in your belt, on your right hand side you can't get at it. You will have to debus from the car and then draw it, so losing much time, not giving covering shots to get the enemy's head down. You could be killed, before you can react.

The car was the most probable place we could be attacked, and so we had to be alert and ready at all times. In the car, like I said earlier, we varied routes, and tried to alter timings (not easy to do) but aside from that, we needed to be watching for anything out of the ordinary, as in Int gathering, and personal safety.

We had to keep our distance from the car in front. Especially in traffic queues and junctions. We kept at least ¾ of a car distance, and at all times calculate 'actions-on' if attacked at that exact moment such as sink the boot, mount the pavement, or smash your way between cars. At junctions, if attacked, rake out of the end of the road without looking – turning left. Why 'turn left'? That way you were running with the traffic. You may collide with a vehicle but could still get away, by turning right, you would quite likely hit a car head on.

The main objective was to get out of 'the killing area'. It was safer to try and escape the killing area, than try to get out and engage the enemy.

Although we may have wanted to engage the enemy, it was unsafe. Just think of this? Stopping the car! It would take a couple of seconds! Undo seatbelt, open the door, move and get out. So much time, time to be attacked, without the change of defence.

Get out of 'the killing area'!

In the training, we went into 'the hollow' at Ballykinler barracks (a live round exercise area – rural) and completed quite a few exercises. One exercise, driving the car along the road, then suddenly there was an illegal V.C.P. (an IRA VCP). What would we do? Try to shoot our way out (blank rounds on this ex) Chat your way out? Accelerate, and get out? We went through various scenarios, and practiced them.

We also fired live rounds in different scenarios, such as approaching an obstruction on the road (a car parked taking up much of the road) and having to debus from the car, fire quick warning shots, dress back quickly to some cover, returning fire (fall when hit targets pop up around the ex-area). We did this both in singles, and pairs. On one exercise I fired some warning shots, and got into cover, I was dressing back in pairs, and was with Timmy. We completed this ex, but noticed that the front windscreen of the car had been shot out. I said it must have been Timmy, and definitely not me. Timmy said it wasn't him! We went into the debrief office, and slow motioned the exercise video. It was me who had shot it out, when I fired the two quick warning shots, one bullet had entered the open driver's door, then out the windscreen. I never got billed, but got a quick telling off (to put it lightly)

Incidentally! There was an officer from a regular regiment, who had come across from England, and had to complete this course, for the role he would be doing in Northern Ireland (perhaps liaison officer?). When it came to doing the IRA illegal VCP's he went into meltdown, started crying. The exercise was just too real looking, felt too real. Nobody chastised him, we were just flabbergasted that it was so real to him.

We were taught better weapon handling drills. Taught how to strip, reassemble, load, unload, clearing stoppages. All using one hand, left and right. This was just in case we were wounded on one side, or perhaps grabbed by the arm, and so, had to use the other!

We were taught how to answer the front door to our homes with a ppw. Let's say you were to go to the door and open it and there was a person with a gun pointing at you? Little if no time to react! We were taught to draw the ppw, make it ready (finger on the trigger), before getting to the door, then opening it. Whatever hand was not opening the door, was holding the pistol behind the door, pointing at whoever was at the other side. That way if anyone was going to engage, we could fire first, and through the door.

We were told about stories of different 'contacts', what happened, and the good and bad of reaction, what happened, and what to think about. For instance, if you get shot first, it happens so quick, it is like getting a blow or thump. It takes a little time for your body to realise what is happening. It is a bit of time before you feel the pain. Just like when I was with a workmate, and he cut the top of his finger off. He was putting wood through the saw, and his hand slipped. He pulled his hand back, and said 'I don't like that happening', he continued to push the wood through the saw, then saw a trail of blood, where his left hand was pushing the wood. Even after he had seen it, it took at least 20 seconds before the pain came.

We were told of a known story of a Corporal Glass (part time 4 UDR), who was engaged by the IRA. There was more than one IRA man shooting at him, there were 4. He ran out of rounds in the firefight, as the pistol he was carrying only had a magazine of eight rounds. He ran back to his van for the second magazine. He was wounded, and killed one of the terrorists, who was trying to kill him

All the drills I learnt, I took them back to my company, shared, and taught what I have learnt. One time a friend from my company who had his own personal ppw, was using the drill for answering the door. A post man was delivering a parcel, he slipped the 'ready' pistol into his belt, covered it with the jumper or shirt, and signed for the parcel. When the postman left, he went to take the pistol back out of his belt, to make it safe, and reholster, but in doing so, when pulling the pistol from his belt, he accidently pulled the trigger. The pistol went off, and the bullet went down his leg like a pole. Luckily it never hit any muscles, just ploughed down the side of the leg. No bone or muscle injury, just (when I mean just, it still was very sore, and he had to go to hospital) skin, and bleeding damage.

20

Shooting

Shooting? The only shooting I had done before joining the army, was a couple of Saturdays I went with my dad (I was about 10 years old), and fired his Beretta under & over shotgun at clay pigeons. It was literally only a couple of times, and I enjoyed it, yes I hit a few (they were easy, down the line, ones). I fired my friend's air rifle, across a small field, at small targets (about 13 or 14 years old). About a year or so after leaving school, I got myself a wee (low powered) air pistol. It wasn't very powerful, and I could hang balloons round the garden, and shoot at them. It could just about bust them!

I always looked in awe at the British Army SLR's, and I remember one time, when I was about 8 or 9 years of age, an army patrol coming into our housing estate, and the soldiers let me get into the back of the land rover, look out the top-hatch cover, and even look through the sights of an SLR. It was brilliant. My dream! I asked if I could shoot at the man who was walking down the street, and the soldier said I couldn't! I then asked if I could fire some shots at one of the parked cars? And wasn't allowed to do that either! Why not? They do it on tv all the time! From memory, I think it was a red dot sight on the SLR?

During the months of June/July, before I went on my recruits' course, our company went on a range day in Ballykinler, which I was allowed to attend. I helped out with bits n pieces, and towards the end of the range day, the company let us recruits (there were about 3 or 4 of us, at the range that day) fire 10 rounds each, at a range of 100 meters. Before we went onto the range to fire the SLR, we were told of the kick/recoil of the rifle. It was supposed to be brutal, if you didn't pull the rifle into your shoulder, or the butt wasn't placed in your shoulder correctly, so I was a little anxious going onto the firing point, carrying an SLR. Oh yes, I had done weapon handling on the rifle, quite a few times in our company lines, on the training nights, which I'd attended. Some of the soldiers said the kick of the SLR was like a shotgun (that I knew) and others said it was far worse.

I fired the ten shots, and got 9 of them onto the figure 11 target. I was disappointed, as I was hoping to be the best shot of us recruits, but two of the recruits, got all 10 shots onto the target. I was so disappointed, as I knew to pass the shooting test on the recruits course, not only had we to get all ten shots onto the target, but achieve a group of under 4"s.

Whilst on the recruits course, weapon handling/shooting was a major part of it, as we were going operational straight after we 'Pass-Out'. And during that week of intensive training, we would be taught/coached into getting shooting groups of this size which I did with ease (well perhaps not that easy, but I was in the first section of recruits (on this cadre) that achieved it.)

After the recruits course, I was still wanting to shoot better, be part of the shooting within the company. Quite often during our training weekends, or on a Camp-Guard weekend, we would do a monthly shoot (we had to shoot quite regularly, and at least once a month, not only shoot, but achieve a tight group) for each person to stay operational. I tried to get shooting as often as I could. I remember once, quite soon after the recruits course, on a Camp Guard weekend, we went to the 25 meter barrack range where we were using the Browning 9mm pistol. I went through the 9mm APWT (annual personal weapon test). That entailed shooting 8 rounds starting from 25m, changing magazine (another 8 rounds), moving closer, then doing another shoot. In all, 3 magazines (24 rounds) were used. I achieved the top score that Sunday morning, and Lead-Balls was amazed, and asked if I had fired a pistol before? I told him about my air pistol, and quite a bit of practice with it. He said he knew I had practiced somewhere, as I had got a good score, and said "I'll remember that Cardy! You'll be with us on the next range-day". More of an order, than an opportunity!

I haven't mentioned it, as during those years I didn't realise it, but the UDR shot far more rounds than the rest of the British Army Regiments (not considering the special forces, Para's and Commando's) by a long shot (excuse the pun). This was because we were on active duty every day, every week, every month, and we had to be skilled, so we could use the rifles proficiently, and not hit an innocent person in a contact situation.

If we had to attend Court, we could state that we were skilled, had completed our monthly shoots, passing every annual APWT (and show it on our army records).

Well! As Lead-Balls said, I attended as many range days as I could. We had range days during our mini-camp weekends (once every two months on average) at Ballykinler or Magilligan Point and the odd one in between. Later in the year, there were far more range days, which were mainly for the company shooting team. Although many came down for monthly shoots, or to pass the SLR APWT, as you had to pass at least one APWT per year (mandatory annual training).

The reason for the range increase was that the Battalion SAAM (skill at arms meeting) weekend was normally in February.

I managed to join The 'D' Company shooting team. The fact I am going to tell you now, is quite amazing, and in a way disturbing now (2025)! We were not allowed to wear ear defenders. The argument being 'How can we hear words of command, if we are wearing ear defenders?'.

After an SAAM weekend, my ears were ringing for about three days. I naively thought it was like having a sprained ankle, and your ears repaired themselves, but I was quite wrong!

After a shooting weekend, or SAAM weekend in addition to my ears ringing, my right cheek was hurt and swollen for a few days, due to the kick/recoil of the SLR. It was fine to shoot one or two matches throughout a range day, but completing shoots the full day, and for two or three days?

I continued on with the shooting and Company shooting team, and improved substantially. During the Annual Camp 1988. Warcop (Cumbria/Lake District) one particular day there were very important officers from the British Army visiting our Battalion Annual Camp, to see how it was run, enquiring about the training directives that year, how our battalion was doing, speaking to the soldiers. Lead-Balls asked me if I'd like to (well more of a 'told me to ') shoot on the FIBUA Range whilst the visitors were coming and going. Of course I said 'Yes', and for that full day, I ran up and down the range. I loved it! It was tiring, as I was jumping into shell scrapings, running from cover to cover, and was continually shooting. This got me recognised (perhaps as someone who didn't need to be persuaded to endure whatever).

During the SLR years I won quite a number of individual prizes (SAAM meetings), and LMG (light support weapon (magazine fed GPMG)). However when the SA80 came along, everything changed!

The SA80 was very easy to shoot, as it was a smaller calibre, less recoil, and every SA80 was fitted with the SUSAT (Sight Unit, Small Arms, Trilux). To the regular soldier, the APWT's became easier to pass. To me the SA80 felt like a drop in weapons. Yes, it was easier to shoot, but had many downfalls compared to the SLR. Having a SUSAT meant you had one eye closed. Although given a bit of time, I learnt to shoot with both eyes open. One eye on the sight, one eye keeping a look out for other targets emerging. You had to reach over the rifle body to cock it and make ready, where the cocking handle is on the left hand side of the SLR, and was quicker to cock. Safety catch was pushed from the right-hand side with your trigger finger on the SA80, whilst on the SLR it was a right hand thumb release. The trigger on an SA80 has a far longer pull and was much heavier. Over a distance the SA80 round will be blown off course far more than the heavier more powerful SLR round.

The SA80? The 7.62mm rifle round is used in the SLR, and the USA also used this calibre. It is the NATO standard round. But then the Vietnam war came along, and a new standard rifle for the US Army – the 5.56mm round, or, imperial measurement (.223"). The 5.56mm round was smaller than the 7.62, and therefore lighter, smaller, with less recoil. This meant an individual could carry more rounds whilst on patrol, and the rifle (M16) was lighter easier to shoot, with less recoil, thus the rifle can be fully automatic without going out of control.

On a different note! A 7.62mm round was so powerful, and would most probably kill, whilst the 5.56mm was more likely to injure a soldier rather than kill him. This was better in warfare, as if you killed a soldier, his comrades could leave him on the battlefield, continue with the battle, whereas if you injured a soldier, then the comrades would have to look after him, and so, you have stopped at least 2 soldiers on the battlefield by injuring one.

I stayed on the company shooting team, when the SA80 came along, but I didn't have as much of an advantage over the standard soldier, and had to work at it quite a bit, to learn the rifle and all its habits. I got better, but found it hard. In February 1991, we had a battalion SAAM, I had been in the UDR for almost 4 years, but not quite, so I was still a 'B' Class shooter (in the army for four years or less), and I was shooting well. On Sunday (the SAAM is shot over the weekend, starting Friday) I had a great score, but level with me, was Honey Monster from 'C' Coy. I hadn't realized that I had a good score, till Honey Monster told me during Sunday morning. He said he knew I was trying to get the 'B' Class shot at that year's SAAM, but I hadn't realized! So from that point I concentrated far harder than I normally did, to keep my score up. At the end of the day, and I mean right to the last shoot, Me and Honey Monster were on pip to the post points. One shoot left and he was ahead of me, and the last shoot, if I remember correctly, was service pistol shoot, I pipped him by about 1 or perhaps two points, to win the 'B' Class shot of 11 UDR.

In 1990 our battalion (11UDR) amalgamated with 2 UDR (Armagh Battalion), and we became 2/11 UDR. With that we got some of the best shots in the British Army, in pistol, and rifle shooting. A Sgt/Major who joined us, had risen through the ranks, and won many medals in shooting, including the best shot in the British Army, and that was in the 1970's.

In 1990 in Mahon Road, Prince Andrew (our Colonel in Chief, of the UDR) came to visit us in Mahon Road, and presented the Sgt/Major with a 'Golden Eagle' Award for his contribution, dedication, skill, and time for his shooting. I met Prince Andrew that day, and talked briefly to him. Little did I know that I would meet him quite a few times whilst being in the R/Irish, and whilst in shooting teams.

That afternoon in Mahon Road, I thought so highly of that award that the Sgt/Major received, as it was such a rare award, and it took so much to accomplish. I would really love to receive one!

The Sgt/Major was an ace with the SLR but also knuckled down and learnt the SA80 when it came along. He was the organizer, leader and coach of the Regimental Combat Shooting Team, for service rifle, sniper rifle, and pistol. I had only seen him once or twice since that day in Mahon Road, and knew little about him. Well. He was looking after the regimental team, and I was just in the company team. It wasn't until about 1993 that I bumped into him again properly!

Whilst at annual camp at Lyde & Hyde, we had a range schedule. Strange? It wasn't an APWT, or a standard shoot like the The Roupell, or the White Head shoot, it was a shooting lesson 'How to shoot better, and pass the APWT easily'. It was being led by the Sgt/Major who had received the award. I had forgotten about him, until now! Today's lesson is about how to shoot the 'SA80' with ease and accuracy! I had won quite a few medals in shoots during our battalion's SAAM weekends, and company shoots, and was becoming accomplished at shooting the SA80 too. My thinking when our rifles were getting 'cleared' before going onto the range was "Who the Fuck was he, telling me how to shoot? I can already shoot, and I'm good at it".

He taught us things that were never done, nor did we do? Like the prone position - place the SA80 magazine on the ground and be directly behind it! This was so wrong with the SLR, setting the magazine on the ground, would give possible stoppages, if you did so, then it wouldn't be a good shot, the bullet wouldn't go where it was meant to go, and to be behind the rifle, instead of being at an angle? With the SLR, our bodies were angled slightly behind the rifle, with the right knee forward, to give the body a little angle and lift your chest above the ground, thus when breathing it does not interrupt in movement on the rifle, but here, the Sgt/Major was telling us to be behind it, chest on the ground, and rifle lower than the SLR would have been, with the magazine resting on the ground. How can this work? This Sgt/Major is stupid! I did not conform. I shot MY WAY. Funny enough, the Sgt/Major did not force me to correct my posture to his position, and we shot on, but my platoon mates were hitting the targets far more than they normally did? In fact, I was having trouble keeping up with their hits. About ¾ of an hour in, I decided to try this 'new' position , and found it is far easier to get the position, aim and shoot, and of course hit the targets.

It showed me how I, and in general (men) think they can do it for themselves far better than anyone else (who is He, that thinks he can teach me anything). From that moment on, I have never let myself think 'I know best, who is he to tell me how to?'. From then onwards, I have always been willing to listen to others, and try out what their version is, and quite often I will adopt the other version. From that range day, I also learnt that 'I' am not the best, and if I am - then someone will beat me, if I drop my training, dedication, or confidence!

I got better at shooting, and was always on the company shooting team, but that was as far as it went. No further! Until1996, when the Sgt/Major asked Ozzie and I to come and try out for the Battalion part-time shooting team. The N.I. GOC wanted part-time members of 3 R/Irish, to take on the full-time battalion shooting team.

The Sgt/Major wanted to make up a battalion part-time shooting team. Anyone from the part-time companies could try out for it, from Ballykinler, Rathriland, Portadown or Armagh. Quite surprisingly, there weren't thousands who applied. Perhaps not everyone heard about it? Perhaps they didn't want to devote so much time and dedication to it? Or other reasons? Out of my company ('F') it was only me and Ozz. I don't think anyone from Armagh companies came (perhaps too far to travel, as the training was to be in Ballykinler). Surprisingly Stop-Watch and Honey Monster from 'L' Coy didn't come either? I thought they would have shown up, as they were keen shooters. I never found out why they didn't apply.

Turning Up at Ballykinler the first Saturday, there were about 24 to 36 participants. Some of these just needed to be there to knock up another range day and APWT shoot for their bounty requirements! The Sgt/Major had to whittle the numbers down to 12. We shot mainly the two main shoots. The Whitehead shoot and the Rupell (which I loved shooting). The Rupell match used 75 rounds total, started at 400m, then down to 300m where we got targets at distances of 100 to 300m. The positions were prone (400m), prone (300m), Running forward and kneeling (1½ meter run) (200m), then firing from the trench (100, 200, and 300m), then prone (300m).

Most of the soldiers that attended, shot well, and the Sgt/Major never sent anyone home, as he knew it would whittle itself down naturally. He wasn't dominating, or controlling, he was very pleasant, and good at coaching.

The training continued every fortnight, and after a couple of range days, the numbers surely enough, had whittled down to about 12-16. They were great training days.

The first few times, I met Ozzie in Portadown, got a car from the MT, made our way there, and back. It was long hours but we enjoyed the shooting so much. I would leave home just after 7am, and meet Ozzie at 0800hrs Portadown. The first to arrive would go over to the MTWO, to sign for the Car. The range was active 9am to 4pm, then we would make our way back to Portadown, sign the car back in. Sign out for the day, and travel home (be back at home about 6:30). After a few weeks, we were allowed to sign in at Ballykinler, at one of the part-time companies there. Ozzie and I had an extra set of rifles (just for this shooting team) in the Ballykinler armoury which made the range days much easier.

The Sgt/Major showed and talked about different ways and shooting positions of which the battalion combat shooting team used, and why they used it. Most of the battalion team (about 8 of) were also in the British Army shooting team. The battalion team had learnt so much, like how to position a rifle in the standing position, to achieve maximum hits, where to place the rifle when wearing combat body armour, how much oil to put on a rifle and recoil mechanism to give no stoppages, and no carbon build up. This information was passed onto the Army Rifle Association (ARA) (the association which looks after all weapons, shooting matches, and recorded scores in the full British Army) which puts this information into the pamphlets for instructors to use.

The Sgt/Mjr never forced these ways onto us, just asked us to try them out, and perhaps improvise and adopt. Our shooting improved so much.

One range day, Ozz and I had finished lunch pretty quickly, and went back to the range. We could take it easy, perhaps lying in the sun until the rest of the team returned. It was only Ozz and I at the range. I was dying to shoot. Ozzie was range qualified, and we decided that I could go on and shoot, with Ozzie running the range. I shot the Whitehead Shoot complete twice, with the rest of the team turning up when I was half way through the third time. The Whitehead Match started off at 400m with various shoots and ends up at 200m. Shooting at the little figure 12c targets.

We thought the Sgt/Major might be pissed off, that we started without instruction, but he was laughing, and asked if we enjoyed ourselves?

The shooting team was great. We got to know one another well, with great chat and banter during the days, and we were improving. So good we thought (and knew) we would beat the full-time battalion team. Word got out how good we had become! The powers above us, decided that the competition would no longer happen. Perhaps there would be embarrassment if the part-timers beat the full-time battalion team? When we heard this, we were scundered, but we had a couple of range days still booked, and were allowed to shoot those remaining times.

On one of the last range days, we were on the 100 meter range, and the Sgt/Major arrived, with two Sniper Rifles (L96's) with him - they were like a magnet to me!

The Sgt/Major had them down, to sight-in the scopes (sight-in is where you shoot a group at 100m, and adjust the new sight so the shot impact is very near the centre of the target, so that when someone uses the rifle, the shots are near the Correct Point of Aim (CPA), and is easy to zero) for the Battalion Sniper Team, as they would be training soon for the upcoming sniper matches in Bisley.

I asked, and asked multiple times to have a few shots with the Sniper Rifle, as it was a 7.62mm calibre, and might take me back to when I shot the SLR's, and I was dying to feel what it is like to shoot a Sniper Rifle. The Sgt/Major would not let me! After a few requests, he directed me to get in touch with Stop-Watch from 'L' Company, as he was shooting target rifles competitively in the battalion. I loved shooting SA80 and Browning pistol matches, but I wanted more, I wanted greater challenges.

Little did I know that at this point, one chapter was finishing, and a full new chapter was beginning.

Within a day or so (perhaps even the next day?) I got in touch with Stop-Watch. I had always known Stop-Watch whilst in the UDR, as he was a well-known Corporal, perhaps not in my company, but next door in 'C' Company. He was a keen shooter, and an excellent instructor in weapon-handling. I knew him and had talked 'Guns' with him many times. We had our ppw pistols, and at times we would talk about what each other held, wanted, and which was better. Once I had a Walther P88, and it was labelled 'the wonder nine'. At that time Stop-Watch had an H&K P7m8 (the character in 'Die-Hard' Hans Gruber has one) which was way ahead of its time. Small to conceal, quick to fire, hammerless, and very safe. When I was on camp guard Stop-Watch was getting keys to the outdoor 25m range, we talked, and we went down to the range trying out each other's pistols. Stop-Watch quite regularly shot on the 25m range. Always training for an off-duty response to an attack.

I asked Stop-Watch about target shooting, and he said they trained every week. I enquired if Ozzie and I could join? Stop-Watch smiled, and would love for us to come along. Shooting was in the 'TA' centre on Charles Street Portadown each Wednesday evening.

We could have shot in the indoor range in Mahon Road, only it had been converted into a 'FATS Room' (Firearms Training Simulation)(No live rounds, bit like a Xbox shooting game), and so! When Wednesday came (lucky enough we were not on ops), we came into Mahon Road, signed in, filled our flasks with coffee, grabbed our combat jackets (Stop-Watch said we would need them), headed over to the TA centre.

There were 4 or 5 soldiers from 'C' Coy there, Honey Monster and Stop-Watch being two of them. It was small-bore shooting. Well it couldn't be 7.62mm Sniper Rifle shooting, as it was an indoor range! Most indoor ranges were not built to take that velocity of bullet. Honey Monster gave us both single-point slings which we were to use with the rifles, and tightly adjusted us in.

Small bore shooting is using bolt action single shot rifles. We shot two or three score cards, and our scores were quite good (for first time). We were both hitting scores of about 89-90 out of 100. Ozz and I were made very welcome, and we continued with the training.

Well I did - Ozzie just went about 3 or four times. Ozzie probably stopped, as the shoot wasn't very exciting, it was quite mundane, but improved your rifle shooting (even on combat rifles) greatly.

I continued. It wasn't the 7.62 Sniper Rifle I was wanting to shoot! But I loved shooting, and the goal was to get onto the Inter-unit shooting team (smallbore target shooting), to compete across the water (in Bordan, near Aldershot) at the end of the winter season (August to April), and hopefully compete in the full-bore season (March to August) with the Sniper Rifle (7.62mm L96A1)?

Smallbore shooting is so skilled, and so precise. I started with a single score of 89-90, and it took me months to get my average (average score is counted over the last 6 cards) up to 94/100.

Stop-Watch got me onto 'Full-bore Target Rifle' course (Bisley), in which we shot out to ranges of 900-1,000 yards, with the L96 Sniper rifle! I thought it amazing to shoot at 1,000 yards, for the bullet to take about 2 to 3 seconds (in flight) to hit the target.

Later, we all (Stop-Watch, Honey Monster, myself and Kenny) went on a 'Target Pistol' course, which meant I got more skilled at the pistol shooting, and am coach qualified!

We also got taking part in the full-bore shoots in May (inter-unit), in which I shot the L96. I enjoyed it, and steadily improved.

The winter season smallbore took place in indoor ranges, where there was perfect light, and no wind movement. But full-bore (outdoor ranges from 300 yards to 1,200 yards) was a thinking-man's sport, where you had to guess how strong the wind was, and off-set your sight to counter it, off-set the sights for brightness or sunlight, watch the heat rise, as when your bullet is dropping, and heat rising, the bullet will roll to the right. Watch the wind strengths at intervals down the range. All this, and make sure you have the perfect shooting position, and the perfect shot.

When we got to the end of the next smallbore season (April) I was able to attend the weekend finals in Bordan as a reserve. I still got shooting, but only as an individual. There were no awards for individuals, just a token mention. I enjoyed that weekend and continued shooting smallbore.

The following year I was in the teams (full-bore & smallbore), but our team was nowhere near the top teams, we mainly got to the finals because we were the only team from Northern Ireland to have competed for the matches. Our main challenge when we went to the finals was as individuals to beat 'Tank'! Tank was one of our team members. He was in Rathriland 'B' Company, and the best shot (as well as Stop-Watch) among us. Don't get me wrong! I enjoyed shooting against the other teams, but they were so far ahead of us, we shot our best, but amongst each other!

A few years down the line, in Bordan, we had another weekend of finals (smallbore), and we shot amongst ourselves. When it came to distributing prizes, we listened to who won the 3rd Place, and we clapped, listened to the second place, and clapped, and listened to the 1st place, and clapped! "But hold on?"," Who did they say?", we were so busy shooting against each other, trying to beat Tank, we never looked at the overall team scores, and WE had won. From then onwards, we improved, and started winning every smallbore competition, and simultaneously, began to accelerate in the full-bore matches also.

Full-bore. We (battalion team) managed to take part in the inter-unit, inter-corps shoots. I was scoring well, and becoming better at reading the wind (guessing how much the wind would blow the bullet off course, on route to the target). In May we were over to take part in the inter-unit shoot (Bisley in Surrey), the regimental team commander did not select me for the team, but chose two other R/Irish soldiers from a different battalion. I think (know) he chose them as they had more rank than me (they were Commissioned Officers). I thought – "I'll sicken you!". I (in that competition) could shoot as an individual (honours only), and I did, I concentrated on those matches so much. I outscored every officer that the Regimental Team Commander chose. From that point on, I was in the R/Irish Regimental team.

During 1997, I had my own rifle for use in the shoots. I excelled in full-bore, and in 1998 I was on 'the British Army shooting team', in addition to the 'R/Irish Regimental team'

By the end of 1998 the full-bore 'British Army team' had 8 R/ Irish Soldiers within the 12 man team, and in the Combat Rifle shooting 'British Army Team' there were more R/Irish Soldiers, as in the full-bore team.

Small-bore. Our Regimental Team was dominating most of the competitions, but the Captain of the army team, didn't invite us onto the team, which I think was because we didn't dedicate all our shooting to the one discipline (smallbore), the next year we were invited onto the smallbore 'British Army Shooting Team', there were 4 to 6 R/Irish Soldiers in the smallbore 'Army Team'.

In full-bore competitions we started dominating and winning every competition we entered. We had (sadly) become so successful that before other regiments even entered a competition, they checked to see if we too had entered, and if so - did not enter.

We (Stop-Watch, Dickie, Honey Monster, myself and a few others) were regularly going over to Bisley, taking part in training and competition shoots, in a Battalion, Regimental, and Army Team capacity. We all loved every moment of it!

Pistol Shooting! We (3 R/Irish Team) thought we would take part in pistol target shooting, in addition to the smallbore rifle shooting. We thought that we were good at pistol shooting as we all had ppw's (Personnel Protection Weapons) which we shot regularly, and at the Battalion SAAM meetings.

Before I took part in the target pistol course, I thought that I was a good pistol shooter, that the army (in general) were good at pistol shooting.

Immediately after the course, I was shooting in an open competition where civilians were also shooting. I couldn't believe the skill, shooting, tight groups, of the competitive pistol shooter. I had so much work to do, to get anywhere near that standard!

21

The Shooting

I had been going out with a girl for about two weeks, and today, the first Sunday in April 1990, I got to spend some time with her.

I had taken my girlfriend to Newcastle, Co. Down. It was lovely day, and I felt so happy. I came back to her house to say goodbye for the evening. She lived in a housing estate about 2 miles away from Lisburn. We were chatting a while in my car, before she went in for the night. I left around 10pm.

I drove home along a country road, towards Lisburn. I wasn't driving through Lisburn, but around the outskirts of the town. I put on a cassette to listen to whilst going home. The cassette was a recording of a CD I had got recently, it was 'Trash' Album by Alice Cooper. I was very happy, had enjoyed a nice day, hopefully would get to know the girl a bit more, was looking forward to a new week, everything was looking rosy.

On the small road I was driving about 55-60MPH, and caught up with a Ford Fiesta, which was driving much slower. No big deal! I waited until we were on a straight, where I could see the road ahead, and overtook the Fiesta. It was still a mile or so before we come into the streetlights of the ring roads at Lisburn. I noticed that the Fiesta has sped up, perhaps I had woken the driver up? Or maybe he had just realised that he wasn't travelling very fast?

I came to the end of the road, and I noticed that the Fiesta was behind me. That's ok. I crossed the staggered junction, onto the next road, and I noticed that the Fiesta was still behind me. Turned left onto Prince William road, car was still behind me. I wasn't worried about it, as it had only been a couple of turns, and I doubt it was following me! I turned right onto Knockmore Road about a mile down the Prince William Road. The Fiesta was still behind me.

The Fiesta then put its headlights onto full-beam, Strange? As we were under streetlights. Perhaps it was trying to warn me there is something wrong with my car? Perhaps it is someone I know? Maybe they wanted a race, as I am driving a SR Nova? Believe me I love a race, and can handle my car really well, but tonight I don't want one, as it's been a good day, I've had a great time, and I am just unwinding – listening to a bit of music, and on my way home for the night.

I turn right onto Ballinderry road, heading out of town, and I still have the Fiesta on my tail, and quite close now, still with the full-beam on. I don't want a race tonight! Just what if this car is following Me? Will I have to sink the boot, and get away from it, or will I have to drive around a labyrinth of roads to shake it off? Is it someone I know? I doubt if it's following me, as someone following me wouldn't have the headlights on full-beam? And again! I don't want to race tonight!

So, along the Ballinderry road I slow down, to let the Fiesta pass. It's a straight bit of road. Why won't it pass? I know, I'll get it to pass, and when it does, the next roads to the left and right we come to, I'll go a different way to the Fiesta. I can go down a few other different roads on my way home!

I'll get it to pass! I slowed away down. But still the Fiesta doesn't overtake me? I'll give it a sickener! So I slow down and stop. The Fiesta then stops behind me (still on full-beam). How strange? What's happening? I see in my passenger wing mirror, the passenger door opening. Who is this? I pull forward slowly so get a better view in my wing mirror, as I can't see anything out my rear screen because of the headlights of the Fiesta. As soon as I start moving forward the Fiesta goes for it, and overtakes me. Great! I can get on with my journey, and unfortunately will have to go a strange route home, just in case this car was tailing me? I doubt it! I let the Fiesta overtake me, and wonder what it wanted, and who was going to get out the passenger door?

After the Fiesta had overtaken me, it then pulled in front of me, at an angle on the left lane, blocking my way. I think I will have to rake my car away, and race out of this situation (whatever it is?), but I can't, there is a car coming towards us on the other lane.

The song playing on my cassette is 'Poison' by Alice Cooper. I am playing it with the volume up (not as high as the kids today). I am ready to rake away, with clutch in, and in first gear. The passenger door in the Fiesta (it's only a 3 door car) is opening again, only this time I see someone getting out of it. Oh dear – I will have to go into my drills (army off-duty drills). I go into drills when answering the front door, when getting out of my car when I get home etc.

I take the car quickly out of gear, pull the handbrake, and then draw my 9mm pistol. I keep it low, as I don't want anyone to see it when I'm running through my drills (it would compromise me).

It is a man, and now he is at the front of my bonnet, leaning on it and shouting, but I can't hear what he is saying, as I still have Alice Cooper 'Poison' playing. Oh no! I will have to get out, and perhaps compromise myself, as I might have to declare that I am in possession of a pistol? I don't want to compromise myself! What does he want? I cock the pistol, and there is a round in the chamber, hammer is back, and will have to continue on with my drills! I was thinking that in this strange situation, it is still good to do the ppw drills. You will never know when you will need them?

I'm not looking forward to this point. I will have to tell him to go away – I have a pistol, and I might have to say that I am a member of the security forces. That should get him away!

I opened my door and was getting out. Straightening up (the man is now coming round the front of the car, and is at the front of the right wing of the car) I feel a blow. I'VE BEEN HIT, I'VE BEEN SHOT. My head bounces off the door sill at the top of my driver's door. I'VE BEEN HIT!

What I thought at that exact moment is 'If I'm going down? I'm not for going down without a fight". I have nearly straightened up, the man in front must have been armed, and shot me. I'm going to take him out!! I raise my pistol with two hands, and the man is along the right wing of my car, about 3 feet or so away. When I lifted my pistol, I see his eyes, all of a sudden, they are so wide, he is in shock, he didn't expect this!

I open fire - and as soon as I start shooting, I hear the Fiesta wheels squealing, as the Fiesta takes off on up the road. I feel the presence of someone behind me, swing round, to see a figure at the back drivers side of my car running away. As soon as he clears my car, he is turning towards the side of the road – and on down the road. WHO THE FUCK IS THAT? My training was going full-blast. He is one of the terrorist's, and I am in danger. He may have been the one who shot me? Where did he come from? He must have got out of the car after the first man?

I chased after him. He is my main threat! He has the gun! I run after him. He isn't on the road long, as there is a gap in the wall alongside the road, it's where the wall had fallen in during the years. He was now running into a field. I raised my pistol and fired a shot at him! But in doing so, I was starting to wonder? If I have been hit on the right shoulder, why can I operate my right arm. Do I have to transfer my pistol into my left hand, when continuing to chase him? Yes! I'll have to do that before I lose power in my right arm. I move the pistol into my left arm. I know it is a bit of time before the pain hits me! As I am on an adrenaline high. I don't feel any bleeding! I can't feel the pain coming!

So I stop briefly to see where the bleeding is, and if the bleeding is bad, I might have to stem it, But I can't find any? Instead of jumping into the field, I stop to quickly examine myself. I have no bleeding! What has just happened?

The man in the field is still a threat. The Fiesta that has left? It is still a threat. It might return? What about the man I shot?

I quickly get back to my car. Engine is still running, driver's door still open. I push my driver's door slightly in, and walk to the right hand wing of my car, pistol still in my hand (back to the right hand again), pistol still cocked and ready to engage! The man I opened up on is still a threat! Where is he? Did I not hit him? Perhaps not? At the right hand wing of my car I see in front of the car, the headlights of my car are lighting the road to the front. There is a body lying face down, face at the side of the road, and legs strewn on the road, with a large pool of blood around his head and shoulders. The body is jerking. He is most likely still alive? Not sure, but he shouldn't be with the amount of blood I see? I can't tend to him, much as I would like to, and administer First-Aid, there is still a man on the loose behind me. And what about the Fiesta? I have to vacate this location.

I get into my car. Still observing just in case I get attacked by the 'loose man'. I have to think very quickly, before I get attacked again. I turn the car, as I can't drive forward. There is a slow bend in the road up front, and I don't know if the Fiesta is awaiting? I'll have to drive back to Lisburn, and to the RUC station on Castle Street.

After I turn and am heading back, there is a car coming towards me. I flashed my lights at him, as the body is still on the road in front of him.

I get to the Police Station, park, decock, and holster my pistol. I walked into the station and saw a police officer at the reception desk. I approached him, and wasn't sure what to say? I just told him that I have just shot someone on the Ballinderry Road, and I am an off-duty UDR man. He started to flutter a bit, didn't know what to say, composed himself, and says 'Right, I haven't heard anything, but will get onto it now!'.

Then I heard the radio behind him start to come in about a shooting on the Ballinderry Road. Things started to click in with him, and he said he'll get someone now, for me. I said, "Do you want my pistol?". He was stuttering, and didn't know what to do. I told him that the pistol was now to be put in evidence. He was still stuttering. I asked if he had any evidence bags, to which he replied 'Yes', and got one out. I asked him if he wanted the pistol 'still loaded' or will I clear it, and make it safe? He didn't know. So I told him that I was going to clear it, and he is to write 'unloaded' on the evidence bag and put my name on it.

I was listening to the police radio, and the police said that they were at the scene, but there was no body there? just lots of blood, skin and empty bullet cases.

Someone more senior came along, and led me into the hallway, where I still got to listen to the radio further. The police on the Ballinderry Road went back to 'Lagan Valley Hospital' as it was the most likely location of where the body may have gone?

They found the man I had shot; he was in 'Intensive Care' and they found the other man. He was the brother of the man that I had shot. He was the 'loose man'. The police found out the identity of the man I shot, and it turned out to be one of the top Loyalist Paramilitaries in Lisburn; his brother was also in the loyalist paramilitaries. The condition of the man I'd shot was getting worse, and he would have to be moved to 'Belfast City Hospital'. "Do you want us to escort him down there". The answer from the controller was "No! arrest the brother, and if someone wants to finish the wounded man, on his way to 'The City', let them"

When the police found out who was shot, I got handshakes from many officers. A few officers asked if I would like a 'Chinese' meal, or a 'chippie'. I said I didn't. The adrenaline was still racing through me full blast. I asked who had attacked me? One or two police officers (whilst still in the corridor) told me he was a bad man who was responsible for a few murders, and other nasty incidents (like shoving a pool cue down someone's throat, in a pub)

A plain clothed police officer took me into a room to establish who I was and what had happened, were if I wanted, I could listen in on the police radio.

The incident was over, and I didn't think there would be much more about it on the police radio! We talked for a while, and once he knew what had happened, he said 'let's go to a better room upstairs', and we left the room. As we were walking back along the corridor, I noticed a couple of men sitting near the doorway, in the inside of the police main desk. One of them looked as though he'd been crying. I asked the officer who was leading me upstairs "who is that?", and he told me that they were the occupants of the Fiesta. I was very surprised! How on earth did the police find the Fiesta so quickly? The officer told me that they had come in of their own accord, to report the incident. They didn't know that I was in the police station and had reported the contact. As soon as they made themselves known, they were arrested!

In the room upstairs, the officer said I could sit down and rest, whilst he noted all the info down (on paper). I still couldn't sit, as the adrenaline was flowing through me. The officer asked me how many shots I had fired, and I couldn't remember. I told him 2 or 3 at the most, but he could check the magazine from my pistol? It was loaded with 15 rounds. I hadn't ejected any. After the incident, when I came into the police station, I unloaded my pistol, and placed the round from the chamber back into the magazine.

We found out more about the incident, as the persons who were arrested told the police what had happened.

When I had stopped the car the first time, saw the passenger door open, and moved forward to get a better viewing. One person did get out. When my car was stopped the second time, the man who had got out in the first stop was running to catch up, and when I was getting out, he had caught up, took a big swing, and thumped me in the head (right hand side), at which my head hit the top sill on the doorway. The shooting then started, to which he turned and ran.

When I got into my car, turned, and went back towards Lisburn, the loose man came back onto the road, and managed to flag down a car, which helped the wounded to be taken to Lagan Valley Hospital.

Once we had collated the information, I asked if he would like a statement. It was almost 12 midnight! He said that he would need one, but not necessarily now, perhaps tomorrow, when things settled? I said I would do one straight away, whilst everything was fresh in my mind.

I had always been told, if anything happened on or off duty, get the Army flying lawyer! I asked the officer if I could get one, he agreed, and got in touch with Thiepval Barracks.

The flying lawyer arrived fairly quickly, and I apologized for calling him so late (whilst he is yawning). He said, "It's ok, it's all in the job". The three of us sat down. I explained and described everything that had occurred and then wrote my statement.

I was leaving the police station after 2am and went home. The adrenaline had worn off, and I was exhausted. When I got home, I went straight to bed. Only to sleep in for work!

I woke up about 8am and should have been in work at this very moment! I threw on my work clothes, and went straight out. No brekkie or coffee this morning!

Got to work about 8:45. Parked the car and ran upstairs to the office. When I arrived, I apologized to dad for being late, and that I'd slept in! He looked at me and said "There was a shooting on the Ballinderry Road last night! Do you know anything about it? Was it you?". I said "No, I don't know anything about it". About 10 minutes later, the business phone rang, dad answered it. He then turned round and said the police were looking for me to go up to the police station again! Then he said "Thought you said it wasn't you?" I replied, "I didn't want to worry you!"

The police doctor was there, and examined me, to look for any bruising on my head from the thumping. There was a bit, but not too noticeable. After getting examined, and a little more questioning, the police told me some more about the arrested men, and I returned to work.

Only for about an hour or so, as Portadown Mahon Road barracks phoned me at work, and asked me to come up to see them! Little did I know that my platoon sergeant, and Section Corporal, had already been out to my house looking for me, and then to my parents' house!

I went up to Portadown, where I made another statement for the Army/UDR. I stayed there till the evening, as I was on duty that evening, and anyway, I had to wait until evening, as I needed a replacement pistol, as my own was in forensics, and I had to wait until the armourer came to open the armoury. I was issued a Walther P5, until I got my own back.

Of course, the army wise cracks started. Within a day or so, I have lost my nickname 'Raggy Doll', and gained a few new ones, like 'Cool Hand Cardy', 'Dirty Cardy' and a few others, but the one that stuck was 'Psycho'. So from that point on, I was 'Psycho'. In a month or so, one of the fellas in my platoon got a number plate made, with 'PSYCHO' on it, and stuck it to my locker. And from time to time, someone new in the platoon asks, "Who's the Physio?", to which I normally replied "I'm the physio, I'll watch your back"

The man I shot, survived, and was on a life support system in the City Hospital.

One of our Sergeants worked in the City Hospital and was able to tell me what injuries he sustained. I had shot him three times. Once just off the centre of his temple, and that shot wiped away a lot of skull, and brain, the second was a flesh wound on his cheek, the third hit him in the middle of the chest. That shot hit a bone, and travelled on into the body, missing all vital organs. How on earth did this man survive? Only God could have saved him! Why didn't God let this man die? Did God want him to live for his sake? Or for my sake? Only God will know the answer?

I started getting threats from the loyalist paramilitaries quite quickly, even on the first week!

Good-Boy Stephen (who works in a main grocery distribution warehouse) came over to me during that week, and told me he had been approached by a man from the loyalist paramilitaries, and Good-Boy was told to pass onto me, that they knew who I was, and they were going to get me! I told Good Boy to pass back "If they are going to get me? bring plenty of them! I want the body count to be big!"

A couple of Saturdays after the incident, I fancied a 'Chinese' take-away, and the one at the outskirts of the loyalist area is a great one. Sure? Who would see me going quickly in and out of there?

So I went into the Chinese take-away and ordered my meal.

I was looking forward to it. Get home, put the tv on, and enjoy a lovely meal, and have a restful evening! I stood against the back wall, so I could see out the front of the shop.

But within about 5 minutes, the Chinese take-away emptied! Except for one man. He was sitting opposite me. Sitting on the low windowsill. Then, after a short time, I recognised him! He was the brother of the man I had shot! He was the 'loose man', the one who had thumped me at the side of my head! He was looking at me! What would I do? What should I do? Should I leave without my meal? But if I did that, it would show weakness. It would show that I was scared (I was of course). I had to stay. I had to get my meal and show no fear! My pins and senses were hitting the roof. I watched outside to see if any others were there, or if any others were arriving. I watched the cars. Were there any cars with a few people in them? The wait was taking forever. I looked at him, as often as he was looking at me! My pins/ senses were going wild. But I could not show it. Not on your nelly. I had to be ready to draw my pistol! I had to be ready to make evasive actions, like run, fight. But not freeze.

The meal arrived. It was in a paper bag. I took it with my left hand. Leaving my right hand free, to act (if needed). When I left, I would have to think of actions to take, if attacked. Use the paper bag of food as quick weapon. A distraction and stopper to give me a split second or two, to get my ppw! I picked up the bag, then I went straight over to the 'loose man' (who was now standing), and I mean close. About 1 foot away – face to face, and smiled, and smile quite broadly, and I said to him "It is lovely to see you! and I hope to see you again. SOON!" I flicked my head up and to the side in a short jerk, to say ok. Then I walked out. Pins alive/ senses going mad, ultra-aware. Got into my car. There was nobody else about. No-one I could see. And quickly left.

If you tracked the route I left Lisburn, you would most likely laugh. Such a labyrinth way, to make sure nobody was following, or if someone was watching, they won't have a clue where I was heading!

I got threats quite often. Even 10 years after the incident, I am mentioned (not by name) in the loyalist paramilitary newspaper, what had happened, and that they have not forgotten about me.

There is always that thought/worry from that incident, to now, and beyond.

22

VIPs and Guests

From time to time we got visitors. Mostly senior officers such as Brigadier and General, and occasionally, Royalty!

If there was a visit, and we are in Mahon Barracks, everyone in the company will be called for a Muster Parade on the Drill Square.

Most times they would walk along in front of us, stopping every two to three soldiers, asking similar questions. In fact, they asked such similar questions, we knew they didn't actually listen to what we said.

During one visit, an Officer from England was inspecting a full-time company in Mahon Road, and each time he stopped in front of the soldier, he would ask "How long have you been in the You Dee Hour", followed by "And what did you do before joining" followed by "and what made you join the You Dee Hour?", "splendid, splendid, splendid", and move onto the next soldier two or three down.

One of the full-time soldiers conversation went like this: "How long have you been in the You Dee Hour", to which the soldier replied "Three years Sir", "And what did you do before joining", "I was a brain surgeon", "And what made you join the You Dee Hour?", and the soldier replied "Cause there aren't any brains to work on in Northern Ireland!", and before the Officer moved on, he said, "splendid, splendid, splendid."

I twigged onto this, and on a few such visits, I said I'd been in the UDR for something like 19 years, and when asked about how long I've had rank, I'd said '20 years'. Each time, I was never listened to, it was just a standard set of questions, to make soldiers think they are well thought of.

Although there was one Officer who visited from time to time, General Jackson, Mike Jackson. He was commissioned in 1963. He asked and listened to what each soldier said. I remember on one of his visits, he came out on the Ground to meet us. We were on Ops in Portadown during the ceasefire period in 1997. At that time our Ops/Patrols were not as overt, in fact we were one of the last units on the Ground in Northern Ireland, so much so that the press would try to find us to take pictures of us. General Jackson came to meet us on the Armagh Road. In conversation with me, I asked him "Why are we being taken off the ground, confined to barracks, when we are becoming so prolific at what we are doing, and now, with intelligence, are defeating the terrorist" "Why are you letting this happen, when you know that if we come off the ground, instead of terrorism being defeated, it will grow!". He listened to everything I had said, and replied "I know what you are saying, and I agree with you, but unfortunately it is out of my control. It is in the Government/political hands!".

I have great respect for General Jackson, as he has done so much for the British Army.

I wasn't a 'Yes' man, and spoke my mind, so quite often when there was a visitor, I would be kept away, or they were never steered in my direction. One time after I caused a Land Rover accident in Mahon Road Barracks, the CO (commanding officer) of our battalion was visiting us on one of our patrols. When he came to me, he asked my name. "Lance Corporal Cardy, Sir", and he said "Oh yes, Corporal Cardy? You're up in front of me next Thursday night, to get charged!". And I said, "I'm not going to accept the charge, Sir", to which he replied, "You will accept the charge!", and I repeated that I would not. He raised his voice, as did I. The conversation became so heated that the Battalion

Adjutant, who was standing beside him, turned and walked away. The row continued, and I was face to face with him, both shouting our pieces.

On that matter? When the Thursday came, the adjutant talked me into accepting the charge. It was only £120, but was the only 'black-spot' on my army record. I changed my mind to accept the charge in the spare of the moment, but no sooner had I 'Accepted the Reward' from the CO, than I regretted it.

I found out since, that I should never have accepted it. The charge couldn't have gone any further. That's another story!

One VIP that I met a few times, was our Colonel-In-Chief Prince Andrew. The first time I met him was when he visited Mahon Road Barracks to award Budd (a Sergeant Major, in charge of the shooting teams and training in our battalion). Budd had risen through the ranks whilst in 2 UDR (Armagh), and excelled in shooting, winning some of the top shooting competitions in the British Army. That day Budd was to receive one of the top awards for devotion, dedication, and glory he brought to the regiment. That award was 'The Golden Eagle', a framed embroidered Eagle symbol. When Prince Andrew awarded Budd the Eagle award, I would have loved to receive that award, but it was an enormous achievement and took many years of hard work and dedication. No surprise that such an award would be presented by our Colonel-in-Chief. Little did I know that around 15 years later, I would receive the SAME AWARD (but with no VIP). The day Budd was awarded the Eagle, Prince Andrew circulated around the room (coffee and bickies) and a few, including myself got talking to him. It unnerved me a bit, as he was actually listening to me. The short conversation wasn't a deep one, but I was impressed that he listened to me. A Lance Jack!

Another time I met Prince Andrew, was when I was over in Bisley (British Army and civilian shooting ranges in Surrey, near Woking) training with the Army Shooting Team (full-bore target rifle) on the 1,000 yard range (Stickledown). This was an out of the blue visit, and Prince Andrew was just chatting freely to us. Chatting about our training, shooting and the rifles we were using, particularly Peter's rifle. Pete was in the army team, and the head of our regimental team, and had not long been in possession of a new rifle, that had a colourful stock. Prince Andrew said that it looked like the striped toothpaste he used to get. From that moment Peter got the piss taken about his rifle stock.

Another time I saw Prince Andrew (but he didn't come near us) was one Saturday, when my company was down at Ballykinler for a range-day. We were shooting the Rupell-Shoot on range 1, an electric target range up to 400 metres long. Behind the range is a flat grass area, sometimes used for football, but was also used as a heli-pad. Helicopters large and small came and went whilst we were still shooting. As they flew in and out behind us, there was no chance of being hit by bullets. That day Lead-Balls came out of the range console and instructed all of us to 'Unload, show clear, ease springs and rest'. "Why are we unloading?" I asked. *cause there's a helicopter coming in!" I was told. "But helicopters fly in all the time! What's so special about this one?". Silence! A Puma came in, and did not look unusual, but something must be up? When it landed, and started to power down, I tried to see who was getting out. I couldn't see it clearly, so I used the Susat sight on my rifle to see. It had a 4x magnification, and I saw Prince Andrew climbing out. I shouted over to the lads "Look! It's Prince Andrew!", at which the others, used their Susat sights.

Suddenly Lead-Balls ran out of the range console shouting for us to put our rifles down. As we were all using our sights to watch Prince Andrew leaving the Puma, all of us (over 12 of us) were inadvertently pointing our rifles at Prince Andrew.

23

After the Army and PTSD

Quite a while before 2007, we knew our roles in the Royal Irish were numbered.

Since 1998, The Good Friday Agreement, 1997 when the IRA called a permanent ceasefire, and the '9/11' attack on New York in 2001. I placed the events in this particular order as this is my personal belief of the order of importance.

The Provisional IRA called a ceasefire on 6th April 1994, which the British public believed was both a new chapter and a fresh start, with the IRA stopping it's violence. This was very short lived, it didn't even last a week! The IRA conducted several attacks. On Saturday 9th April, the IRA attacked two army checkpoints near Newtownbutler; fired an improvised rocket at an army patrol in Stewartstown Road, Belfast; threw a coffee jar bomb into Oldpark RUC station in Belfast, and mounted an attack on a permanent border check at Aughnacloy, County Tyrone by blocking the road between the checkpoint and the border. Here they transported and fired a Barrack-Buster Mortar at the checkpoint, luckily the mortar missed the checkpoint.

Like during so many of the so-called IRA ceasefires in the 1970's, we had not stepped down our patrols and security.

On Wednesday 31st August 1994, the Provisional IRA announced a 'cessation of military operations', but continued Active Service Unit attacks. 16th October the IRA fired shots at Woodburn RUC station. 10th November the IRA murdered a Post Office worker in Newry, and intensified attacks in 1995, but after Wednesday 31st August 1994, the IRA stated that the ceasefire was still going on, and the attacks were not sanctioned by the IRA Army Council. It made our patrols and security at security bases quite difficult, as the politicians and media viewed our patrols as an insult to the IRA ceasefire, and the British Army as trying to keep the 'Troubles' going.

At this time we were instructed by our superiors to maintain a low profile, not on overt patrol, but to continue patrolling in a background manner. Our patrolling methods changed. We started conducting a new type of VCP's, scaling down the frequency of VCP's whilst out on patrol. We still completed them, when needed, as a deterrent to stop terrorist movement and activities, but had to scale down, as the public, media, and politicians wanted Northern Ireland without conflict and military presence.

Nevertheless, as everyone knew from the previous ceasefires, they didn't last, and if we (the security forces) didn't continue patrolling, collating information on players, threats, activities, movements, when the ceasefire ended (and we knew it would), it could bite us in the bum when we least expected it. If that happened, and we were not on top of it, then the public, media and politicians would blame us for not halting/stopping it.

Our latest VCP's were to park-up, with the Land Rovers and personnel visible to the public, but we were not stopping vehicles, or the public, and so it looked like we are scaling down, but unknown to the public, and terrorist movements, I was sitting in the Land Rover noting down every registration plate (VRN) that passed. Every make, model, location, direction and time. At the start of the evening before we headed out on patrol, I got half a dozen or so sheets, that were columned out for completing all the vehicle descriptions. At the end of the patrol, along with my de-briefing documents, I left the completed sheets into Int-Cell, for them to log all details of movements into the computer. I returned with about 300 to 600 VRN's. One patrol I returned with over

700. It wasn't just my patrol doing this, it was all the R/Irish patrols from Mahon Road. Even whilst conducting VCP's, I had someone sitting in the Rover recording every VRN that passed.

We continued showing our presence whilst doing certain patrols, like GDA's around our barracks and police stations. If the RUC needed us to show presence we were there. We stayed mobile around the areas, so we could react immediately if anything happened. Morale was still ok, but we all felt as though we were being curtailed from our duties in stopping the terrorist.

Off-duty we never dropped our guard, or security measures, as intelligence informed us that the terrorist threat still loomed. So our everyday life of work and army duties continued as normal, well our normal!

On Friday 9th February 1996, I came in for an ops patrol night, changed into uniform, down to the armoury, left my pistol in, rifle out, along with 50 rounds and two magazines, loaded up the mags, and returned to the company lines.

Having signed for kit for my team, I prepared the flap-sheets of soldiers on the patrol and other documentation, and we loaded the kit onto the Land Rovers, and headed out on patrol.

For the past year or two, I brought a ghetto blaster (stereo radio) with us on patrol, which I put in the back of the Land Rover. It was good for morale. A little background music playing, and we sometimes sang along with the tracks (making fools of ourselves, as none of us could sing) and listened to the news. It was never played at a high volume, as we still had to be alert doing our job.

Our patrol had just left Mahon Road barracks, and we were heading into Portadown along the Armagh Road, when the stereo gave a news interruption stating that a massive bomb had exploded in London, in the Canary Wharf area. About a minute later, the ops room came over the net saying what had just happened. The IRA ceasefire had ENDED. 2 people died in the explosion. We were now on full alert. That night we were so vigilant. All town centres and around security bases had to be checked for any suspicious vehicles or people, we didn't know if we would be driving into another bomb. As on 9th April 1994, when the IRA broke the ceasefire, it had many attacks planned. Patrols had to be increased, we were on full alert for more bombs and attacks, as we expected many more incidents imminently or within the next few minutes, hours and days.

The threat was now so heightened, that we (the part-timers) were now on 'Call-Out'. This was where we have become full-time for the duration of the threat and active terrorist activities. We were not to go to our civilian jobs until 'call-out' passed. We were now 24 hour soldiers. We only got home to sleep, change of clothes etc. This was the first 'call-out' I had experienced and will (as I found out) experience more. This 'call-out' lasted just over a week. The IRA were back to being active (even though they were always active, without attacks).

The Canary Wharf bomb was a 3,000 lb bomb, brought to the site in a Ford truck. In addition to killing 2 people, it caused £150 million worth of damage.

Following this ceasefire, we knew we could get attacked. Army and police were on high alert whether on patrol, or off-duty. Whilst the IRA were on ceasefire, we knew they still engaged in activities, planning, training, making IED's, and now the ceasefire had broken, the IRA would put that planning and preparation into action. Over the following few months, we were so careful on and off-duty. Watching and reporting everything. On the 15th June 1996 the IRA detonated a 3,300 lb bomb in the centre of Manchester injuring 212 people and causing £700 million of damage.

July 1996 Drumcree, Portadown. The previous year there was trouble with Orange Order parades marching down the Garvaghy Road, back into Portadown following the service in Drumcree Parish Church Sunday 9th July. The march was permitted on the 11th July, but 1996 year was different. No compromise was reached. Sunday 7th July the Orange Order marched up to

Drumcree Church, and it was not allowed to return down the Garvaghy Road to Portadown. There was another stand-off, which lasted until 11th July, when RUC Chief Constable (Sir Hugh Annesley) allowed the Orange Order parade to march down the Garvaghy Road.

We (3 R/Irish) didn't get involved in the Public Order, or confront any protest or protesters on either side. Our R/Irish command managed to keep us away from all confrontations. But we (full-time and part-time) played our part. The part-time companies patrolled around the Portadown suburbs, completing VCP's on the roads leading in and out of the Drumcree/ Portadown area (still keeping a VRN Trace), whilst the full-time element were going more in-depth, and doing lye-up positions, overlooking vulnerable points, and active points, taking notes, and giving continued 'sit-reps' of what was happening, and any known 'players' or politicians entering or leaving.

Drumcree 1998 was more vicious. 1,000 soldiers were brought in, also about the same number of police from Yorkshire, and other districts. There was much violence from both Republican and Loyalist sides, this was the second time we (part-time Companies in 3 R/Irish) were on 'call-out'.

During 1996 and 1997 the British and Irish Governments (and Sinn Fein) were in talks about a ceasefire. On Saturday 19th July 1997, the IRA announced the renewal of its 1994 ceasefire, as of 12:00pm on 20th July 1997.

The Secretary of State for Northern Ireland accepted the IRA ceasefire as genuine. Talks and negotiations continued, with pressures from the media, public and other country governments, and pressures by the government for a loyalist ceasefire also. We knew that if Sinn Fein were involved, then there were most probably talks for a military withdrawal from Northern Ireland, and the Royal Irish coming off patrols, and be barrack bound.

In January 1998 the Prime Minister Tony Blair announced a new inquiry into the 1972 'Bloody Sunday'.

There were quite a number of attacks by the IRA since the 'ceasefire' agreement, however the British Government chose to ignore it, as the IRA stated it was breakaway groups that had conducted the attacks, and not the IRA. Breakaway groups such as 'Continuity' IRA (CIRA) and the 'Real' IRA (RIRA).

The Provisional IRA is also a breakaway group (PIRA) from 1969.

During February 1998 the RUC could prove that some attacks and murders (two men killed in Belfast on 9th and 10th February) were by the IRA and proof means that the British and Irish governments had to stop talks with the IRA/Sinn Fein because of the attacks which were clearly by the IRA.

20th February 1998 the IRA detonated a 500lb car bomb beside the RUC station in Moira, which destroyed the building. On 23rd February the IRA detonated a 300lb car bomb near Portadown RUC Station.

10th March the IRA launched a 'Barrack Buster' attack on a RUC station in Armagh, five mortars launched, three exploding on impact (no injuries).

We thought that Ulster, was back to normal (what I have known since birth) and the normal patrols and attacks were back. However, pressure for ceasefire and normalization was still wanted by the public and government. In March 1998 Sinn Fein/IRA agreed to rejoin talks.

10th of April 1998 'The Good Friday Agreement' came into being. On 22nd May 1998 the Northern Ireland public voted in the 'Good Friday Agreement Referendum'. The Government was happy to announce that it was a 70/30% vote for 'The Good Friday Agreement'. Although I think this was a fixed result. Personally, I have never met anyone who voted for the agreement, as it meant releasing from prison, all IRA and loyalist prisoners (428 prisoners released. both Republican & Loyalist), clearing all their criminal records, and settlement for them, as in money and houses.

I knew after the Good Friday Agreement that our days on the ground (operational role) were numbered. We knew in our hearts that the British Government would appease the IRA/Sinn Fein (to stop the bombing that was causing so much damage (£) in the UK) and that IRA/Sinn Fein wanted rid of the Royal Irish and the RUC. On 4th November 2001, the RUC ceased to exist, and the new police force came into being.

The PSNI (Police Service of Northern Ireland) was part of the 'Good Friday Agreement'.

Our operational role was reduced over a short space of time. British Army regiments were removed from Northern Ireland, and our roles reduced. So much so, that we (3 Royal Irish, Portadown) were the only patrols on the road, journalists were out and about the Portadown area to get pictures of us (as we were the last!)

01st August 1998 the IRA (the IRA say's it was the 'Real IRA' which conducted the attack) detonated a car bomb (500lb) in Banbridge, 35 people were injured. £3.5 million of damage. My company was on operations that day in Banbridge (I unfortunately was at Bisley, Surrey, shooting for the army), and was on cordon when it exploded. It was Saturday 1st August, my company were patrolling the Banbridge area, when there was a threat of a IED Attack. The IRA gave a very short warning, and we (RUC and our patrol) had limited time to clear the streets. We thought it was a hoax bomb, or a hoax warning.

The Main street was almost evacuated, the timed explosion occurred. 500lb of explosives were in a Vauxhall Cavalier parked in Newry Street. It was later claimed by the 'Real Irish Republican Army' (RIRA)

At 1419hrs, on 15th August 1998, a red Vauxhall Cavalier carrying 500lb of fertiliser-based-explosives, parked in Omagh. There were two IRA members in the car, they armed the bomb, set the timer for 40 minutes, left the car, and walked to 'Market Street' to meet the 'scout car'. The same scout car which had been in front of them whilst transiting the 'bomb-car' to the target site (Omagh).

The scout-car had travelled a distance in front to warn of any Vehicle Check Points (by mobile phone). The IRA phoned in the bomb-warning at 1430hrs, giving the bomb location as 'Main Street in Omagh' and that the bomb would explode at 1500hrs.

The IRA did not have a bomb designated for 'Main Street, Omagh', they had the bomb designed and designated for where the RUC/Royal Irish Regiment would set up an ICP (incident control point). The aim was to kill as many security-force and agency-workers as they could (as in Warrenpoint Bomb of 1979).

The bomb detonated just after 1500hrs. The red Cavalier containing the bomb was on Market Street. Murdering 29 people and injuring more than 200. The IRA had either guessed an incorrect ICP location, or the pair of IRA members in the bomb-car got spooked or got the bomb location wrong, but still the 'Good- Friday Agreement' remained. Even though the inquiry ('No stone will remain unturned' Tony Blair) shows that PIRA planned the attack, PIRA made the bomb, PIRA was scouting and moving the bomb into location, and suddenly the inquiry stopped, as it would upset the 'Peace Process'

Bombs, shootings, targeting and plans still went on, and of course with release of the prisoners under the Good Friday agreement, going back to the paramilitaries. Our job of looking after the people of Northern Ireland was becoming increasingly difficult. Especially as the government, politicians, and public wanted us demobilised, and to trust that the 'Peace Process' will work.

The river of operational commitments, became a stream, that was drying up. We tried to keep the training commitment high, but morale in all the companies (full-time and part-time) was getting lower.

Our battalion was still providing the best rugby and shooting teams in the British Army, and those commitments and individuals remained busy.

I was in the shooting teams (Regimental and Army Team).

Much as I tried to pretend, my morale was dropping. After the year 2000 our battalion (I can't speak for the rest) was getting officers joining, and they were making our army lives hard. There became more and more monetary training needed, to stay in the army, and to receive an annual 'bounty'. The new 'mandatory training' subjects was one of things we never needed before, and subjects that never aided in our training or operational role.

The full-time companies started to have very little time off. They would be away (perhaps in Crumlin Road prison, or at the border ops) and straight after, had to go to training areas in England for two weeks, this placed increased pressure on us, the part-time element. Bring morale down, make life hard, and get us to leave without getting pushed. We thought our roles were coming to an end, we just didn't know when, and as a part-timer, I was thinking we would become a T.A. (reserve forces) Regiment, perhaps the full-timers would go into the Roulement Battalions (overseas, general army).

By 2003 our duties had dwindled to 6 per month, but being in the shooting team, some months I was permitted more. My personal life was getting a battering as well. My marriage was disintegrating under my nose. If I was honest, I knew it was hitting rock bottom long ago, but I chose to ignore what was going on in my marriage, and put more time into the army, to hope the problem would go away. I had always put too much time, commitment and dedication into the army and shooting. I believed I was ok, as I wasn't going out drinking, didn't go to the football and other social events, all I seemed to do was work. Work at the kitchens, and work in the army. I was giving my family a good standard of living. But I was never there! I was putting the army first, I was putting the army second, I was putting the army shooting third; marriage and family after that. I never realised that I had lost attachment to my wife, and didn't have an attachment to my two children (never to get a close relationship back). In 2004 I thought I was losing my marriage and losing the army. My family and marriage were far more important than the army, so I put my family first! I dropped my duties down to practically nothing and put my everything into my family/marriage. My marriage survived another 7 years, but was so broken, I could not fix it.

During 2004, manpower in the battalion was dropping. Morale wasn't great, and it wasn't joyful coming in for duties.

In the UDR we were 11th Battalion, and we amalgamated with Armagh 2nd Battalion, and we were 2/11 Battalion UDR. In 1991 when we became the Royal Irish, we left the Armagh Battalion and joined the Co. Down Battalion (which were 3 UDR) and briefly were 6 Royal Irish (for about 2 weeks) then (as we now were) 3 R/Irish. 2004 we were getting ready to amalgamate once again with Armagh Battalion (8 R/Irish). Through the 'Peace Process' our operational commitment was dwindling, and we were under no illusion what was happening.

We were to be leaving Mahon Road and moving to Drumadd Barracks in Armagh. During 2004 administration was getting ready to move to Armagh. Tonnes and tonnes of documents were getting burned.

Sanjay was in during the daytime burning 'our company' documents. Burning the documents? There was so much paper, to bring it up to Armagh was deemed silly, as it was all now computerised, and records are held in York. Sanjay was destroying all the personal documents, when he came across my 'army records'. They never made it to the burning barrel; Sanjay passed them back to me and I still have them! The documents note every duty I have ever completed (ops and training), every course, and awards (and the one charge I have had).

In early 2005, we moved to Drumadd - not a pleasant company lines. They were very basic and run down through years of operations. It took a wee while to get our bearings and establish what all was happening. It was a higher risk barracks, which had been attacked quite a number of times. The barracks wasn't situated in a dominant/tactical area. It was in a large hollow. A farmer had donated the land to the UDR, who built the barracks in 1975 for 2 UDR, and wasn't the easiest to defend. One thing I noticed when entering the barracks was the GPMG (bren, belt-feed machine gun) poking out of the front sanger.

Our roles now? Training, camp guard, GDA's, and now and again mobile patrols around Armagh City centre. The number of duties we could do was still 6 per month, so it was very difficult to get yourself established there.

Having reduced my duties in Mahon Road to try to fix my marriage, I lost much of my status in 'F' Company. Many of the soldiers in my company gained rank within the last year. Some comrades with rank had left within the past year or so, because our duties had reduced to so little, our operational role had taken a dive, and morale had sunk to a depth, which I had never known in the R/Irish.

I had been out of the picture for the last year or so, as I was trying to patch up my marriage and family, so when I came back and moved to Armagh, most of my team were under other team commanders. I used to be involved with helping training within the Company, but training had been reduced, and other Corporals now conducted the training which previously I would have done.

Whilst at Armagh, I managed to get most (if not all) my team back.

We occasionally did Camp-Guard, but not as regularly as in Mahon Road. The GDA's around Drumadd Barracks were a bit wider afield than Mahon Road. You could drive about 5 miles around the barracks, whereas it was about 3 around Mahon Road. We could conduct mobile patrols in and around Armagh centre, and outskirts.

Men, full-time and part-time were continually leaving, and what was previously the largest battalion in the British Army, was shrinking month on month. In June 2006, everyone (It was a scale 'A' parade, where everyone had to attend) in the battalion turned out for a battalion photo. I was quite sad as I knew that so many of our important soldiers of all ranks, were not there, as they had left (some never turned up for the photo, as they were pissed off at what was happening and how we were now treated). Some that were there had never seen active service in Ulster.

As our company marched over to the pitch where the photo was to be taken, I noticed how low our numbers were in comparison to the numbers in the 1990's, and I knew it was the same across all companies, all battalions. As we marched over for the photo, and returned we already knew that we had just a few months left in the army.

From early that year we heard more and more of what was to come. We weren't continuing OR going into 'Reserve', but we were being disbanded. Political appeasement meant we were not going to exist. Individuals in the part-time companies, could request to go into the 'TA Reserve Forces', and full-time individuals could try to transfer into another regiment. The day of the battalion photo, we knew we were being paid off, morale was low, and many were glad it was coming to an end.

I still have that battalion photograph, which hangs proudly in my upstairs hall (away from public view).

Spring 2007. Everything was nearing the end. We had our company mini-camp February/March. We had a few lecture evenings, regarding what was happening, explaining where we could go, or join if we wanted to remain. The T/A came a few times, encouraging us to enlist with them, or we could request to go full-time into a regular full-time regiment. However, in doing so, you forfeited the payoff we were due to get when the Royal Irish Regiment finished. We never knew how much we would receive. We knew that if the government had their way as they were planning to do – there would to be NO payout, as our part-time R/Irish contract said – when we were needed no more, the 'contract' just stopped, but some of the unionist politicians made sure we got a 'Pay-Off'. By around March we found out it was to be a sum of £12,000 each.

We were called to company Scale 'A' parades during March,

were formed-up on parade, and marched down to one of the main halls, were we were brought into single file, and into the hall, with our Army ID's (MOD90's) out, ready to hand in.

We quickly went from table to table. The first table was to identify your 'paper' with your name and number on it, go to the next table, and show the paper, and your MOD90 (to make sure they match), the next table, you handed over your MOD90, and signed the bottom of a printed sheet of paper. We didn't get to read this form, just had to sign it. We never got to read the script on it, but were told we were forfeiting our claim for a pension, which we never thought we would get as we had been continually told we did not qualify for a pension, as we were part-time and in our contract were only paid for what we did and the hours we worked.

I later found out that the form we had signed, is not forfeiting the pension, but forfeiting any other claims regarding health, and physical injuries.

We were brainwashed into believing we had no rights to a pension. We did not get a chance to read what was on the form. As far as we knew and were told – if we didn't sign the form, we would not receive the £12,000; and if we didn't sign the form, we had no chance of a pension anyhow, as we were part-time. After that table, we made our way back to the company lines in two's or three's.

Once we left the barracks that evening. That was it. No longer would we be allowed into any British Army barracks (no MOD90), No longer in a part-time company or regiment, No longer in the army, and no longer to be together with The Muckers.

Through the 'Good Friday Agreement' all the convicted terrorists were released from the prison, and the much hated political prison (the Maze) was closed. Each of those convicted terrorists that were released received £14,000, and if they didn't have homes, the government give them homes too, and much more.

On Saturday evening the 7th March 2009, four off-duty soldiers of 'The Royal Engineers' walked out of the front gates of Massereene barracks at the edge of Antrim. They walked out of those front gates to receive a pizza delivery, which had been ordered.

It was usual for the soldiers to do this, as it was a treat at the weekends, but as this was a weekly routine, it heightened the risk level. Regular soldiers that hadn't lived there long, didn't realize the risk of routines! The men were looking forward to the pizzas, however as they were receiving the pizzas from the delivery drivers, two masked IRA gunmen came from a nearby parked car, armed with AK47 type assault rifles and opened fire. The shooting lasted over half a minute (which felt like a lifetime) and more than 60 rounds were expelled. After the immediate bursts of gunfire, the IRA men walked over to the wounded soldiers lying on the ground, and shot again at them in close range, murdering two of them (Sappers Mark Quinsey and Patrick Azimkar). The two delivery drivers were also wounded.

The soldiers were in Desert DPM clothing, but were unarmed. The car used by the IRA men was found near Randalstown (8 miles away) and had only partially burned. As the vehicle had not fully burned, the PSNI found evidence.

Two days after the Massereene Barracks shooting, Monday 9th March 2009, the IRA murdered PSNI officer Stephen Carroll in Craigavon. The IRA manufactured a 'come on' attack, by smashing a window in a Craigavon housing estate, and forcing a member of the public to phone for the police. Two police cars responded and went to the scene.

When the police stopped their cars, and were getting out, they were shot at by an IRA man, that was around 50 meters away with a AK47 Type Assault rifle. Stephen Carroll had not yet got out of the police car, and was shot in the head.

The evidence found in the partially burnt-out car in Randalstown, was a pair of latex gloves, which had the DNA of a well-known IRA player from Lurgan (the same player who had been arrested for the murder of Johnnie Lyness), DNA on an abandoned mobile phone, and a partially burnt-out matchstick.

The PSNI went to arrest the player in Lurgan, but he could not be found. He had not been in his own area/home for a quite a few days. When he did turn up, he was arrested, and detained. Arrested for the murder of the two soldiers and attempted murder of five others.

Another player from Magherafelt (who was the driver) was also arrested. Both men got out of prison, as the DNA findings may have been in the car by circumstance. As the trial had to be done by Diplock, the evidence MUST be 100%. Was it possible that the known player was in the car at a different time and had left the gloves there by mistake; the same was said for the mobile phone and partially-burnt matchstick that was found. It had the DNA of the second (suspected IRA) man.

As soon as we were decommissioned, I felt the 'spark' had left me. Difficult to put into words, but it was as though my engine had stopped. Even though I was married with a family, I felt as though I was alone. One of the things I missed most, was the 'wavelength' of our army minds. The army wasn't a job, it was an institution. We all had the same mindset, understood each other inside out, had the same sense of humour (which a normal civilian wouldn't find funny. Perhaps a bit sick).

When I said that I had lost the spark, I know that this has happened to quite a percentage of the R/Irish that got booted out. I, like most of the ex-soldiers that I have spoken to, or heard on tv, have lost our purpose, lost our identity in life. Over the following year quite a few marriages came apart, and I think that is because we lost our spark. We stopped being pro-active in gathering terrorist information out on the street, we lost our aim of 'killing or capturing' the terrorist, lost the 'being alert 24 hours a day'. Lost 'the danger zone'. The anticipation of going out on patrol.

Have we been brought down to earth and are now everyday boring people. And as the last sentence applies, I have lost my self-esteem.

I was watching tv, and watching the Channel 4 program 'Who Dares Wins' and ex SAS man Jason Fox said something that hit the nail on the head. He said when he left the armed forces, he felt like a nobody! Whilst in the army I was somebody. Now I am a nobody. It hit an exact chord with me. So much that I recorded that bit of the series, and watched it repeatedly, whilst watching his face, his lips, watching his body talk. I felt exactly the same as he spoke about.

I was respected in the army, I respected others, I trained and taught others, I commanded sections and teams, I was commanded, I listened and was listened to. I looked after my men, and they looked after me. The list goes on and on. But now it had STOPPED.

PTSD? Not many men, especially soldiers say they have PTSD. In fact most of us, including myself don't think we have it. I mean, I'm not sitting on a chair rocking back and forth foaming at the mouth, I don't want to blow the world up, I have no anger issues, I don't want to dive into drink. I don't have PTSD? It was years later (after 2020) that my wife recognised that I have PTSD, and I should go and see about it. It was then, that I started to look at myself. From early in my service years, I began to have nightmares, and they escalated as time went on. It began with dreams of getting chased and ambushed, and escalated to not trusting anyone, even family, they were all out to get me in my dreams. They are so frequent, that it is like a series, like EastEnders, occurring 3 or four nights of the week. So vivid that I could write a book based of my dreams. Each dream I am in combat or ambushed on, and mostly off duty. Fighting and shooting, trying to protect and save others, and most times at the finish (about 90%) I get killed or shot. Sometimes when I have saved someone, I am so pleased, and hug them, as we have escaped, only to have them stab me in the back or chest. And the moral? Trust no one!

Following my own shooting incident. I find it so uneasy to go into any loyalist estates, pass any loyalist areas. I can go into them, but if I do, I am on pins. Looking everywhere for the threat, analysing everywhere, everything, and everyone, and can't wait to get out. With all the murders of my friends and colleagues, they are constantly on my mind. I still avoid any situation that happened, and if I am there, I try to be so very prepared for 'actions-on'.

In a car, whether driving or a passenger, if someone else is driving, I hate the car travelling closer than a car length in distance behind another car whilst at traffic lights, or a queue of any sort. When stopped at traffic lights etc. I constantly think of 'actions on'. As in, if I am attacked, how do I get out of this killing zone. Mount the pavement to the left or right? Drive at the attackers? Debus from the car?

Flashbacks! They can happen almost anywhere. Something I see, hear, or think can trigger flashbacks. I can be sitting at my desk in work, and I hear banging outside. Quite often the banging does not affect me, but sometimes the banging is on a frequency or regularity that triggers, and as soon as I hear it, I am thinking 'Where is the contact coming from, where is the device, are there any casualties, will I need to Casvac, what is the sequence of the casvac report, Who are my flank teams? Where will I send them, where will I set up my ICP (incident control point). All these thoughts hit my mind at once, it's like a flash of thousands of mega bites per second. Every time the banging continues, the spark of thousands of mega bites hits my mind. I can taste the adrenalin in my mouth, and my head pounds!

We (very close friends and colleagues from the shooting team, and the two part-time companies I was involved with) keep in touch. We keep in touch with one another almost on a weekly basis. It's good for the mind to keep in touch and talk to each other. I go back to Stop-Watch's house on a weekly basis, and there are normally one or two others from the R/Irish there too. Stop-Watch still has connections with the police and army and relates the weekly threats that come out. For instance, threat of an off-duty shooting, threats of attacks on the PSNI, threats of an under-vehicle booby trap (UVBT). It was good to be kept up to date of the threats. Why did we need to know these? If we had left the R/Irish? Because we are still under threat! Although the government/state says there is no longer a threat? We, in the real world know that that is not true. Perhaps we are no longer the first choice of being attacked by the IRA, but if the attack that is planned can't or doesn't happen, then a soft secondary target like us, will happen.

The RUC changed to the PSNI in 2001, and the main objective was to keep the peace, and to be accepted by the catholic community, some of whom deemed the RUC of being sectarian. Soon after the PSNI came into being, it wanted a 50/50 protestant/catholic workforce. But the IRA didn't want this, as it would mean that there were more Police personnel living in their communities, which would weaken the IRA's control. Information seen by an off-duty officer could result in convictions. So, the IRA had to threaten the catholic communities (especially republican areas) not to join the PSNI, hence there was a large threat on catholic police personnel. We knew of this threat and kept a look out.

On Friday morning 08th January 2010 PSNI Officer Peadar Heffron (age 35), left his house in Randalstown (near Antrim) to go on duty in Woodburn Station, Belfast. About half a mile from his house, Peadar felt a bang, and the car spun around. It was a UVBT, and he had his legs blown off. Peadar had joined the PSNI, as it was a new turnaround for Northern Ireland, and his thoughts were that someday the PSNI would join forces with the Gardai (Southern Ireland Police Force) in the run to a united Ireland. Peadar was also a GAA member, he survived that attack by pulling himself out of the car by using his arms, and rolled onto his back on the ground, and waited for the ambulance to arrive. At that time, we didn't know of a specific UVBT threat, but knew that catholic police officers were being targeted.

We did know about a year later (start of 2011) of specific threats, for an attack on an off-duty catholic police officer, using an UVBT. We began checking our cars again daily, not wanting to be a statistic of a secondary target. We knew that the PSNI officers, were at this time vigilant checking their cars before heading into their stations, and so we too continued to check our vehicles, as we knew that if the police are checking their cars, and a UVBT was made to be placed under a car, we could be secondary targets.

As far as I know, if the bomber made a bomb, it most likely had a 'best before date' home-made explosives had to be used soon after being made, or they wouldn't work! Perhaps moisture got into it, or it just faded out? But Semtex? I don't think it had a 'to be used by' date. Rather, the person who has made the bomb would want it used sooner rather than later, as the longer it hasn't been used, then the more chance it would be found by the police or army and would offer up forensics and evidence. So, on this note - we still remain vigilant, despite no longer in the security forces. There may be (probably) more than one UVBT made? We don't know where, and we don't know when, it will happen.

On Saturday afternoon 2nd of April 2011, an explosion was heard in the village of Killyclogher, near Omagh. It was a UVBT explosion that murdered Constable Ronan Kerr, as he was leaving his home.

Constable Kerr was aged 25, a Roman Catholic and a member of the Gaelic Athletic Association (GAA).

The location the BBC and Ulster news reported from, was a cul-de-sac overlooking Ronan Kerr's home. I suspect that location was used as a vantage point by the IRA, whilst watching Ronan leave the house time after time without checking for a suspicious device under his car.

Thursday 1st November 2012, A Prison Officer who worked in Maghaberry Prison was on his way to work, along the M1 from Dungannon towards Moira. He was travelling alone, and just as he was about to pass Junction 10 (the Lurgan Junction) (Moira junction is No 9) a car was gradually passing him. When it came alongside him, David Black was shot, from the passing car. The car was hit many times, and David veered off the motorway, over the hard shoulder, and tumbled down the bank. David Black was murdered. There is very strong suspicion that the terrorist gunman was none other than our main 'player' from Lurgan IRA Active Service Unit. David Black was a lovely man. When talking to friends who are fellow prison officers in HMP Maghaberry, they said he was a gentleman, making no enemies with inmates, and always helping people of all abodes. He was murdered, as he was an easy target - he had made no enemies.

There is a ceasefire, and the IRA should not be active? (Good Friday Agreement)

Life continued on, we kept in touch with each other, but that faded as time went by. However, as is the case with at least three of my army friends, we still have flashbacks, something or some dates, trigger memories of the incidents, or murders of our friends.

Come the 2020's, all of these things I could keep within myself, but my wife noticed that I could become pretty absent, and give the thousand mile stare, when an incident appeared on the television or news. It flashed me back to an incident/incidents.

In my mind I was replaying what happened, what went wrong, and what should have happened, what did happen, and who died. I was staring at the tv or out the window, and I didn't want to be disturbed. My wife also noticed that sometimes when we were out, something triggered, and I was analysing everyone and everything. Perhaps in a large clothing shop, something triggered, and I was analysing everyone, to see who the threat was, looking for exits, but not to take an exit that the terrorist has anticipated that I would take.

It was situations like this that my wife thought I should go and see about PTSD counselling. I always thought of PTSD as a condition where a person can't control anger, or would drink too much, but in fact I am the opposite. I have no anger; I have no emotions. I am emotionally vacant. And I noticed that nothing excites me. It sounds quite random, but nothing excites me. I must have lost that during my first year or so in the UDR. Like My shooting incident! It just felt like a normal day, and the day after, just a normal day.

Don't get me wrong! I look forward to things, like a holiday, or watching the latest film that's right up my street. But nothing excites me. I never get angry.

In the army the perfect soldier does not lose control of his anger. We learn to subdue it. Over the years in the army, I learned how to switch on, and switch off aggression in the snap of fingers. And over time you can control aggression more and more, to such a point that anyone who is with me asks "Did that not affect you?", "Why did you not punch him?", "Have you got no feelings?".

Since I was 18, I was in the army, on patrol, training, threats and risks whilst off duty, always active. Life was so alive. Now - Life is a lukewarm steady stream.

My hearing now lets me down. When I joined the UDR, we were using 7.62mm SLR's, and we weren't issued ear defence. In fact, we were not allowed to use them, if we had them. "How the Fuck can you hear my words of command, if you're wearing ear defenders?"

In a crowded room, or in a public bar, where there are lots of people talking, I cannot join in a conversation, as I can make out few words that are spoken, even talking one to one in a place where there is background noise, I find problems hearing the words spoken. I either say "what?", "what?", "what did you say?", or pretend to hear hoping to piece it together, as we go. My wife noticed this, and said when we socialised, it was as though I'm a loner. I don't join into conversations. At home I turn up the tv volume to hear what is said. I always blame the tv series or film, as having muttered speech. Can nobody talk clearly anymore? My wife arranged an appointment in the local hospital, to have my hearing tested. I left work early and went to the hospital audiology department for 1630hrs, and at 1800 I was going home with 2 hearing aids that have been programed to amplify the frequencies that I have lost.

Regarding the PTSD, my wife persuaded me to get an appointment to see if they can do anything about it. Ordinarily, I don't believe in counselling. I think it's a weak way for todays society in dealing with things. But I do know I have PTSD, so I got in touch with 'Walking with The Wounded' via my mobile phone and made an appointment for someone to come out and talk with me.

In August 2022 a girl called Louise came and met me (during working hours). I'm always pessimistic about such meetings, but it went really well. Louise was with me chatting for about an hour to an hour and a half, and collated all the information, about my service, and how I thought I had PTSD. Louise left, and kept in touch by texts, letting me know about progress at her end. Her superiors referred me to 'Combat Stress' where I was to make an appointment for them to assess.

During mid-September I received one. The first interview was my assessment, to see what if anything would follow on. Texts between myself and Louise continued, and I had to send her details of incidents I was involved with, and those which affected me. Further texts went back and forth and mid-way through December I received an appointment. The first interview had been via telephone, and was on a Friday whilst I was at work. I wasn't very optimistic about this, as I thought they probably wouldn't take me on, and just think that I was pulling their leg, and trying it on, and drop me.

It was a clinical psychologist called Laura. I expected to get the usual questions like 'How much alcohol do you drink?' 'Do you have nightmares' 'Do you get flashbacks?' When the conversation started, Laura asked my name, how long I was in the army, where I served, and after the getting to know me questions, asked me how much I drank. I told her that I took alcohol every day, but only as a glass of wine with my tea (dinner for those who live in the South of England), with equates to about 1½ to 2 bottles a week. Guinness – a flat of Guinness would last almost a year. Laura then asked me about flashbacks, dreams and nightmares. But she didn't just ask me if I had them, she asked me to describe them. I said that I was hyper-alert, and hyper-vigilant, and sometime analyse places and people. After about 40 minutes, Laura asked me a question I never expected. "Does your hyper-vigilance alertness, not tire you out? Are you tired by the end of the week?". I had never thought of it. Since 1987 when I joined, I was taught, and am hyper-alert, vigilant, and analyse so much, but it does tire me - I just never realised it!

Laura then asked, "What do you want us to do about it?". Another question I never expected. I said that I didn't want to lose the hyper-alertness, as that is ME, that is what I have become, I didn't want it taken away, and to become like a Zombie. I didn't want to be brain dead walking the earth, 'This' is who I am. "I don't want you to take all these things away, I just want to be able to manage it. I don't want my past to disappear, I just want to be able to live a normal life, enjoy normal things, without having to look behind me, watch for risks and threats. I don't want to forget about army and police personnel that I knew and had fallen. I want to remember them. I would just like, if they came on the TV, to remember them, without my mind going back to the very incident that killed them, and relive it." The conversation didn't last one hour, it lasted an hour and a half, and it was really good, and really deep. It felt great to be able to pass the information on to Laura, good that she listened and understood what I was talking about, and good that I was not asked the usual 'cop-out' questions.

Laura said she was to have a meeting the following week, and would get back to me in about a week or so. She did keep in touch, and I went to the offices of 'Combat Stress' in Belfast in the middle of January. This time it was a face to face interview. It was very similar to the phone appointment, but more personal than the phone appointment, since Laura had records they had archived from the army, and notes that were taken during the phone appointment. She asked in depth about everything (service, incidents, personal problems, nightmares, flashbacks etc). By the end of that meeting, she said she thought I was eligible for therapy with 'Combat Stress' but it had to be discussed in detail with the rest of the team, and I would probably have to come in again soon, to be assessed by a Doctor, for PTSD.

I didn't have long to wait, as there was a meeting within a few days and by the end of the week, Combat Stress contacted me (the afternoon after the morning's meeting in Belfast), to confirm that they would like to provide me with therapy, and I would receive an appointment, for a meeting with the Doctor. Again they came back to me very quickly, and I had an appointment for the morning of 14th February 2023, which would take about an hour to two hours.

I arrived for the appointment very early, and walked the nearby streets until the allotted time. The meeting was very casual, it felt like two muckers just chatting. Instead of asking me questions about service, flashbacks, nightmares and hyper alertness, we chatted about it. I told the doctor that I am always hyper-aware, when I am in Northern Ireland, no matter where, and even if I am on holiday somewhere, I am always hyper aware. It is so strange, because even if I go over to Scotland or England, the stress, pressure just lifts. I was telling him about the previous year, when my wife and I went on holiday around the north of England, then to Bath, staying in various hotels in which we got good deals. I felt no stress or hyper alertness the full holiday, and it really gave me rest and enjoyment. I related this story to when I used to go over to Bisley every other weekend during the summer to shoot with the army team. My colleagues from Mahon Road and I had so much rest and relaxation each time we went, even though we were working hard at our shooting. The appointment was relaxed, and we chatted about other aspects of PTSD. About three days later I got a duplicate letter from the Doctor at Combat

Stress, of one he had sent to my own GP, confirming the diagnosis that I have PTSD, and would receive therapy to help me.

It did not take long to hear back from C/Stress for an appointment in their offices in Belfast. During the first week in March, I was contacted to arrange a mutually agreeable time for appointments. I asked for first thing in the morning, to avoid going to work, leaving for my appointment, then returning to work.

I am always wary of who I meet. Not in a threatening way, but how could someone understand what I am talking about, if they have never been in the army? How could you empathise about something, if you have never been through it? I soon found out that the person conducting my therapy has also served in the army, and that most personnel in Combat Stress have served somewhere in the armed forces.

My initial appointment was 28th February, I arrived early, long before C/Stress opened, in fact long before most of Belfast opened. Why? because I go to work early, and if I wanted to get up a little later than usual, I'd probably sleep in and miss it, also I wanted to get a parking spot before people started parking for work. Being early was good also, as I walked many of the streets in the city, looking at the architecture and history. Some buildings dating from Victorian times, some post war, some from the 60's. and I also looked at some businesses that no longer exist, like the Nambarrie Tea Factory, founded in Belfast in 1860. The Belfast Factory closed about 2010, and the building is falling into disrepair. It's amazing how much history can be seen in the buildings, and what great industries have come and gone. Walking about thinking about places and things is so therapeutic, and I enjoyed this before each appointment.

At my appointment I met Mark, he introduced himself, over the sessions we got to know each other. He explained what the therapy involved, and what the objectives were, and how long it would continue for, and we began the first session. The therapy wasn't to brainwash me, or forget my past, or make me into a zombie, it was to understand what PTSD is, what triggers it, how to identify and manage it, and learn to control my hyper alertness, and hyper vigilance. There were 6 sessions in the course, and each session might take more than one or two appointments to go through. There was no rush, it went at whatever speed I needed. The first session was about understanding how PTSD affects us, how the body responds, and what are the causes, the other sessions were about understanding what triggers it, the body and mind's response to it, how to manage when the trigger goes off, how to place the thoughts into today's reality and not in the reality of when I was serving. How to manage flashbacks and nightmares, and how to manage my body and minds responses. Combat Stress were really understanding. Mark asked me how frequently I wanted the appointments? Once a week? I said that I would like to meet every other week, so it wouldn't interrupt work too much, and also wouldn't set up routines that others could see me taking (old habits). This worked out really well, as it wasn't too fast, and gave me two weeks between appointments to think about our previous appointment and the next one. Each appointment day, I went to Belfast (very) early, parked my car, and walked around another small part of the city. This habit was under rated, as I benefited greatly, it was so relaxing. Walking around deserted streets before the mainstream of people came into the city for work. AMAZING. My last appointment was at the end of November 2023, and I missed when it ended. Throughout the sessions, we quite often went off key, and talked about other aspects, like walking in the Mournes, walking along the coast which freed up our mind and is good mentally. We chatted about music. I know that everything we talked about had importance, as it was looking into ME, and how I work.

The therapy really helped me. No longer am I having the continual series of nightmares that I have been having for decades (in a way I miss them), I just get the occasional one now and again. When I get hyper aware because of tv news or footage, I have the techniques to rationalize it, switch it off, and manage it. The good thing is that I can become hyper aware if I want to, and just stay in that zone for as long as I want to. I can control it, and it is no longer in control of me, and my mind. All the therapy still hasn't made life exciting! Life now is still just lukewarm.

I watched a programme on BBC, it was the fortieth anniversary of 'The Falkland's War', and there was something that a few of them did that resonated with me, perhaps empathy? They said that after a battle or traumatic bombing, they wondered how and why they got out of it. They felt as if they had died in that battle/ war, and although they are still alive, they had died in that battle, living after that battle is just a bonus. I feel similar thoughts. So many friends/colleagues were killed during my service years, but I got out unscathed. I feel as though I died somewhere/ sometime during my service years. I can't pinpoint any exact time or incident, but somewhere in my patrolling years I died. Perhaps it was my own shooting incident, perhaps the overload of threats, perhaps the near misses, comrades getting murdered, or perhaps a collaboration of all the above, or maybe because I have no purpose and identity? Please don't get me wrong - I still enjoy life, and look forward to things, and am happy. Just life out of the Army, with no risks and no threats on continual movement, and no patrols in dangerous places, no comradery with fellow soldiers. Who would miss that? I DO!

24

Pensions and Questions

I joined the part-time UDR in 1987. We could do as few as about 5 duties (8 hours per duty) per month, and as many as 19¾. But on various conditions, like call-out, special training assignments, or other special conditions, we could complete as many as 31 duties. From the start we were told that there wasn't any pension provision, and that they could cease our employment anytime either I, or we, are were no longer needed. Most months I carried out at least 19¾ duties, and many more hours, but I only got paid the 19¾ duties. We got paid for what we did (like I said – up to 19¾ duties per month), but never did we receive holiday pay, bereavement leave, days off with the family at Christmas or any other public holiday! Terrorism didn't stop for holidays! We were expected to cover our platoon patrols the full year. Well? except for when all our part-time companies in our battalion were away in May for a week, to fulfil the annual camp exercises.

We were not reserve forces such the T.A. We were regular British soldiers. We didn't have Reserve Forces numbers, we were given regular forces numbers (personal ID number). We did not just train to be ready for war, we were in a conflict EVERY moment, and most of our duties are operational, patrols. In fact, until the Iraq/Afghanistan war, we were completing more operational duties than all the rest of the regiments put together. We were on military law 24 hours per day.

I remember hearing stats in the late 1990's, saying that the R/Irish did over 90% of searches and V.C.P. ops in Northern Ireland. Not only that, but 3 R/Irish did 90% of the 90%. Additionally, the part-timers did 90% of that, as most of the part-time patrols were V.C.P. orientated. The full-timers mostly did border patrols, Crumlin Road prison duties and security, training on the mainland, and lie-up ops.

The majority of our part-time patrols were on week nights, and so it was V.C.P.'s to collate information on movement, deny the terrorist movement and activity, and hopefully kill or capture the terrorist.

It was bled into us from the start, that we had no rights to a pension (army), and so we believed it. However, the British Army, like the Fire Service, has a non-contributory pension scheme. I did as normal, at least 20 duties per month, which equated to over 40 hours per week. More hours than a normal working week that civvies carried out.

The UDR – R/Irish part-timers were not on a zero hours contract. We had to conduct (I think) at least three full duties each month, or we might get kicked out! We had to do our mandatory training. For instance, we had to complete and pass all the mandatory tests throughout the year, such as fieldcraft, first aid, map reading etc. and complete and pass the physical requirements, 2 basic fitness tests (B.F.T.'s), pass all required shoot complete the C.F.T. (complete fitness test), have attended for at least 8 days continuous training days (preferably on mainland Britain) plus weekend mini-camps, and completed at least 75 duties through the year (25 training, 50 operational days). Why should I not be entitled to a pension? I began thinking about these things a few years after I got dispatched from the army. Why didn't I start to think about it immediately after I left?

As soon as I left, the shock to lifestyle, you put the army to the back of my mind and close it. It was the easiest way to try and move on with life.. It was the easiest way to try and move on with life; to try and fill that empty box space with other things (it actually is not possible). The army box opened now and again and was hard to shut. Around 15 years after leaving the army (about 2022) I thought I should try and push doors, to see if I was entitled to an Army Pension, let's face it, I'd been doing a full-time job for 20 years, and did not leave, but was disbanded from it.

By 2022 I had joined an ex-service support group (Decorum NI) for RUC men, UDR men (and women of course), R/Irish, prison officers, who had been working throughout the troubles in Northern Ireland, and needed the support of comrades who have been through the same thing.

I enquired through Decorum if I was entitled to an army pension and was told that there were many other UDR soldiers who had chased after the same thing, had completed as many duties as myself, only perhaps a few years earlier. It came to nothing, they never got any response.

This was about the time Uber and Amazon delivery drivers were asking for holiday pay and demanding it, as was written in the law. With this information, I decided to up my chase.

I got in touch with a local MLA (local Minister that attended Westminster, on a weekly basis), and asked him if he would pursue it for me. He agreed he would, and that I might be DESERVING of it. I have most of my pay chitties (payslips) and have my army personnel records to confirm it. I provided him with some photocopies, spoke with him, and he went on his way. A few weeks later, he returned and asked if I'd signed the form when I was leaving the R/Irish to say that I was forfeiting my pension. I replied that I had, but that it was a moment of madness, where we never got to read the form. Just hand your MOD90 over, sign the form, and move on, and that we were advised before we entered the hall, that we were not entitled to an army pension, and if we did not sign the form, we will not get the £12,000, when we leave!

Nowadays, legally if the small print is not explained and highlighted, the document becomes useless, and not worthy

- I found this out quite a few years ago! When I'd paid off my mortgage in full a few years earlier than term length, I went to lift my house deeds from the bank, they said it would cost me £500 to lift my house deeds. I said that I had been faithful to the bank and not remortgaged with any other bank. I stated that at the time I took out the mortgage I was not shown this cost. They told me it was in the small print. I stated that I was not shown this small print. I never got my deeds out without any cost, but it was reduced considerably.

When it comes to an Army Pension, I served in the Regular Army, how could they not give me a pension?

The Northern Ireland part-time Fire Service were in the same predicament, and a few years ago they won their right to a pension.

I am still chasing the pension. I hope to get another MP, who will listen to my claims, and pursue it.

Last year (2024) it came to light, and the news and media of the Post-Office scandal. Pursued by Alan Bates. Although Alan Bates devoted his time (his life) into winning.

During 2024, the Reservists (new name for the T.A.) had a right to qualify for the pension, as they were sometimes on active duties, as in Iraq and Afghanistan. Following the invasion of Iraq in 2003, the T.A. were permitted to take tours of duty, as the British Army were becoming so thinly spread across Iraq, it was very happy to receive assistance from the T.A. (Reservists), and the Reserve Forces have been helping since. The Reserve Forces are now in the pipeline for getting a pension, because they were operational, and not just a training role. Well! The part-time UDR and R/Irish were operational, as soon as the individual joined, and were fully on operational role until they left the army (although the risk and threat to that ex-soldier will never end). The operation name was 'Op Banner'. Night after night we were operational, and out on patrol. Not just going to a war zone and helping out with logistics! Sorry, I know that a number of reservists did go to the front line in Afghanistan, and were fighting.

However we were under Military Law 24 hours a day, every day.

I hope quite soon that an MP, will takc up my offer and pursue the right for pensions for the soldiers of the UDR and R/Irish. That MP will get as much respect/identification as Mr Bates of the Post Office scandal.

Epilogue

Thank you for reading about my time serving in the UDR and Royal Irish Regiment. I am sorry I could not give you full names of the people I was serving with, or even their nicknames, as there is still threats, either on a personal bases, or in general to veterans of the Police or Army. Quite a percentage of us got nicknames in the army, and it spilled over into everyday life, so I couldn't mention many of them also.

Nicknames. I never covered that topic during the book. Nicknames were given to each soldier so not to show/reveal the identity of the soldier whilst out in operations. My nicknames (as you know) were 'Raggy-Doll' and 'Psycho'

Nicknames were easily come by. I remember a young soldier who was telling a joke – "What do you get hanging from a banana tree?", and he then quoted "Saw Ams" (his accent and dialect). So from that moment on, he was known as 'Saw Ams'.

Throughout the book I have shown how we relied on each other, trusted our lives with each other, and most probably given our lives for each other.

I would have given my life for my comrades, as in a mobile patrol one evening in Craigavon.

We were patrolling around the suburbs of Craigavon. I was the team commander of the second team, good boy Stephen was driving the Snatch.

On driving around an open area (Flats to the right) I heard what sounded like a machine gun going off. It was to the right of us. 'Bang, bang, bang, bang'. I shouted 'CONTACT', and Stephen hit the brakes.

Before the Land Rover came to a halt, I was around the front of the L/Rover, cocking my SA80, trying to locate the firing position from the flats! At that moment I was thinking of the men in the back. I didn't want them to get hit. I would rather be hit myself, than them. I was just hoping to get to the firing point before I get mowed down.

Paul and Colin were in the back, doing Top-Cover, and I was hoping that on my way across the green, the firing point could be located by them, and they could return fire. I was the decoy!

I was running as fast as I could, whilst weaving left and right. Still looking for the muzzle flashes of the gun that is on us.

I had covered a fair bit of ground, when I heard shouts from behind me "Psycho, Psycho. STOP", "Psycho – STOP!", to which I came to a quick stop, turning round, and shouting "Waa? Whats up?". Colin and Paul shouted to me "It's Fireworks!"

After that, my team and others knew, that I wasn't for backing down, when it came to the punch. I was there to back them, and fight for them.

Civilian life is on a different dimension where it comes to the trust, looking after each other aspect, and so it is also psychologically different.

I am glad that I admitted to myself and others that I did suffer from ptsd, and got the therapy so as to manage the hyper-vigilance, annualizing everyone, and flashbacks. I hope that other comrades/veterans will recognise that they also have ptsd. Perhaps not quite like mine, but similar.

I recommend and thank 'Combat Stress' for all the help they give, and they have empathy, as they themselves were soldiers.

Acknowledgements

I would like to thank:

My friends, family and comrades for their assistance and continued support in the writing of this book

Karen for her patience, whilst I was writing, also for proof reading.

Army comrades, for opening up about incidents that are described throughout.

Doug Beattie M.C. for his personal forward.

Alexa Whitten from 'The Book Refinery' without whom I couldn't have completed this book.

The many men and women with whom I served, and in remembrance of those who paid the ultimate price.

About the Author

Mark grew up in Northern Ireland, and at age 18 joined the part-time Ulster Defence Regiment.

He was based with 11th (Craigavon) Battalion, with operations and patrols in the most dangerous towns and areas of Ulster, including South Armagh.

He excelled in commanding, looking after his teams, and relished the most dangerous of tasks.

Serving for over 20 years, he has vast personal experience of the atrocities which occurred during 'Operation Banner'.

An accomplished marksman, he gained a place in both battalion and British Army shooting teams, earning him the distinguished 'Eagle Award'.

No longer serving, he wishes to ensure future generations remember the sacrifice and risks those who served endured during those monumental years in Northern Ireland.